Great Western Castle Class 4-6-0 Locomotives 1923–1959

Front cover photo:
Rebuilt 'Star', the original 4000 *North Star,* at its home depot of Wolverhampton Stafford Road, c1956. (Colour Rail)

Back cover photo:
Newton Abbot's 5059 *Earl St. Aldwyn* departs from Teignmouth with the up *Devonian* for Bradford, c1956. (R.C.Riley)

Great Western Castle Class 4-6-0 Locomotives 1923–1959

DAVID MAIDMENT
&
BOB MEANLEY

First published in Great Britain in 2022 by
Pen and Sword Transport
An imprint of
Pen & Sword Books Ltd.
Yorkshire - Philadelphia

Copyright © David Maidment and Bob Meanley, 2022

ISBN 978 1 39909 530 3

The right of David Maidment and Bob Meanley to be identified as authors of this work has been asserted by them in accordance with the Copyright, Designs and Patents Act 1988.

A CIP catalogue record for this book is available from the British Library.

All rights reserved. No part of this book may be reproduced or transmitted in any form or by any means, electronic or mechanical including photocopying, recording or by any information storage and retrieval system, without permission from the Publisher in writing.

Typeset in Palatino by SJmagic DESIGN SERVICES, India.
Printed and bound in India by Replika Press Pvt. Ltd.

Pen & Sword Books Ltd incorporates the imprints of Pen & Sword Books Archaeology, Atlas, Aviation, Battleground, Discovery, Family History, History, Maritime, Military, Naval, Politics, Railways, Select, Transport, True Crime, Fiction, Frontline Books, Leo Cooper, Praetorian Press, Seaforth Publishing, Wharncliffe and White Owl.

For a complete list of Pen & Sword titles please contact

PEN & SWORD BOOKS LIMITED
47 Church Street, Barnsley, South Yorkshire, S70 2AS, England
E-mail: enquiries@pen-and-sword.co.uk
Website: www.pen-and-sword.co.uk

or

PEN AND SWORD BOOKS
1950 Lawrence Rd, Havertown, PA 19083, USA
E-mail: Uspen-and-sword@casematepublishers.com
Website: www.penandswordbooks.com

All royalties from this book will be donated to the Railway Children charity [reg. no. 1058991] [www.railwaychildren.org.uk]

Other books by David Maidment:

Novels (Religious historical fiction)
The Child Madonna, Melrose Books, 2009
The Missing Madonna, PublishNation, 2012
The Madonna and her Sons, PublishNation, 2015
The Reluctant Traitor, PublishNation, 2021

Novels (Railway fiction)
Lives on the Line, Max Books, 2013
Steamy Stories, PublishNation, 2021 (Short stories)

Non-fiction (Railways)
The Toss of a Coin, PublishNation, 2014
A Privileged Journey, Pen & Sword, 2015
An Indian Summer of Steam, Pen & Sword, 2015
Great Western Eight-Coupled Heavy Freight Locomotives, Pen & Sword, 2015
Great Western Moguls and Prairies, Pen & Sword, 2016
Southern Urie and Maunsell 2-cylinder 4-6-0s, Pen & Sword, 2016
Great Western Small-Wheeled Double-Framed 4-4-0s, Pen & Sword, 2017
The Development of the German Pacific Locomotive, Pen & Sword, 2017
Great Western Large-Wheeled Double-Framed 4-4-0s, Pen & Sword, 2017
Great Western Counties, 4-4-0s, 4-4-2Ts & 4-6-0s, Pen & Sword, 2018
Southern Maunsell Moguls and Tank Engines, Pen & Sword, 2018
Southern Maunsell 4-4-0s, Pen & Sword, 2019
Great Western Granges, Pen & Sword, 2019
Cambrian Railways Gallery, Pen & Sword, 2019
Great Western Panniers, Pen & Sword, 2019
Great Western Kings, Pen & Sword, 2020
Great Western & Absorbed Railway 0-6-2Ts, Pen & Sword, 2020
Drummond's L&SWR Passenger & Mixed Traffic Locomotives, Pen & Sword, 2020
Southern 0-6-0 Tender Locomotives, Pen & Sword, 2021
LNER 4-6-0 Locomotives, Pen & Sword, 2021
Midland & LMS 4-4-0s, Pen & Sword, 2021

Non-fiction (Street Children)
The Other Railway Children, PublishNation, 2012
Nobody ever listened to me, PublishNation, 2012

Other books by Bob Meanley:

Non-fiction (Railways)
LMS locomotive Profile No. 11 – The Coronation Class with David Hunt, Bob Essery, Fred James and John Jennison, Wild Swan, 2008

CONTENTS

	Preface & Acknowledgements	6
	Introduction	8
Chapter 1	The Engineers	17
	G.J. Churchward	17
	C.B. Collett	17
	F.W. Hawksworth	18
	K.J. Cook	18
	R.A. Smeddle	19
	R.A.G. Hannington	19
Chapter 2	The Design	20
Chapter 3	Construction and operation, 1923–27	56
Chapter 4	High speed in the 1930s	84
Chapter 5	The Second World War and its Aftermath	134
Chapter 6	Resurgence in the 1950s	159
Chapter 7	A New Beginning and the Beginning of the End	208
Chapter 8	Personal recollections	230
	Castle Portraits for Modellers	252
	Colour Section	265
	Appendix	281
	Bibliography	302
	Index	303

PREFACE & ACKNOWLEDGEMENTS

This is the first of three books I really wanted to write. One of my early childhood railway memories is of standing on Bristol Temple Meads station in the winter of 1944 and, after being evacuated with my mother and toddler sister, seeing my journey home start on a train hauled by 4087 *Cardigan Castle*. When, like most young boys of that era, I became a trainspotter in 1947, the first number underlined in my new GWR Ian Allan ABC book was that of 4087. My love of the 'Castles' was further enhanced during seaside holidays in South Devon in 1952 and 1953 and finally embedded in me during five years of vacation work and railway training at Old Oak Common between 1957 and 1962.

More than a few books have been written about these well-known engines, but because they are the favourites of so many, I persuaded Pen & Sword to let me write three books that not only bring together all that is known about the history, operation and performance of the 'Castles', but to permit me to include my own personal experiences of the engines, and to crown it all, to work with Bob Meanley to include his account of the engine's design and technical history, as I'm not an engineer. He contributed part of the Introduction, all of Chapter 2 and has checked and amended my text where appropriate in the rest of the book.

I owe much to many – those who have trodden this path before and whose books I researched and are acknowledged in the bibliography at the end of the book. To Bob Meanley above all, who has written the chapters indicated, and to John Hodge who also reviewed and commented on the text and provided many of the photographs taken in South Wales of both his own and his splendid collections of F.K. Davies and J.G. Hubback's photographs from the 1930s. Thanks to Brian Stephenson and the Rail Archive Stephenson, to Eddie Johnson, Paul Shackcloth and the Manchester Locomotive Society for access to their vast collection of photographs and Barry Hayward who gave me access to Kenneth Leech's 12,000+ photos – I'm grateful for them all allowing me to use them free of any publication fee as I'm donating, as is my custom, all the royalties to the Railway Children charity (www.railwaychildren.org.uk). I founded this international charity in 1995 which supports street and runaway children picked up on railway and other transport terminals of the world – at the current time in India, East Africa and the United Kingdom. I've tried to trace and contact the copyright holders of all the photographs but if I have missed anyone, please get in touch with the publisher so I can make amends. Not all of the photographs from the collections identify and credit the original photographer.

I'm also grateful to John Scott-Morgan, friend and Commissioning Editor of Pen and Sword, Carol Trow my editor and Janet Brookes and the Pen and Sword design, production and marketing team for their encouragement, support and professionalism. I commend the book to all those who, like myself, had a special soft spot for these engines, and to those who like to model particular examples as there were so many varieties and differences among the 171 locomotives of the class – some individual engines managed in their first thirty-five years to sport at one time or another 'joggled' frames, straight frames dished to clear the bogie wheels, renewed straight frame front sections, two, three and four-row superheaters, tall, short and double chimneys, outside slim steam pipes as built and chunkier steam pipes, hydrostatic lubricators, mechanical lubricators in front or behind the outside steampipe or even half-way up the smokebox side, Collett 3,500 and 4,000 gallon or Hawksworth tenders.

So here they are, all 171 of them, sixteen rebuilds from the 'Stars' and the GW's sole Pacific, and 155 built new between 1923 and 1950.

I saw every one except 100A1 *Lloyds* which was withdrawn before my first day's trainspotting round the London termini. Between 1957 and 1962 I worked during college vacations and in my railway management training at Old Oak Common. I travelled behind 156 of them, some 25,000 miles, 36 times behind 5043, not all of them since preservation, 15 times behind 7029, 14 behind 5025, 12 behind 5039. I've ridden the footplate of 28 different Castles, some more than once, for nearly 2,000 miles. I've been inside the warm firebox of one with Old Oak's boilersmith, I maintained the record cards for some 35 Old Oak Castle residents for six months, I've proposed them for Swindon Works overhaul, I've been in 5043's support coach several times including on the GW 175 anniversary *Bristolian* run. I believe I have sufficient authority to tell their story. The story of the first thirty-five years or so from their conception to the end of the 1950s is here, whilst the story of their final years and their restoration and exploits in the preservation era will follow in other books in a few months' time.

David Maidment
August 2022

INTRODUCTION

The story of the Great Western Railway's Castle class locomotives really starts at the end of the nineteenth century, when a young up and coming Great Western Railway engineer called George Jackson Churchward began experimenting with new types of boiler to improve the capabilities of the railway's locomotives. Churchward was deeply interested in the developments that were taking place with locomotives in the USA and a number of modifications were made to existing designs of GWR locomotives in pursuit of greater power and efficiency, mainly centred around their boiler designs. By the turn of the twentieth century the GWR's locomotive superintendent, William Dean, was showing increasing signs of illness, and it gradually became obvious that Churchward was taking more and more responsibility within the department, and that he was ultimately destined to be the new chief. This delicate situation was handled with great skill. During this period, Churchward was able to consider what the railway's future requirements were likely to be and to lay down guidelines for a future policy of providing the GWR with a whole fleet of bigger and more powerful locomotives of a range of types which nevertheless used many standard components in their manufacture. In February 1902, the first signs of this policy became apparent with a startling new design of locomotive. The locomotive was numbered 100 and it was the first ten wheeled, or 4-6-0, passenger locomotive that the company had built and for that time it was a very large locomotive indeed. It completely blew away any pretence of traditional Victorian appearance, in fact its outward aspect was considered by many commentators of the time to be stark in the extreme, but nevertheless it was the very important prototype of what was to follow.

Soon after, in June 1902, Churchward succeeded to the top job in the GWR's locomotive department, and it became obvious that things were now moving at a fast pace, for in little more than nine months after his taking high office, Swindon locomotive works produced a second 4-6-0 to Churchward's specification. It was however not a mere copy of No.100 but incorporated a great number of modifications which had been discovered to be necessary in the intervening period since No. 100 took to the rails – including better proportioned valves and tapered back ring of the boiler barrel. The new locomotive was numbered 98 and it contained all the basic features of the GWR's standard 2-cylinder locomotives which were to endure to the end of steam traction on British Railways' Western Region in 1965. The Belpaire firebox originated from Belgium, the tapered boiler from the USA, the cylinders and smokebox design from principles described by Professor Goss of Purdue University in a paper entitled *Master Mechanics – Front End*. Piston valves with a 30in stroke were found in a locomotive on the Stockton & Darlington Railway in 1871 and long lap valves had been used on Caledonian Railway engines in the 1856-76 period. Churchward brought all these elements together in a harmonised and effective way. Over the ensuing months further similar locomotives were built containing detail developments and these ultimately formed the genesis of the 'Saint' class of locomotives. From the design of these locomotives, it was becoming apparent that Churchward possessed a certain genius for bringing together various design features from around the world and moulding them into a unique style of his own, and the resulting locomotives were beginning to demonstrate that they were actually rather good.

The first Churchward 4-6-0, No. 100, that startled the railway engineering world in 1902, the austere high running-plated locomotive with Belpaire boiler and other design improvements developed from his experience of American engines. (MLS Collection)

The second of Churchward's 4-6-0s, No.98, built in 1903, that incorporated further modifications and a tapered boiler and was the prototype of the GW 'Saint' Class that was so influential on British locomotive design over the next half century. (Locomotive Publishing Co./ MLS Collection)

Churchward then experimentally constructed some of his new ten wheelers as Atlantics for comparison with the French compounds, one of which was No.184 *Guy Mannering* seen at the head of an express at Paddington station, c1905. (R.W. Miller Collection/ MLS Collection)

Not content with progress so far, Churchward saw an opportunity to purchase and test a locomotive of French design which was being hailed as something of a world leader in power and efficiency. The locomotive concerned was built to the design of Alfred de Glehn and worked on the compound principle, whereby the steam first passed through a high pressure cylinder, followed by passage through a low pressure cylinder before being exhausted to atmosphere. *La France*, as the test locomotive was named, quickly demonstrated that it was indeed powerful, but in fact no more so than Churchward's new 'Saint' class locomotives, which were also able to compete with the French loco in efficiency terms.

The French De Glehn compound that was brought over by Churchward for testing alongside his 4-6-0s and 4-4-2s, No.102 *La France*, as new in 1903. (F. Moore/MLS Collection)

The second and larger De Glehn compound, No.103 *President*, that was purchased by the GWR together with a similar engine numbered 104, seen at Old Oak Common, c1905. Note the copper capped chimney. (R.W. Miller Collection/MLS Collection)

103 was rebuilt in 1910 with a Churchward No.1 standard taper boiler and received a superheated boiler in 1914. It is seen here at Old Oak Common. (R.W. Miller Collection/MLS Collection)

Two more French compounds of a slightly larger design soon followed, and perhaps the greatest impression that these locomotives made was the smoothness of their riding which was ascribed to their use of four cylinders as opposed to the two cylinders of the 'Saint' class.

A subsequent period of testing and consideration caused Churchward to decide that the GWR would build a four cylinder simple expansion locomotive to compare with the Frenchmen, and in 1906 his first four cylinder locomotive, number 40, was unveiled to the world. To make any comparison fairer, No. 40 was built with the same 4-4-2 wheel arrangement as the French engines. No. 40, which was named *North Star* after the GWR's first broad gauge passenger engine, soon established a reputation for similar smoothness of its ride, and the decision was quickly taken to build ten more engines of the type, all as 4-6-0s, and named after further celestial bodies, and these duly appeared from Swindon works in early 1907. Given the naming policy for the first ten engines, the class quickly became known as the 'Star' class and further batches of these locomotives were built both up to and after the First World War, the final batch in late 1922 bringing the class total to 73 engines.

No.40, the four-cylinder Atlantic built by Churchward to test alongside the French Compounds, constructed at Swindon in 1906. (R.W. Miller Collection/MLS Collection)

No.40 with a down express passing Old Oak Common West, c1907. (F. Moore/MLS Collection)

No.40, renumbered 4000 and named *North Star*, rebuilt as a 4-6-0 in 1909, at Old Oak Common, seen shortly after the end of the First World War and before further rebuilding as a Castle in November 1929. (MLS Collection)

4005 *Polar Star* on test on the LNWR, working the 10am Euston-Glasgow on Bushey troughs, 20 August 1910. The exchange with an LNWR 4-6-0 had been arranged by the LNWR management with the GWR's acceptance and the 'Star' performed all that was required of it with ease and economy. (LCGB/MLS Collection)

The 'Stars' continued to feature in main line work until the 1930s and a few could still be seen on passenger work in the 1950s. Five were rebuilt as Castles in the 1920s and ten more of the later 'Abbey' series built in 1922/3 were similarly converted in the late 1930s. Any plan to rebuild further 'Stars' as 'Castles' was abandoned at the onset of the Second World War. With superheating added from 1907, swing-link bogies being replaced by side-bearing with lateral spring control in 1908 and topfeed added in 1910, the 'Stars' and the two-cylinder 'Saints' became the backbone of the GWR express passenger services for the following twenty years and were, frankly, ten to fifteen years in advance of comparable locomotives running on other British railway companies. Their performance on the road was regularly recorded in the Charles Rous-Marten and Cecil J. Allen articles in the *Railway Magazine* of the century's first decade, with examples such as 2903 reaching Plymouth, 225.7 miles in 225 minutes; 2942 bringing 520 tons up from Badminton (100 miles) in 105 minutes; or 2915 touching 90mph on an up Birmingham

train. 'Star' 4042 took 525 tons to Westbury before the first coaches were detached and its achievement of producing 40 dbhp per square foot of grate area on the climb to Savernake was some 10 per cent higher than that achieved by any other UK locomotive at the time. 4005 demonstrated its prowess to the LNWR authorities in 1910, on the main line from Euston to Carlisle, cutting the scheduled times with ease and at a running cost well below that of the LNWR's own engines.

One of Churchward's 'Stars', 4021 *King Edward*, working King Edward VII's funeral train past Subway Junction, Paddington, en route to Windsor, 20 May 1910. (MLS Collection)

The Stars worked all over the GW system in the 1920s and 30s and roamed onto other territory. 4004 *Morning Star* is seen at Nottingham Victoria with a train from the Southern Railway to Sheffield, 22 August 1937. (G.A. Barlow/MLS Collection)

As late as 1950 'Stars' could be seen on important expresses as here at Exeter St David's where 1907 built 4007 *Swallowfield Park* (renamed from *Rising Star* in 1937) is at the head of the down *Torbay Express*, 27 June 1950 (the wrong train identification number is being displayed – 180 was the 9.10am Paddington-Birkenhead!).
(G. Newall/MLS Collection)

By the 1950s, they would be found mainly on secondary services as is 4043 *Prince Henry*, on a Bristol-Taunton stopping train near Worle Junction, 1951.
(G.A. Coltas/MLS Collection)

4056 *Princess* Margaret, the last 'Star' in action, departing from Bristol Temple Meads with a stopping train for Taunton, 6 June 1957. 4056 was withdrawn in September 1957. (MLS Collection)

4061 *Glastonbury Abbey* of the final series of 'Stars' built in 1922/3 and one of the two 'Abbeys' that were not rebuilt as Castles in the late 1930s, seen here at Wolverhampton Stafford Road, 9 October 1955. (MLS Collection)

With the eventual upsurge in traffic following the First World War, the 'Star' and 'Saint' classes had become the GWR's principal express passenger locomotives, but even so there were many older types of express locomotives that were no longer up to their duties as train loads were constantly increasing due to both the heavier vehicles and the longer trains needed to meet demand. In 1919, shortly before his retirement, Churchward had proposed fitting the much larger Standard No.7 boiler to the 'Star' class, but this suggestion had been vetoed by the railway's civil engineer on the grounds that it was too heavy for the infrastructure. This situation was not resolved before Churchward was succeeded as CME by Charles Collett in January 1922. Whilst Collett was happy to continue the construction of the final batch of Churchward's 'Stars' later that year, the Swindon drawing office was soon engaged in scheming out how they could increase the power of them within the weight limits that were permitted by the civil engineer. Their solution was to turn out a locomotive that was a brilliant compromise, and which was to become the principal express passenger steam locomotive in the West Country for the next 42 years – the 'Castle' class.

The preceding timeline of Churchward's output on which Charles Collett built was:

- 1902: Construction of No.100
- 1903: Construction of No.98 and 171 and purchase of De Glehn compound 102
- 1904: Conversion of 171 to 4-4-2 Atlantic
- 1905: Purchase of De Glehn compounds 103 & 104. Building of 173-178 as 4-6-0s & 172, 179-190 as 4-4-2s.
- 1906: Construction of No.40 4-cylinder 4-4-2 and 'Saints' 2901-2910. 2901 was the first British loco to be built with a modern superheater.
- 1907: Building of 2911-2930 & 4001-4010, rebuilding of 171 as a 4-6-0. 4010 was the first superheated Star.
- 1908: Building of 4011-4020
- 1909: Building of 4021-4030, rebuilding of 4000 as a 4-6-0. 4021 was the first engine built with a standard superheater.
- 1910: Building of 4031-4037. This was the first lot built entirely as superheated engines.
- 1911: Building of 2931-2940 & 4038-4040
- 1912: Conversion of 172, 179-190 to 4-6-0s, building of 2941-2950
- 1913: Building of 2951-2955 & 4041-4045
- 1914: Building of 4046-4060
- 1922: Construction of 4061-4066 'Abbey' series of 'Stars'
- 1923: Building of 4067-4072 & first 'Castle', 4073

Chapter 1
THE ENGINEERS

George Jackson Churchward, 1902-22

Churchward, William Dean's successor and virtual co-manager during the final five years, was born in 1857 in Stoke Gabriel on the River Dart between Kingswear and Totnes and joined the South Devon Railway at Newton Abbot in 1873. After absorption of that railway by the Great Western in 1876, he transferred aged just nineteen to the Swindon Drawing Office, and after a few rapid promotions, was appointed as Carriage and Wagon Works Manager in 1885. Ten years later, he became Swindon Works Manager and identified as Dean's successor when he became his Chief Assistant in 1897. Although he was not appointed as Locomotive Superintendent until 1 June 1902, he had been developing his ideas within the ample scope given him by Dean and had already written a paper on a scheme for a limited number of 'standard' locomotive designs by January 1901. However, in the interim he maintained a steady production of Dean designed engines, albeit showing an increasing influence of his own ideas, especially boiler design.

His interest in locomotive design developments in other countries, particularly those in France and America, influenced him. He was very open to new ideas and brought together the best in his design of the two and four-cylinder 4-6-0s in the first decade of the twentieth century. Although he was not directly involved in the production of the Castles, his work was the bedrock of Collett's design, and he had already been attempting such a development only to be thwarted by the company's civil engineer.

Churchward had an even temperament and a dignified bearing suggesting a 'country squire', strengthened by his interest in country pursuits. But he was also a good administrator and leader of men. He drew out the best from his staff and created a culture of good teamwork, a tradition and practice he inherited from Dean and his predecessors. In 1916, his title was changed to that of Chief Mechanical Engineer, he was awarded the CBE at the end of the war and in October 1920 he was the first Honorary Freeman of Swindon, of which he'd been the first Mayor as far back as 1900. It is well known that his life ended run down by one of his successor's Castles (4085 on a down Fishguard express) whilst crossing the line from his home to the Works, nearly twelve years after his retirement.

Charles Benjamin Collett, 1922-41

Charles Collett had come to Swindon in 1894 as a draughtsman and was spotted by Churchward and appointed as Assistant Manager in the Locomotive Works in 1900, and Works Manager in 1912, becoming Churchward's deputy in 1919. The far-seeing strategy of Churchward was the foundation of Collett's design programme and his involvement in the management of the Works during the production of the standard GW locomotives gave him a clear insight into the background of the basic designs, which he continued from his appointment to the senior post in 1922.

However, the severe reduction in coal output following the 1921 and 1926 miners' strikes, the reduction in peacetime requirements and then the impact of the Depression required him to reduce annual costs by £500,000, a colossal challenge, in excess of £25 million in today's currency. Some workers were laid off, but Collett sought savings from improved methods in the Works and keeping most essential new builds to existing designs. He is best remembered for the 'Kings' and 'Castles', but his Works experience played a significant part in the cost savings he brought about.

Collett was a very different character to Churchward. Although he'd had a privileged initial upbringing in the family home of Grafton Manor, he'd lost his elder brother when he was only ten, then his father died in 1884 when he was just thirteen and a pupil at Merchant Taylors public school. He was, perhaps because of this, a more private person, devoted to Ethelwyn, his wife, and he was greatly affected by the tragedy of her premature death at the age of forty-seven in 1923. He was never significantly involved in civic affairs though he was a magistrate for a number of years. He retained charge until over seventy and only retired under pressure from the GWR Board and government after his reluctance to permit conversion of much of Swindon's activity to munitions manufacture, a reflection of his experience of the impact of such work on the maintenance of GWR engines in the First World War.

Frederick Hawksworth, 1941-49

Collett eventually retired in 1941, handing over the reins to Frederick Hawksworth, a CME in waiting then already fifty-seven years of age. The latter had therefore little choice but to recognise the need for the Works to become heavily involved in munitions production as decreed by the Board and look elsewhere for help with the massive freight requirement that developed during the war. He was able to continue the build of the GW 2-8-0s and met the Ministry of Transport demand to use Swindon's facilities to build the Stanier 8Fs, a design chosen for the international role that the Dean Goods 0-6-0s and the Robinson RODs had undertaken in the First World War. In 1943-4 he benefited from the short-term availability of 175 USA built S160s prior to their shipment to the continent after D-Day, and later oversaw the temporary allocation of the Riddles WD 2-8-0s, which became permanent after nationalisation in 1948.

Hawksworth, although he designed and built thirty two-cylinder 'Counties', reintroduced the building of Collett's Castles from 1946, albeit with higher superheat for post-war conditions. Although he retired a year after nationalisation, his 5098 series and 70XX Castles continued as part of the BR steam construction programme right up to 1950. He died aged ninety-two in 1976.

Kenneth John Cook, 1949-51

By the time of Hawksworth's retirement, the role of CME at Swindon had changed with responsibility now devolved from the Railway Executive rather than the Board of Directors of the GWR. The new occupant of Churchward's chair at Swindon was Kenneth Cook. Cook had begun an apprenticeship at Swindon in 1912 and after war service had served in the Swindon drawing office for a period before being promoted to the role of assistant to the recently promoted Swindon works manager, Robert Hannington. Cook was thus heavily involved in works activities at the time of construction of the first lot of Castles. He was deeply involved in measures to improve the productivity, accuracy and output of the works and worked alongside Hannington until the latter's tragic death in 1937, upon which Cook was promoted to

Works Manager, a position which he occupied until January 1950, when he was appointed Mechanical and Electrical Engineer, British Railways Western Region. He was thus in charge when the final lot of Castles were turned out in 1950, and had been in positions of authority during the entire period of Castle construction, but his tenure was only to last until the following year when BR politics caused him to be moved to take the role of M&EE of the Eastern and North Eastern regions. As one of the principal architects of Swindon's famous optical alignment system, he naturally took it to Doncaster and Darlington in an effort to improve the durability of the Gresley pacifics in particular.

He was the author of several authoritative works including the Institute of Locomotive Engineers paper entitled 'The late G.J.Churchward's locomotive development on the GWR' and his seminal book *Swindon Steam 1921-1951* (Ian Allan 1974).

Robert Alfred Smeddle 1951-64

Alfred Smeddle was not a Great Western man by training. His father John Henry Smeddle was a North Eastern railwayman who rose to the position of Locomotive Running Superintendent of the London and North Eastern Railway's North Eastern Division. Alfred Smeddle joined the NER as a pupil in 1919 and following completion of that pupilage rose through various positions at Cowlairs, Darlington and King's Cross to be Mechanical Engineer, Darlington. Following nationalisation, he was transferred briefly to the Southern Region before being appointed M&EE (WR) in mid-1951. Roland Bond is on record as stating that:

> At Swindon, Smeddle soon found himself absorbed into the Western Family presided over by Keith Grand, the Chief Regional Officer at Paddington. It was not in Alfred Smeddle's nature to tear up trees or bash his head against brick walls, but for all that, to him should go much of the credit for pressing on with the work of equipping Castles and Kings with high degree superheaters and double blast pipes which improved their performance so much during the last days of steam on the Western Region.

It really does seem that Smeddle became fully embedded in the Swindon family and is on record in various institute papers of extolling the virtues of Swindon processes and accuracy of work. His belief in the upgraded double-chimney four-cylinder engines was strongly held and apparently the sudden drive to displace steam with diesels launched by Stanley Raymond in 1962 was a great disappointment to him. Sadly, he died at an early age in 1964. Happily, the results of his time at Swindon can still be enjoyed in the continued operation of double chimney Castles on the national network.

R.G. Hannington, Works Manager 1922-37

Robert Hannington is not a name which will be instantly recognised by many GWR enthusiasts but were it not for his death by a deeply unfortunate accident, he might well have succeeded to the CME position upon Collett's retirement in 1941, if normal protocol of promoting the incumbent Works Manager had taken place. Indeed, had he not been killed it is perhaps possible that Collett may have retired earlier. Hannington was born in 1884 and joined the GWR as a pupil in October 1903, after which he worked as a junior inspector and then assistant to W.A. Stanier who was at that time the Locomotive Superintendent of the Swindon division. After Hannington's war service, Churchward appointed him to be Locomotive Superintendent of the Worcester division, a position which he held until appointed Swindon Works Manager in succession to Stanier in 1922. He presided over many significant improvements to equipment and process within the works over the next fifteen years. Sadly, he was killed in a tragic swimming accident in June 1937 at the early age of 53. He was apparently highly respected within the works and was a great believer and upholder of Churchward's principles throughout his life. It is said that Hall class engine No 5930 *Hannington Hall* was always a favourite when in the works for repair. We can only speculate what may have been had he not been killed, but his name should be better remembered as a major contributor to the story of the Castles and Kings and indeed all their lesser brethren.

Chapter 2
THE DESIGN

Over the years there have been many books published on the Castle class locomotives, starting with the GWR's own famous publication *Caerphilly Castle* which was tremendously popular with the enthusiasts of the day when it was first published in 1924. Originals of the book are now collectors' items and there have been several reprints since. Several of the book's chapters detailed the design and construction of the locomotives and, given some of the detail contained within this current book, it is felt worthwhile to take a virtual walk around a Castle class locomotive to describe something of its design and construction.

Looking at the weight diagram for a Castle class locomotive reveals that the engine and tender combined are 65 feet 2 inches long, just over 8 feet 11 inches wide across its cylinders and 13 feet 4 inches high at the tallest point. The combined weight of the engine and tender in working order is shown as 127 tons 3 cwt. During the life of the Castles, various modifications, particularly superheating, would have increased the total weight of the engines by a small amount. The class was officially designated as the 4073 class in company records but became widely referred to as Castles after the naming policy adopted by the company. The nationwide search for suitable ruins to provide names was somewhat alleviated by many engines subsequently being named after Earls, Second World War aeroplanes, and members of the Great Western's hierarchy.

The first lot of Castles built were in essence little more than Stars with frames extended to the rear to accommodate the new Standard No.8 boiler which was somewhat bulkier and longer than the Standard No.1 boiler fitted to the Stars. That extension enabled a less spartan cab of new design to be fitted. The cylinders were slightly enlarged to give a greater tractive effort figure and on that alone the Great Western publicity department was able to claim that they were the most powerful passenger locomotives in the country. The final external clue was the adoption of outside steam pipes feeding steam between the smokebox and the outside cylinders, very much as was done with the French compounds when fitted with Swindon standard boilers. It seems that these started as an idea put forward by Stanier, but whether that is so or not, they certainly removed some of the complications from the inside of the smokebox, that of the Star having been quite crowded. The drawing schedules for the first Lot 22 of the engines show that a very great number of the drawings used were in fact those of the Star class and that allowed not only commonality of parts but meant that a very great deal of tooling, casting patterns and production jigs were available to enable the new engines to be rapidly and economically produced. One of the drawings created to enable construction to start was one showing the alteration and extension to a Star frame plate to the rear of the trailing coupled axle, together with details for the rear dragbox. No other frame plate drawing was undertaken until the advent of the new pattern frame plates in engine 4093.

The foundations of the Castle are the two main frame plates which are made from rolled steel plates some 38 feet 3 inches long, 3 feet 4 inches wide and 1¼ inches thick. Earlier engines had frame plates which had the same joggle as the Star class to reduce the width over frames in the area of the inside cylinders in order to provide clearance for the bogie wheels on sharp curves. Later engines after No.4093 had frames which were dished in the area of the leading bogie wheels. Whilst this avoided certain difficulties in ensuring correct alignment of the joggles, it involved pressing the 'dishes' into 1¼ inch thick plates which is no mean engineering process. The two frame plates are held together by a number of components which, working from front to back are: the front steel buffer beam; cast steel corner blocks and pressed steel dragbox tray; the cast iron inside cylinder and front smokebox saddle combined; the cast iron exhaust channels and rear smokebox saddle combined; the inside cylinder motion 'cradle' which supports the inside cylinder slidebars and valve spindle guides, and which is also the location for the bogie centre pin; the fabricated steel frame stay at a position between the leading and driving coupled wheels and another similar frame stay just in front of the firebox throatplate and a third one just to the rear of the firebox; and finally a fabricated steel dragbox at the rear end of the frames which locates the rear engine drawbar for connection to the tender. The frame is further stiffened by the fitting of the platform plates via a number of frame brackets. These plates together with their outer platform angles or 'hanging bars' as they were known, add considerable lateral strength and rigidity to the frame assembly. The splashers fitted to the platform were of a quite new pattern which were fabricated by welding and bolted directly to the platform plates rather than the hitherto built up type using angles and rivets. This type was actually first used on the last batch of Star class engines built in 1922/3.

Like many of the other components, initially the wheels were completely standard with those of the Star class engines. The wheel centres were steel castings which had very tough steel tyres shrunk on to the outside diameter of the cast wheel centre and they were retained by a 'Gibson' ring (a form of circlip), which was fitted to prevent the tyre from coming off the wheel centre in the unlikely event of it becoming loose or fractured. The coupled wheels were 6 feet 8½ inches in diameter over the tyres which were 3 inches thick and could be progressively turned down when worn over a period of time to just under 2 inches in thickness. The wheels fitted to the bogie were 3 feet 2 inches in diameter and also had tyres of 3 inches thickness. All wheel centres were pressed on to their forged steel axles using a large hydraulic press, the coupled wheels requiring a force of around 110 tons to finally press the wheels into position. The axles ran in axleboxes made of cast steel which in turn had bronze bearings which had their bearing surfaces coated in white metal (an excellent bearing material formed from an alloy of tin, lead, copper, and antimony in varying proportions) which ran on the highly polished journal portion of the axle. The axleboxes were located in position by cast steel axlebox, or hornguides which allow the boxes to move up and down to accommodate the usual irregularities in the track, whilst at the same time keeping the axleboxes the correct distance apart from its next coupled wheel – essential if the coupling rods are not to become bent! The leading coupled wheelset (often referred to as the inside driving axle) had a special axle which is formed into a crankshaft for connection to the two inside cylinders.

Later lots had modified coupled wheels with larger central hubs, or bosses, which provided increased support against the increased alternating forces on the crankpins. At the same time, the shape and size of the balance weights was amended, and in later years it was entirely possible, due to workshop practice, to see engines fitted with a mixed set of early and late pattern wheels, several of the preserved Castles exhibiting this feature still. Other modifications came with an increase in the diameter of the leading crank axle (inside driving) journals from the standard 8¾ inches to 9 inches. In due course, modifications took place to the design of the axle bearings culminating in the 1930s with the later design of coupled axleboxes featuring enclosed oil wells in the axlebox underkeeps, felt pads to apply oil to the axle journals, and the associated deletion of oil feed to the axlebox crowns, together with the large four feed oil boxes which were to be seen adjacent to the splashers and in the cabs of earlier engines. The 1930s also saw the introduction of stamped steel axlebox horns to replace the previous standard cast iron items. These were easier to produce and cost less, as well as being stronger and less prone to cracking than the earlier pattern of horns.

The bogie fitted to the leading end was of exactly the same pattern as those fitted to many of the Star class. Often referred to as the French or De Glehn bogie, that is actually something of a misnomer, because the initial design of bar farmed bogie for the early Churchward 4-6-0s of the 1900s was very much influenced by American design. Initially control of lateral displacement was achieved by means of an American feature known as swing links, but these were not totally satisfactory at the higher speeds which Churchward's engines were being run and when the French compounds were placed in service, it was quickly realised that their ride characteristics were much better than the new GWR 4-6-0s and that was rapidly ascribed to the superior sprung side control mechanism used in the bogies of the De Glehn compound Atlantics. The trial fitment of a similar system was first made in an experimental plate frame bogie fitted to the Atlantic Saint class engine No. 184. The first Star to be fitted was No. 4011 of 1908 which had a standard bar frame bogie with its steel centre casting modified to accommodate helical coil side control springs in a similar arrangement to that of the French compounds, but it certainly was nothing like a complete copy of the French compound's bogies. From the outset, the bogies of the Castles, very much as the Stars, had brake gear fitted to them. The brake gear was actually quite complex and very much shoe-horned into the available space around the bogie centre casting. The first ten engines were built with this brake gear fitted but it appears that the gear was deleted from the production schedules for the next ten engines (4083 to 4092) at a late stage, although photographs suggest that later batches still had bogie centre castings carrying at least part of the brake hanger brackets. It is often suggested that this deletion was due to a decision that the gear was unnecessary, but an additional factor is the likelihood of the bogie wheels 'picking up' in greasy conditions with the attendant skidding causing flats on the tread of the tyres. The brake gear was removed from the first ten engines within two or three years from their entry to service, and no more examples were ever fitted with it.

The Castles had four cylinders, each of which had a piston of 16 inches diameter having a stroke of 26 inches length. This was an increase of one inch on the 15 inch diameter cylinders of the Star class and accounted for the increase in nominal tractive effort of the Castle class. Individual cast iron outside cylinders were bolted to the left and right hand frames, whilst the two inside cylinders were combined in one iron casting which also served as a frame stretcher at the front of the engine. Steam was distributed alternately to the front and back of each piston by an 8 inch diameter piston valve working in the steam chest immediately above each cylinder. The valves were of the by now standard GWR pattern of 'semi plug' piston valve. Cast iron covers were fitted at the front and back of the cylinders and valve chests, to retain the steam pressure, and at the rear cover where the piston rods emerge to drive the wheels via the connecting rods, special glands were fitted to prevent loss of steam whilst allowing the piston rods to slide backwards and forwards at quite high velocities. In order to prevent the piston rods from being bent by resultant forces in the connecting rods, cast steel crossheads were fitted to support the outer ends of the piston rods and connect them to the connecting rods. The crossheads were originally assembled from three parts bolted together (often termed 'built up'), but later engines had crossheads again from separate parts but assembled by welding them together. Crossheads worked between pairs of forged steel slidebars, which in turn were supported by the strong cast steel outside motion plates (often called 'G' irons) to prevent any deflection.

The coupling rods which connect the wheels together were made from forged nickel chrome alloy steel for additional strength and fatigue resistance, as were the connecting rods which couple the pistons and crossheads to the crank pins fitted to the wheel centres, and the pins of the crank axle. The valve motion which was fitted to drive the piston valves in time with the movement of the pistons is of the Walschaert type, and it was all accommodated between the frames out of sight from outside. Drive was derived from a pair of eccentrics fitted to the leading coupled (inside driving) axle between the cranks, one eccentric for the left hand cylinder, the other for the right hand. This motion directly drove the inside cylinders' valves and had a 'rocking lever' which was cleverly arranged to drive the valve of the outside cylinder from the same set of motion, thus negating the need for independent valve motion for the outside cylinders. The reversing gear was very similar to that of the Stars, having the standard GWR screw reverser mounted on a substantial box structure in the right hand front corner of the cab, and connected to the reversing lever by the long reversing rod which had a steady bracket midway along its length and mounted at the rear of the right driving splasher. All the major components of the valve motion were manufactured to exactly the same design as that for the Star class, and as such all were interchangeable.

The boiler for the Castle class was of a completely new design which had something of an unusual gestation. Around the end of the First World War, it became clear that Churchward had been considering the idea of providing more power for his larger locomotives to meet the growth in train loads. Increased power does not necessarily require substantial increase in the size of locomotives, and one way of dealing with this issue is to provide a boiler of increased capacity capable of supplying greater quantities of steam which permitted the locomotive to be steamed harder on taxing portions of the line without exceeding boiler capacity and 'winding' it. Churchward's answer to this problem was to develop a larger version of his standard No.1 boiler which had the same barrel and tube lengths but possessed a firebox which was 1 foot longer, thus providing an increase to the grate area of just over 3 square feet. Furthermore, although tube lengths would remain the same as that of the No.1 boiler, the barrel would be of larger diameter enabling more tubes and superheater flue tubes to be accommodated. In turn the larger barrel would also enable an increase in firebox dimensions providing additional firebox heating surface as well as greater firebox volume to assist the combustion process. All of this resulted in an outline design which eventuated as the No.7 standard boiler. It was originally proposed to fit this boiler to future examples of the 29xx Saint, 40xx Star, and 28xx freight classes, and this is where it ran into problems. The increased dimensions of the No.7 boiler brought an increase in the weight of materials in it, and together with the weight of additional water, coal and longer firebars; this led to all of the proposals going above the maximum weight which the Civil Engineer would permit to run. The boiler would eventually find limited use fitted to the 4700 class 2-8-0s, but those nine engines were the only ones ever fitted with it. All was not lost however because all of the flanging blocks needed for forming the flanged plates for the firebox found use in 1927 when the No.12 boilers for the King class were produced, that boiler effectively being a lengthened version of the No.7 boiler.

What became clear in 1922 however was that the Civil Engineer's weight restrictions still precluded the use of the No.7 boiler on the proposed new passenger engine, and as a consequence this restriction resulted in the design of the No.8 standard boiler which was solely used on the Castle class. In essence the lengths of the No.8 corresponded with the No.7, and it is often questioned as to whether this may have been with the intent of perhaps retro fitting the No.7 at some future date when the Civil Engineer might relax weight restrictions. What differed was that the barrel diameter was some 3 inches less compared with the No.7 and this resulted in a consequent reduction in both firebox volume and heating surface. One other feature of the new No.8 boiler was that the firebox side water legs were narrowed somewhat from standard, which had the effect of a marginal increase in the internal width of the firebox resulting in an increase of grate area of around 0.9 square feet, to above 30 square feet. This feature was subsequently found to have little additional value whilst causing increased difficulty in clearing scale and sludge from the firebox water legs at washout periods. Only the first sixty boilers constructed had fireboxes of this size and the subsequent 190 boilers for the class were built with standard width water spaces and reduced grate area. The first new engine fitted with a boiler with reduced grate area was No.5013 in June 1932.

The outer shell of the boiler was manufactured from steel plate, rolled and pressed to shape as required and then riveted together. The inner firebox which contains the fire and directly boils the water is made of copper containing small amounts of arsenic (0.5 per cent) which improves the strength of the copper at the high temperatures encountered in the firebox. The outer firebox is some 10 feet long by 6 feet wide at the top and 4 feet wide at the bottom where it fits between the locomotive's frames. The inner copper box is somewhat smaller as there is a water space all around between the inner and outer boxes, and the inside is 9 feet 1 inch long by 3 feet 2 inches wide at its base, giving space for a fire grate which has an area of some 29.36 square feet, and you can get a lot of coal on that! The boiler works at a pressure of 225 pounds per square inch and due to this, considerable forces exerted on the shell of the firebox would normally distort and burst it. In order to prevent this, almost 2,000 threaded stays are screwed between the inner and outer boxes all around the sides, ends and top (crown) to resist such forces and maintain the shape of the firebox under pressure. The circular tapered boiler barrel is some 5 feet 9 inches in diameter at the rear and 14 feet 10 inches long. It is closed at the front end by a tubeplate some 5 feet in diameter which has numerous holes in it for the fitment of the tubes which carry the hot gases from the firebox to the smokebox at the front of the boiler where they are ejected to the atmosphere by the action of the exhaust steam as it is exhausted up the chimney. Later the development of a double chimney was added to enable the power output of the loco to be increased, and to better enable it to burn the inferior coal which was often supplied during the 1950s. The steel boiler tubes are of two types. Early boilers had 201 (later 197) 2-inch tubes and 14 superheater flues of 5⅛ inch diameter, whereas the last boilers built had 138 2-inch diameter tubes to carry the hot gases, but also had 28 superheater flue tubes of 5⅛ inch diameter. These flues have smaller 1¼ inch diameter tubes called superheater elements inserted in the bore of the flue, and these carry steam which is passing from the boiler to the cylinders. Their purpose is to take extra heat from the hot gases and add it to the steam to provide extra heat energy for use in the cylinders, in some ways a similar sort of idea to supercharging a motor car. The addition of superheat was found to improve fuel and water consumption by around 10 per cent, so its use became universal in the twentieth century for locomotives such as the Castles. Finally, in order to prevent heat from being wasted needlessly, the boiler was encased in around 8 cwt of a form of asbestos insulation known as plastic magnesite and covered with thin steel sheets which gave the smooth appearance and provided a good base for the well known GWR green paintwork.

The brake system fitted to the Castles worked on vacuum. Air was exhausted from the brake system by a powerful 4 cone brake ejector, the system working on a vacuum of 25 inches of mercury, some 4 inches higher than that used by other railways in the UK. This gave a very powerful brake force to the locomotive and the coaches in its train. Brakes were controlled by an air valve mounted in the cab close to the driver, and operation of this valve admitted air to the train pipe along the train, thereby pushing the brake cylinder pistons against the full vacuum retained on the reservoir side of the pistons and applying the brakes by the levers and links connected to the piston. Additionally, the locomotive was fitted with an air pump driven by the right inside crosshead which was used to maintain the train pipe vacuum against any leakage whilst running. The use of this mechanical pump negated the need to use the steam powered ejectors whilst running, resulting in something of an economy in steam usage. The brake cylinder on the locomotive is a massive 30 inches in diameter whilst the tender has a slightly smaller cylinder of 22 inches diameter. The locomotive brake cylinder is capable of generating a maximum force of over 3.5 tons at the piston rod at a full brake application and this force is magnified by the levers of the brake shaft. The brake system is often considered to be complex, but it became standard across a large proportion of the fleet and was proven to be durable and powerful.

Perhaps the most popular point of interest on any locomotive is the driver's cab, as most small boys have harboured a desire to be an engine driver at some point in their life. On the Castle, the driver is situated on the right side of the cab, and all of the controls are conveniently grouped close to his station. The rudimentary tip up wooden seat will be noted and it is good to remember that the construction of loco 4073 in 1923 heralded the introduction of this last word in comfort for GWR drivers, who were previously required to stand in the belief that it maintained their alertness. In front of the driver is the reversing handle which is used to control the action of the valves. Over to his left is the brake valve with its associated valves for operating the vacuum brake ejectors. Above the brake valve is the gauge indicating the vacuum in the brake system. Usually, the space below the brake valve would be occupied by the quite bulky standard GWR 'hydrostatic lubricator', but on many locomotives during the 1950s there was just a simple pressure gauge, which indicated to the driver that steam was being supplied to the mechanical lubricator atomisers fitted to the engine. Further levers for the cylinder drain cocks, and the sand valves for putting sand under the wheels to make them grip the rails better in damp or greasy conditions, are arranged on the floor in front of the driver. The all-essential firehole is set in the middle of the firebox backplate quite close to the floor. This firehole is fitted with sliding doors and a hinged flap which is used to minimise cold air being drawn in to the firehole between individual shovelfuls of coal.

The fireman has a range of controls which he uses from time to time. Up at the top of the firebox are the steam valves which supply steam to the exhaust and live steam injectors, which in turn supply water to the boiler, as well as the important valve which supplies steam to keep the passengers warm. Over on the left side is the single water gauge with its glass tube indicating the water level in the boiler. It is surrounded by a 'protector' having thick glass lenses, the purpose of which are to retain the bits, should the glass tube ever be shattered by the steam pressure – very rare, but it did happen. In the event of gauge glass breakage, two small 'trial taps' are carried to enable the water level to be tested until the glass is able to be changed. The fireman has two pressure gauges on his side, one for the steam pressure in the boiler and the other for the carriage warming steam pressure. Down on the floor are control levers for the damper doors which control the supply of air entering the firebox ashpan, and there are also controls to regulate the flow of water from the exhaust steam injector.

Behind the driver and fireman on the tender front are the coal doors for access to the tender's coal bunker, the handbrake handle situated on the fireman's side – used to secure the engine when stationary, and the handles to control the tender feed water cocks which supply water to the injectors on the locomotive. High on the front of the tender is the brass water gauge dial plate which shows the amount of water contained in the tender tank. Finally, the handle used to lower the tender's water pick up scoop is located at the tender front on the right side just ahead of the tank gauge.

Castles were fitted with a number of different tender types throughout their long careers. The early engines had what were officially termed '3,500 gallons tender with well bottom', more popularly known as the 'Churchward' type. It was in fact a somewhat developed version of the last tenders built during the Dean era. These normally carried 7 tons of coal. By 1926, some engines were coupled to modified 3,500 gallons tenders which had a deeper coal space holding around one extra ton of coal. Ten such tenders were constructed and became known as the 'Intermediate type'. These tenders are sometimes confused by certain commentators with the later Collett 3,500 gallons flush bottom tenders. By the end of 1926 the Castles were being coupled to the new '4,000 gallons tender with flush bottom' again better known to enthusiasts as the 'Collett' type, the first of which was coupled to engine 5000 for its exchange trials with the LMS. These tenders had a coal capacity of 6 tons. Over the years, this type was universally fitted to all Castles at some point during their history. Following the Second World War, the GWR introduced a further type of tender, the '4,000 gallons welded tender with flush bottom' or 'Hawksworth' type and this too made an appearance on numerous Castles over a period of time. It was basically unknown for a tender to remain with a specific locomotive for any length of time and locos usually left Swindon with a completely different tender to that which they had taken to works on every visit there. The tenders were all of the same basic length and many components such as axles, axleboxes and brake gear were standard to all varieties of tender. The tanks grew in size to accommodate greater supplies of water and the tank and bunker of the Hawksworth type was constructed by welding, which gave a smooth surface devoid of the usual rivets to the exterior of the tank. Prior to the introduction of the Hawksworth type, a small number of Collett type tenders were built with welded tanks in order to prove the acceptability of welding, and these can be recognised again by the lack of rivet heads. All tenders were fitted with water pick up gear which had a scoop arranged under the tank which picked up water whilst the train was moving by being lowered into troughs filled with water laid between the rails at specific locations known to the driver and fireman. Water was also able to be added to the tank from track-side water columns by using the manhole located on the top of the tank.

The class eventually extended to 171 engines, constructed in one form or another between August 1923 and August 1950. 155 engines were new builds whilst 15 engines were rebuilt from Star class engines and one was the rebuild of the lone Pacific No.111 *The Great Bear*. The first withdrawal was engine No.4009 (renumbered 100A1) in March 1950 leading to the interesting fact that the class was never complete as the last ten engines were out-shopped after its withdrawal. The last engine to be taken out of traffic was No.7029 in December 1965, giving a class life span of some 42 years and 4 months. It is inevitable that over such a length of time the design of the class would evolve in its details, and this led to a lot of small variations over the years. Many variations were quite noticeable, others less so, and some were quite minor details, often in the course of experiments being carried out to test new ideas developed by the drawing office or development section of the testing team. There was however no standard regarding application of all modifications to all engines and there were widespread variations in what would be called the Modification (or Mod) Status of the engines in modern parlance.

It has been said, half in jest, that of the 171 Castles the only truly standard feature was that they were all different!

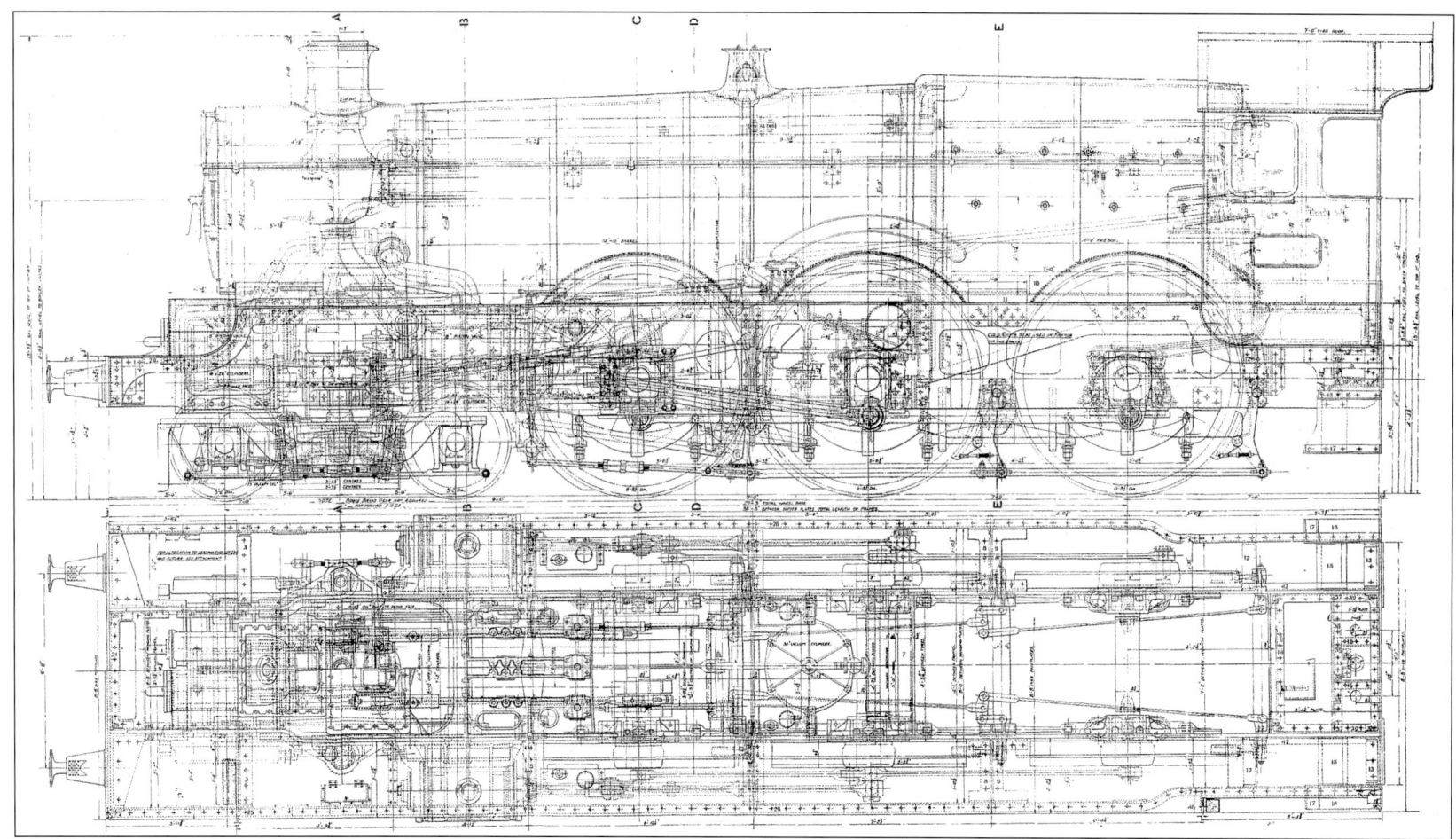

FRAME PLAN GWR DRAWING No. 72265 NOV 1925
Lesser concerns called them General Arrangements but at Swindon such drawings as this were called Frame Plans. To any draughtsman asked to make such drawings it was an indication of standing within the drawing office. This drawing shows the engine from its left side and contains much detail shown in broken lines which indicates parts that would otherwise be lost from sight when normally viewed from the outside of the locomotive. The top elevation, known as a side elevation, shows several notable details such as the complications involved in the bogie brake gear, the smokebox steam pipes, and superheater header, the first arrangement of oil boxes between the leading and driving splashers which fed oil to the axleboxes and the new style of cab sitting on the extended rear frames.

The lower plan view is interesting in showing the mass of components crammed between the locomotive's frames, including the 30 inch diameter brake cylinder, its associated brake shafts and rods, the valve motion, crank axle and connecting rods, inside cylinders and the Star type sanding gear which would see subsequent modification. Not included in this view is the ashpan beneath the firebox. Whilst the rear end appears somewhat bare by comparison, the complex pipework associated with feed water injectors, steam heat and vacuum brake pipes is similarly excluded as pipework was always shown on separate pipe arrangement drawings to avoid unnecessary complication.

The Design • 27

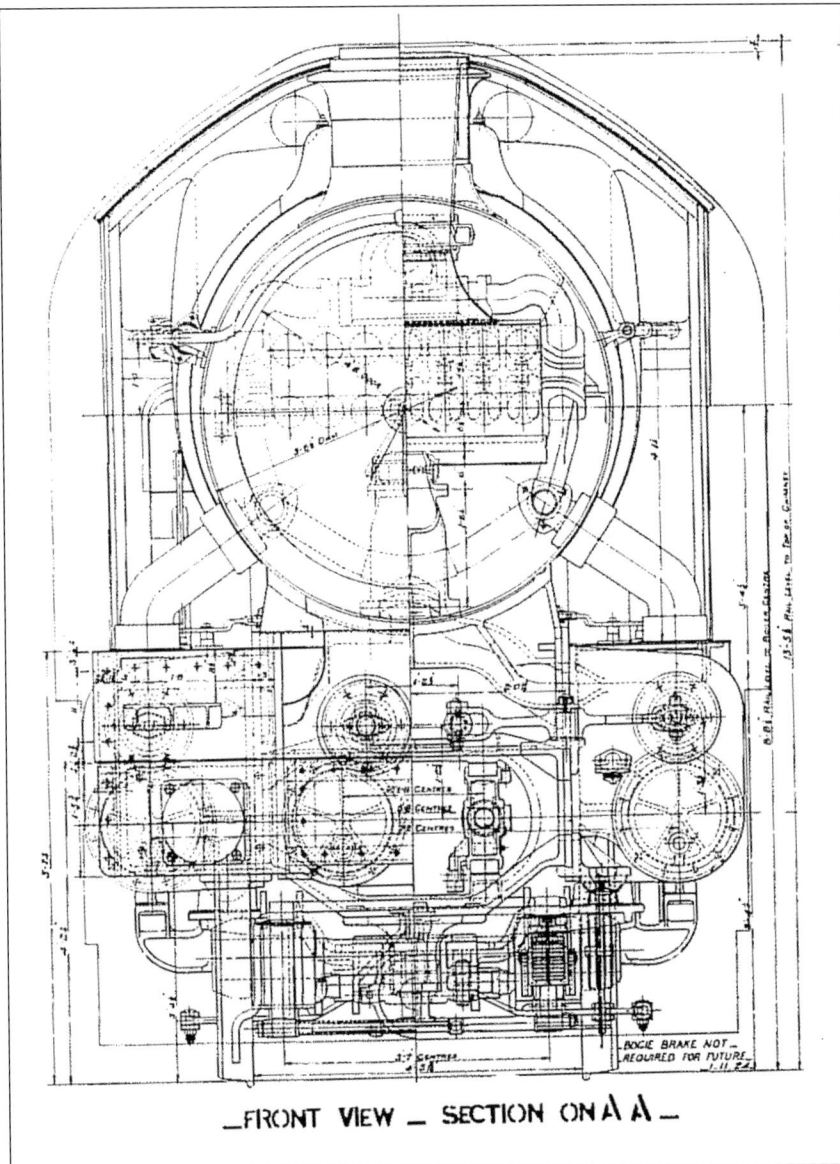

_FRONT VIEW _ SECTION ON A A_

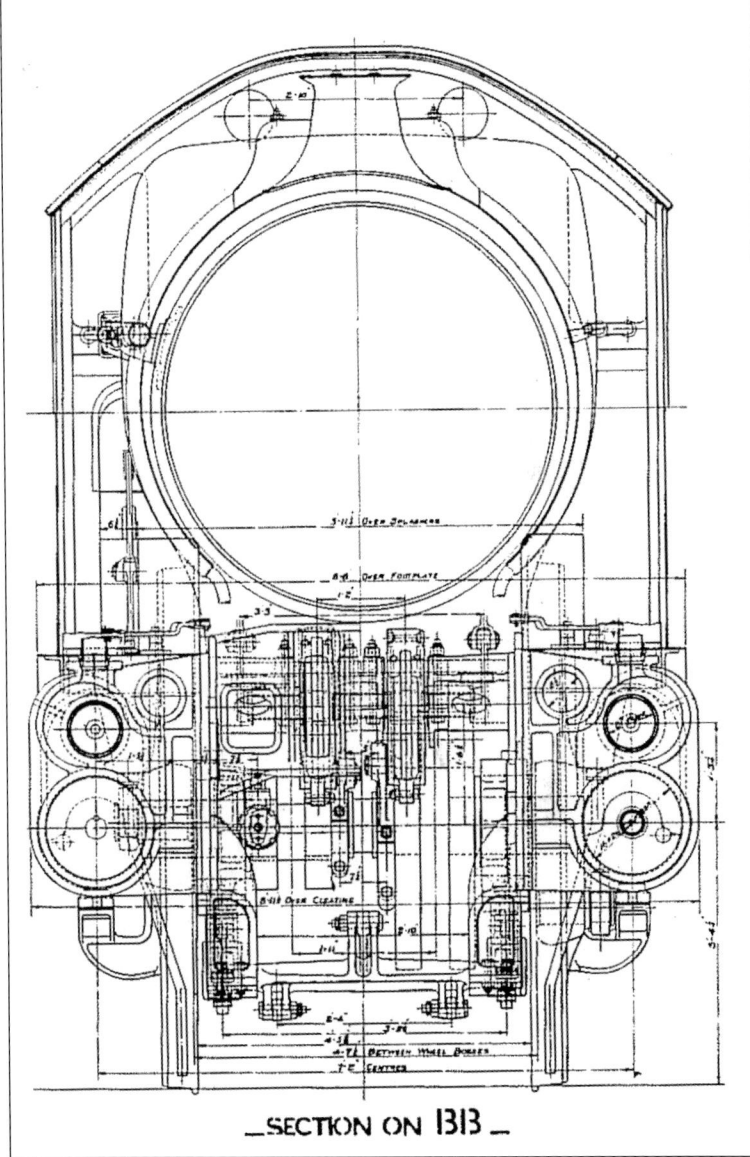

SECTION ON B B

Above left: **FRONT VIEW AND SECTION A-A**
As well as the main drawing for the side elevation it was standard practice to produce another showing views of the engine from both front and rear as well as what were termed sections, which were effectively a slice through the engine at various points of interest. In later times it became customary in engineering drawings to mark components cut by sections, with diagonal lines known as hatching, but Swindon never took to this practice in the GWR era. Consequently, reading such drawings is something of an acquired art which demands a certain familiarity with the product. The left half of this view shows the front of the engine with much hidden detail again shown in broken lines, whilst the right hand side is a section taken along the line marked A-A on the side elevation. This particular line is at the centre of the rocking lever operating the outside valves and also shows the inside cylinder motion as well as detail of the superheater in the smokebox.

Above right: **SECTION B-B**
This view is taken in a line through the outside cylinders and shows how the cylindrical steam chests for each cylinder are eccentrically arranged relative to the valves working inside them, necessitated by the valve gear arrangement and space constraints. It again emphasises the array of items located between the frames, in this instance the expansion links of the valve motion, brake shafts, crank axle and sundry other items.

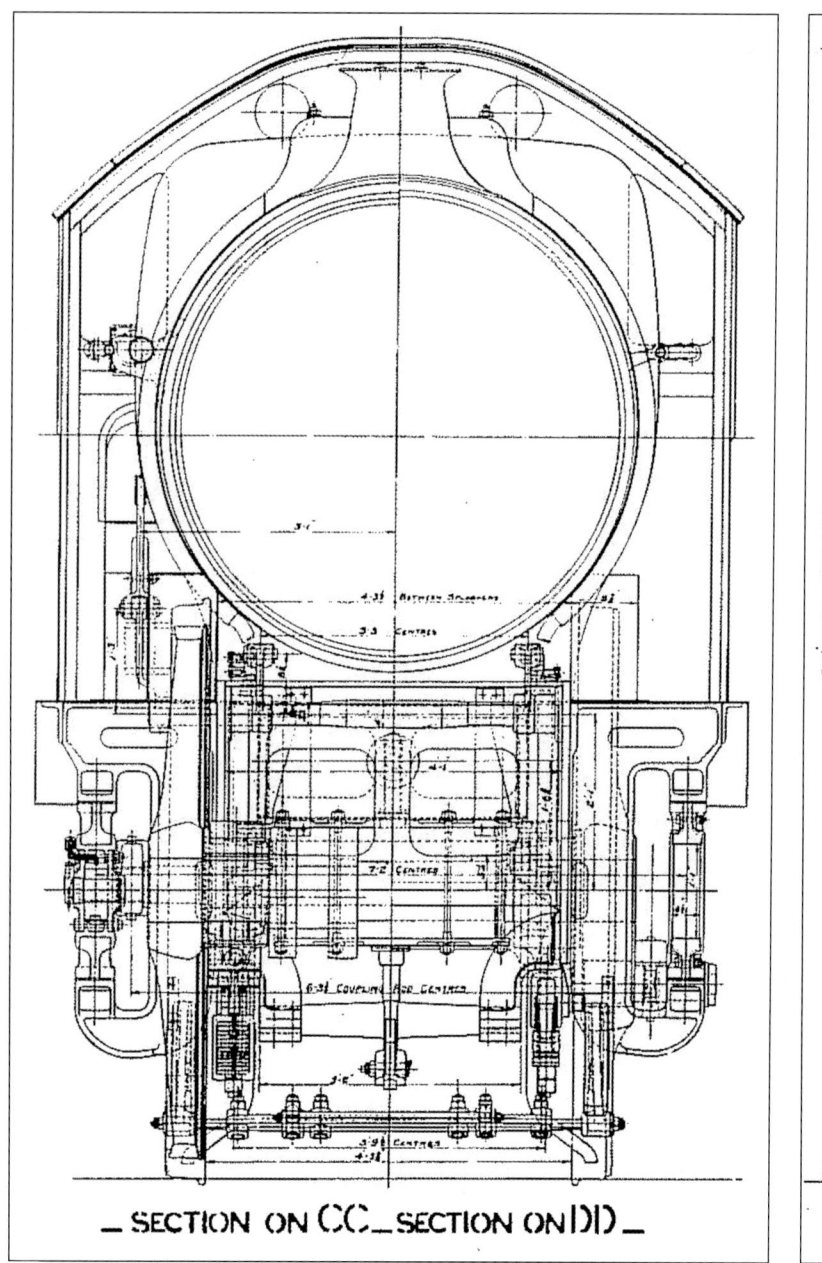
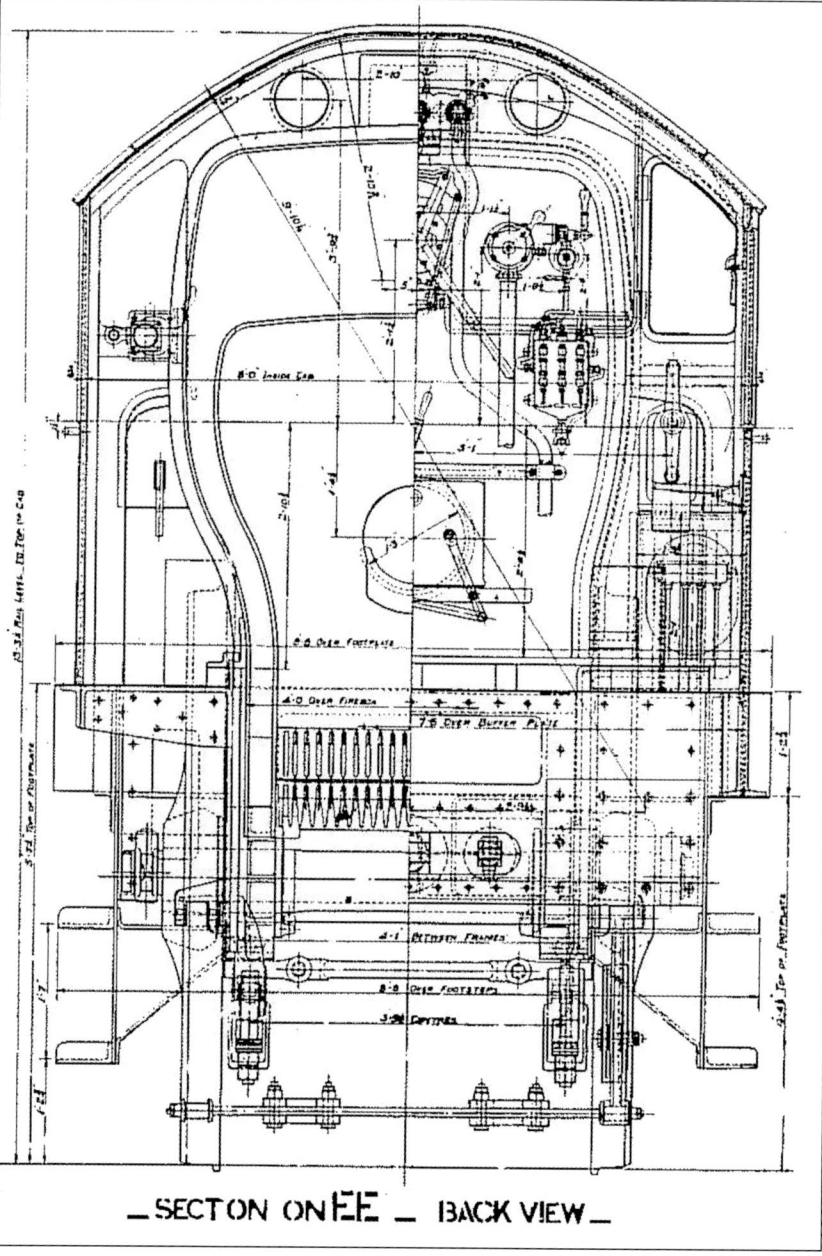

Above left: SECTIONS C-C & D-D
This drawing is a composite section, the left side of which is taken on line C-C and the right side on line D-D. Prominent details here are the brake cylinder and its associated brake shaft, spring gear, sand boxes and the outside slidebars, crossheads and motion brackets (or 'G' Irons as they were often known).

Above right: SECTION E-E & REAR VIEW
Section E-E gives a view of the slice through the firebox, illustrating the carefully arranged Churchward inspired curvature of the inner and outer firebox, which accommodated differential expansion between inner and outer boxes, and which also encouraged water circulation around the water spaces leading to increased evaporation rates. The right hand side shows a view on the rear of the locomotive. Whilst showing details of the basic construction, a bare minimum of detail is included for many of the controls which were shown on supplementary drawings showing the 'arrangement of boiler mountings' as it was known.

The Design • 29

DRAWING 72300 MAXIMUM CROSS SECTIONS
This rather rudimentary front elevation of the engine was intended to illustrate the maximum size of prominent features such as buffer beam, cab, chimney and cylinders, to provide the civil engineer with some assurance that it would not collide with various items of infrastructure such as platforms and bridges. It has become modern practice to claim that Great Western engines, and Castles in particular, are too wide for the current network, but it may be worth noting that the GWR standard dimension for rail to platform edge was exactly that specified by current Railway Group Standards!

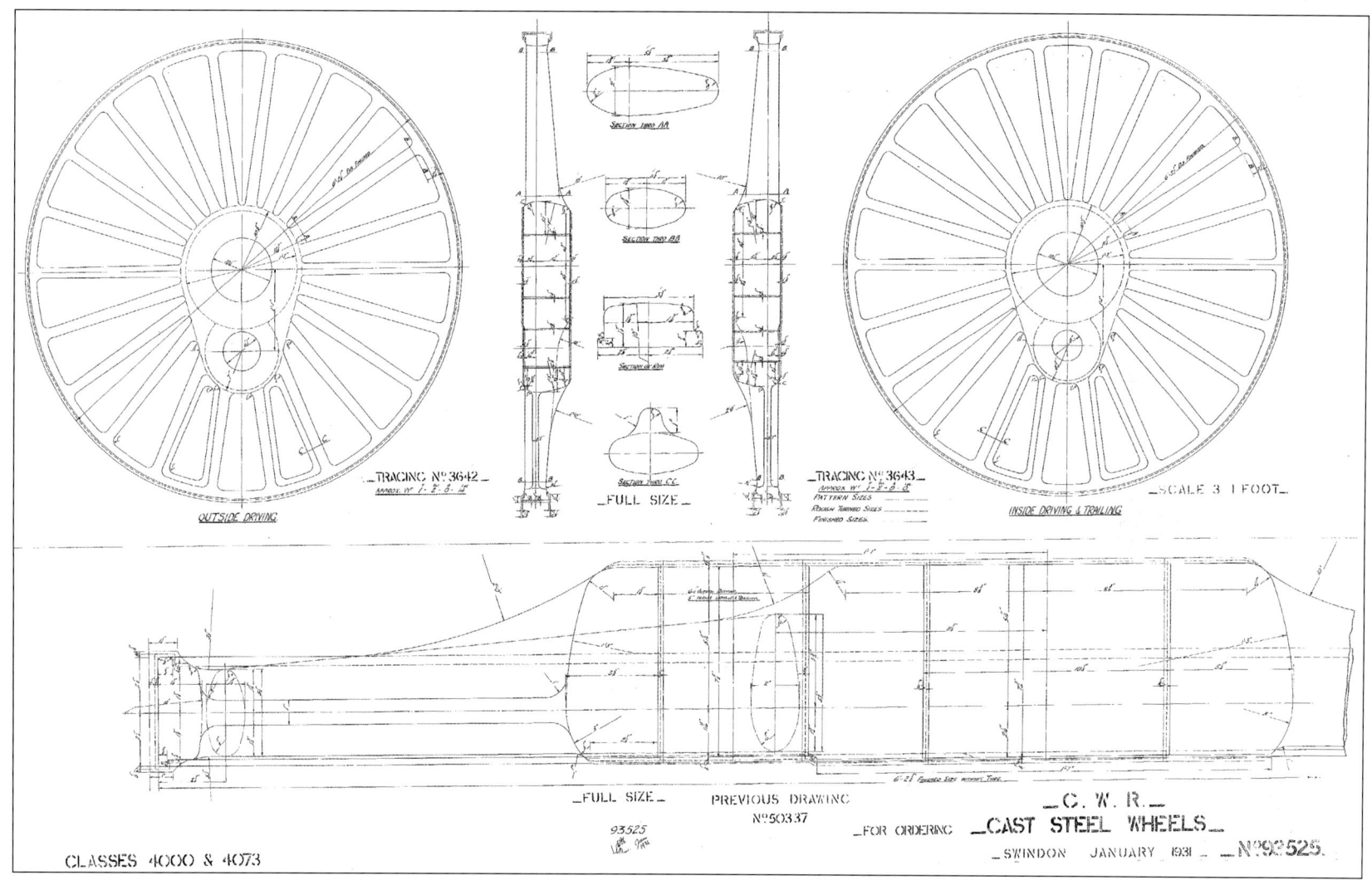

DRAWING No.93525 CAST STEEL WHEELS

Early Castles were fitted with cast steel coupled wheels to the Star pattern. They can be distinguished by the crank pin being in line with the adjacent spoke on the centre line of the quarter piece. The later pattern wheels shown in this drawing had somewhat larger centre wheel bosses, and the spokes at the quarter piece were disposed either side of the centre line rather than on it. Balance weights 'too' varied and it was not unusual to find mixed early and late pattern wheels fitted to individual engines.

The Design • 31

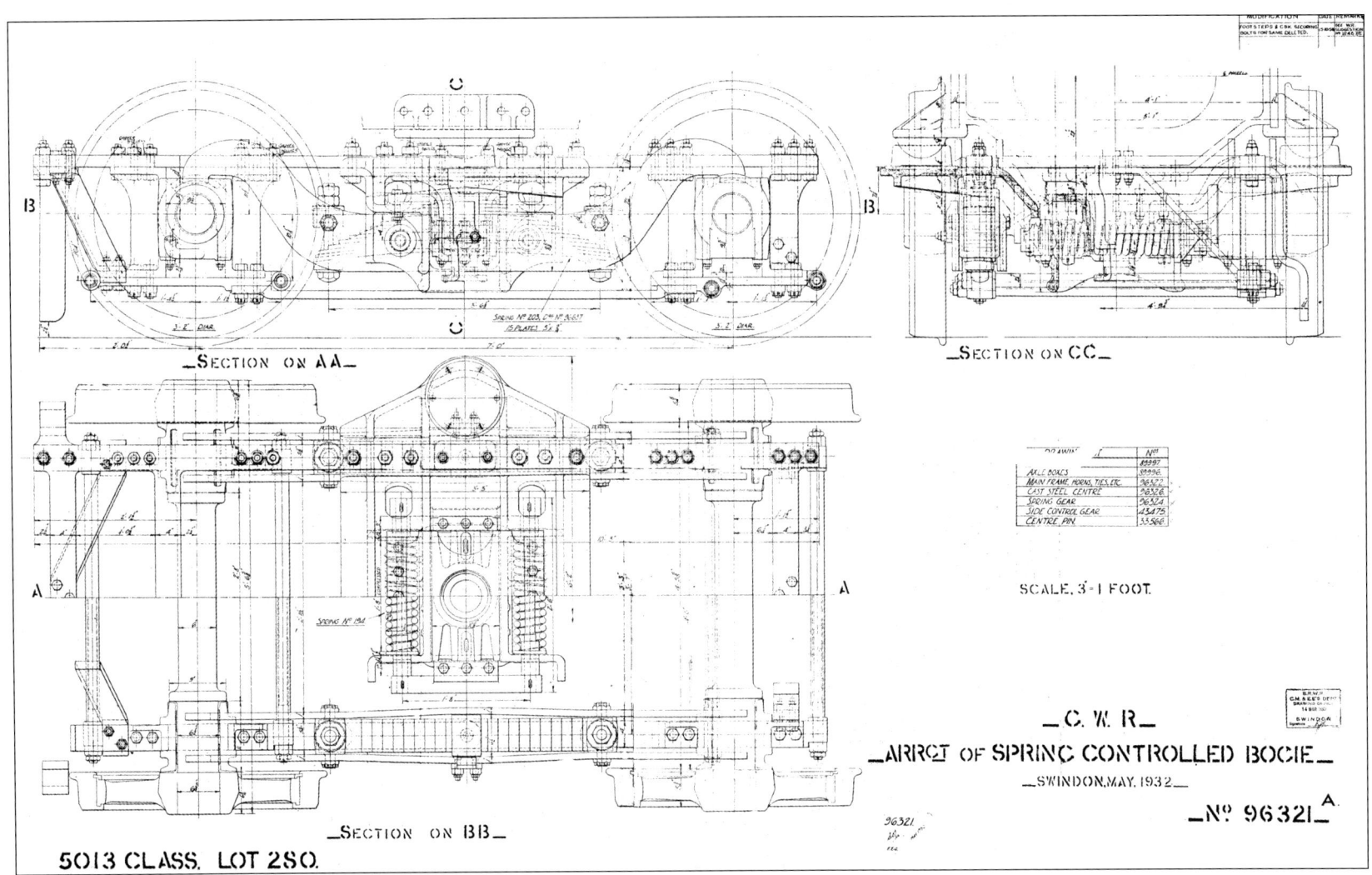

DRAWING No. 96321 ARRANGEMENT - SPRING CONTROLLED BOGIE
This drawing shows the later design of bogie fitted to the 5013 series and subsequent lots. The term 'spring controlled' relates to the provision of a clever arrangement of springs to provide sufficient resistance to sideways movement and provide forces to guide the bulk of the locomotive into curves. Whilst commentators refer to these as De Glehn bogies, they are not of De Glehn design being based on American bar frame principles, and it is solely the spring control and side bolster supports which resulted from the De Glehn influence. Earlier lots had a somewhat different bogie centre casting which had the Star class arrangement of side control springing and also brackets cast on for support of the bogie brake hangers.

Details of some of the modifications are as follows:

Main Frame Plates

The early members of the class continued the use of the Star class frame plates which had a 'joggled' section at the front end adjacent to the inside cylinder in order to narrow the width over the frames to permit sideways translation of the bogie wheels on curves. This joggle was a difficult piece of plate working to carry out and ensure that the frame in front of the joggle was in perfect alignment with the main portion of the plates. Consequently, revised thinking determined that

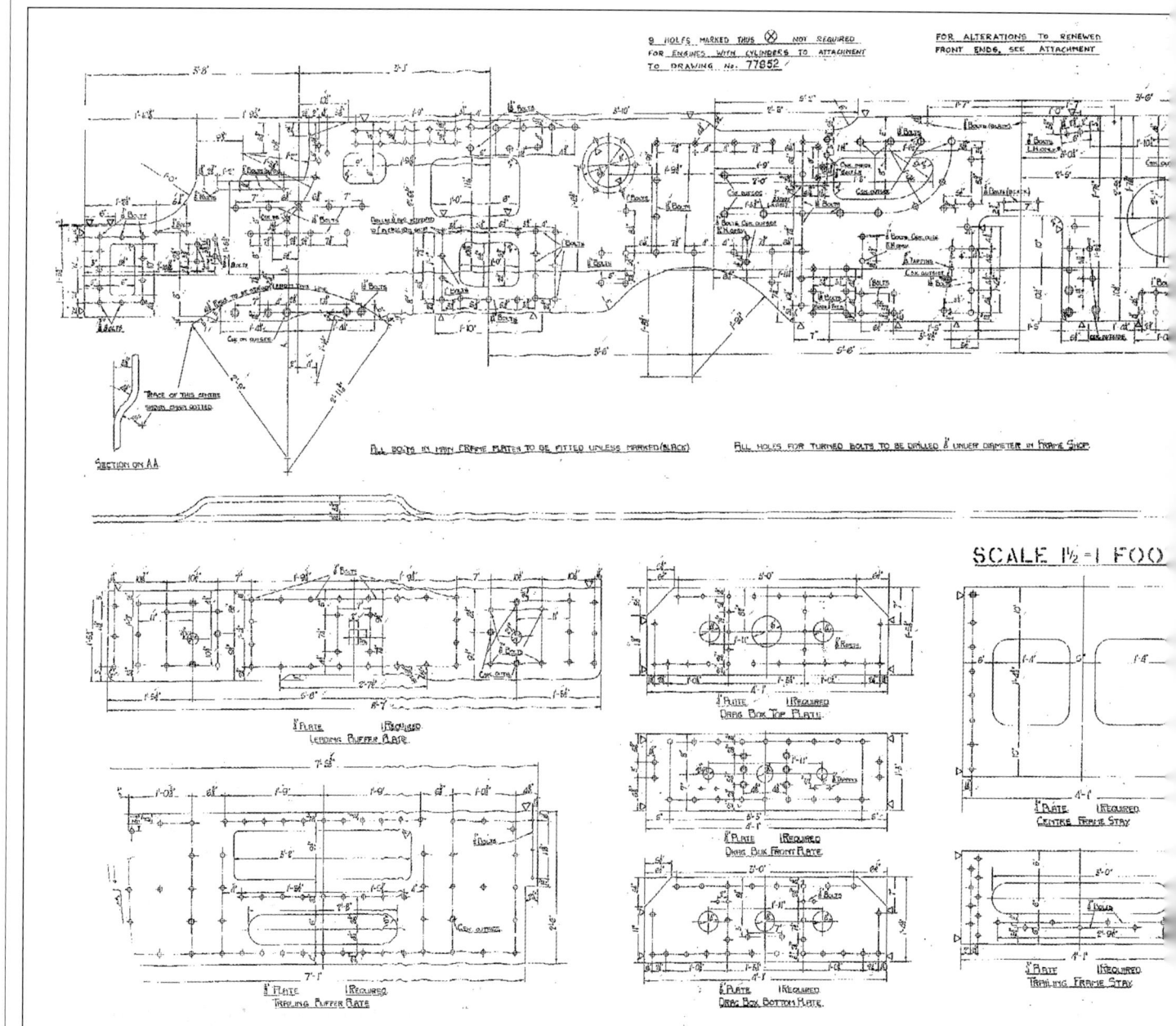

DRAWING 96053 FRAME PLATES Swindon DO traditionally produced a drawing which showed all of the major plates which made up the locomotive frame. This is a later version of the original drawing which clearly shows the depression at the front of the frame plates provided to give lateral clearance to the leading bogie wheels. Other plates include the front and rear buffer beams and various stretcher plates, and even the step backplates.

a significant depression could be made in the frame plates to form what might effectively be described as a wheel arch, and that this would enable the frame plate to otherwise remain straight. This in itself was a very heavy piece of presswork carried out in Swindon works; a depression of this size in 1¼ inch thick steel plate is no easy task. The first such frames were used in engine No.4093 built in May 1926, and all subsequent engines with the exception of Star class rebuilds were built with these frames. At a later date, certain engines including some of the ex-Star class 'Abbey' series were rebuilt with new front

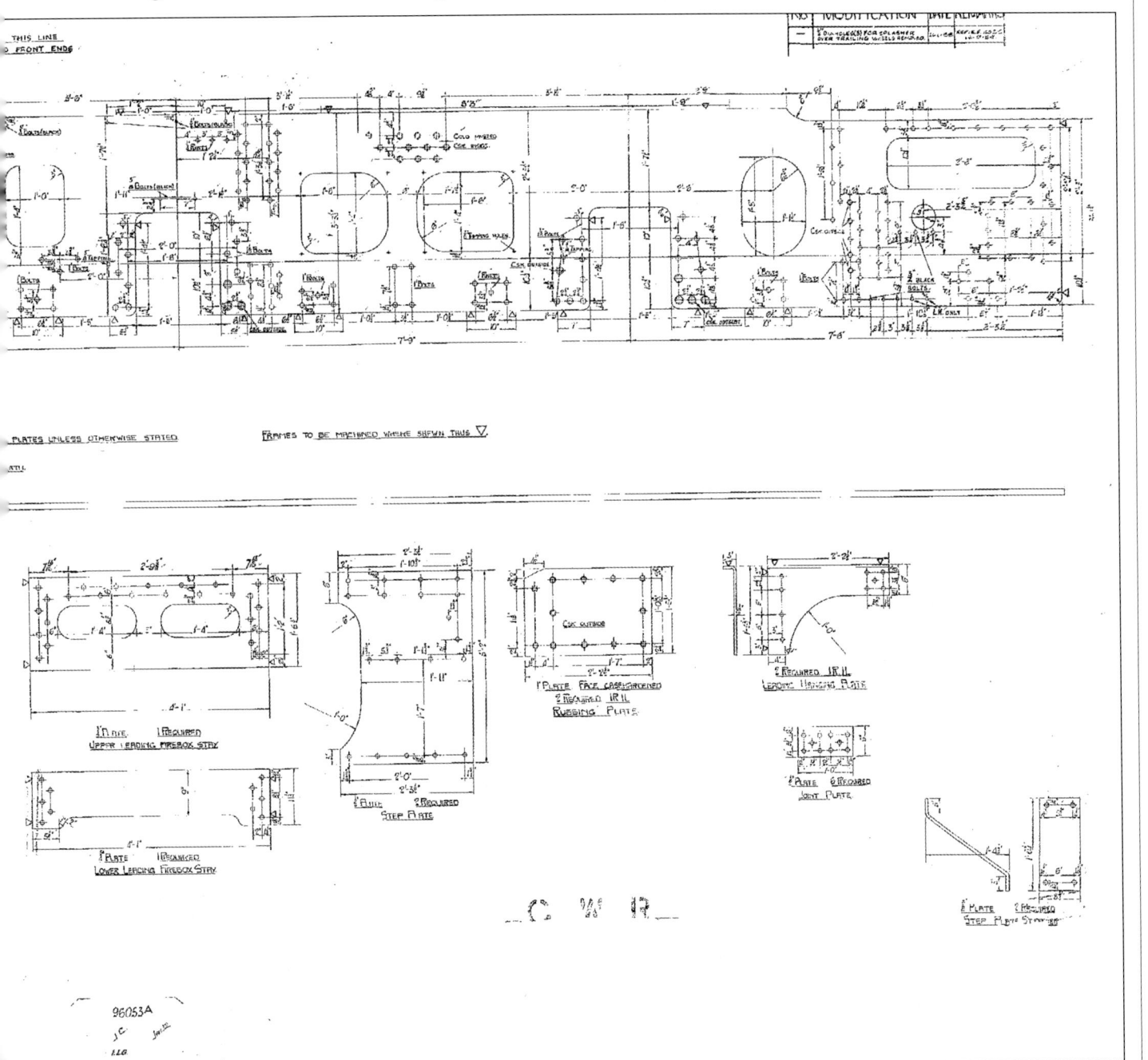

end frames and cylinders to this pattern, as indeed were some of the original twenty engines of the 4073 series. One effect of this change is that a new pattern inside cylinder was required, the width of which was increased to suit the increased 'between frames' dimension of the straight frame plates. Perhaps the most obvious sign of this change was the noticeably increased width of the inside cylinder cleating at the front end of the locomotive ahead of the smokebox.

Axleboxes and Springs

The coupled wheelsets were equipped with axleboxes of the

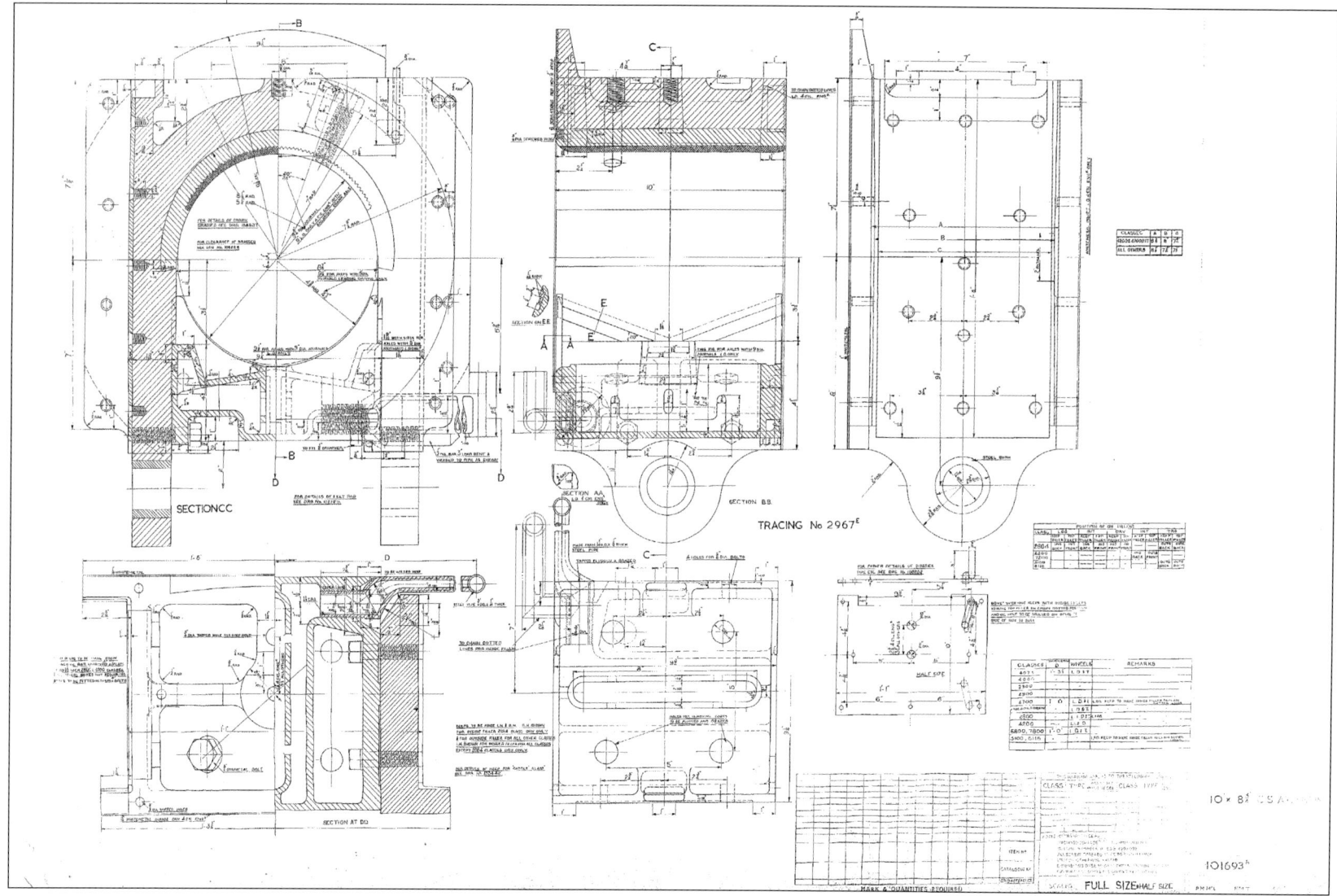

DRAWING No. 101693 CAST STEEL AXLEBOX

Churchward engines were renowned for their high level of freedom from hot axleboxes. He had earlier developed a robust design of axlebox and standardised axle journal dimensions at 8¾ inch diameter by 10 inch length. These sizes remained standard until construction of GW designed tender engines ceased in 1950. Over the years, various arrangements of the axlebox brasses, their white metal lining, together with underkeeps and associated oil pads came and went as development took place, and this drawing shows the later thoughts on bearing formation and the lubrication arrangements for it. Basically, the actual white metal lined bearing brass has become a plain bearing with no oil channels cut into it, lubrication was solely provided by the felt pad which was carried in a slot in the enclosed underkeep. Oil channels were included in the keep to recycle oil which was ejected from the bearing into the reservoir, which had the benefit of reducing the oil consumption from such axleboxes.

standard 8¾in diameter by 10in type. These boxes were of cast steel fitted with pressed in bronze bearings having white metalled bearing surfaces. They were fitted with underkeeps having large wool and horsehair lubricating pads. Oil for these boxes was fed from large four feed auxiliary oil boxes which fed the axlebox guides as well as the bearing crown. They had proven to be very successful in service during the Churchward era but developments in manufacturing during the early 1930s led to a revised design of bearing which had enclosed underkeeps containing felt pads for lubrication of the axle journal. The auxiliary crown feeds were deleted and the plain white metalled bearings depended solely on the felt pad for lubrication. Many of the original engines were subsequently fitted with the new type axleboxes but, as with other standard classes, modifications appear to have been carried out on a random basis.

Early engines of the class had the original Star class arrangement of springing which included equalising levers between the three coupled axles. Equalisation of springs was a feature of American practice designed to cope with the irregular track encountered in American railroads of the era. It may well be that Churchward felt that it was prudent to adopt this feature as anecdotes indicate that the GWR track of the early 1900s was not all that it might be. Certainly, it seems that the LNER crew engaged in the 1925 exchange trials had expressed concerns regarding hard running on some sections of the line to Plymouth. Be that as it may, conditions seem to have improved by the early 1930s, and saw the introduction of more flexible springs and the deletion of the equalising levers in the 5013 class. The equalisers were subsequently removed from the 4073 class and the new type spring gear fitted.

Bogie axleboxes also benefited from improved lubrication with enclosed underkeeps having felt pad lubrication of their journals. From engine 5033 the leading bogie axleboxes had substantial lugs cast on them for attachment of the ATC pick up suspension beams.

Boiler

The boiler underwent a number of changes over the years. As briefly mentioned earlier, the first sixty boilers were constructed with waterways which were slightly reduced from the standard width used in all of Churchward's standard boilers. Various reasons have been put forward over the years, but it seems likely that it was done for no other reason than to squeeze the nominal grate area to a figure above 30 square feet. Experience with these boilers indicated that circulation may have been inhibited and that they could become more easily choked with scale, so perhaps the 'Old Man' had been right and subsequent boilers reverted to the standard width of water way with a consequent but in reality inconsequential, decrease in grate area of just under one square foot. These first sixty boilers had 201 small tubes of 2-inch diameter and 14 superheater flues and were referred to as the HA type. The next 90 boilers with reduced grate area had 197 small tubes of 2-inch diameter and the same fourteen superheater flues, and these were also classed as the HA type. From late 1954, any of the first batch of boilers fitted with new fireboxes and tubeplates were equipped with tubeplates having 197 small tube holes. Many of these boilers were scrapped after this period following construction of new HC boilers throughout the 1950s, the last not being built until 1960.

During the period from 1946 to 1950 a further fifty-four boilers were built having an increase to 21 superheater flues and a consequent decrease to 170 2-inch tubes, these were classed as the HB type. A further development came in 1947 when an experimental boiler having 28 superheater flues and 138 small tubes was constructed and fitted to engine 5049. Extended trials of this boiler proved to be successful and so, from 1950 onwards, the final 46 boilers constructed were all of this pattern referred to as the HC type. All of these HC boilers were gradually fitted to repaired engines and were widely distributed around the class in the 1950s and 1960s as many of the class were rebuilt with double chimneys. Prior to the fitting of double chimneys, the HB and HC boilers could be quickly distinguished by the existence of the small hand hole bonnets placed just to the front of the safety valve bonnet near the top of the boiler casing.

The increase in the number of rows of superheater elements meant that the standard pattern of superheater header in the two row arrangement was not able to be employed. Consequently, the headers were changed to a similar

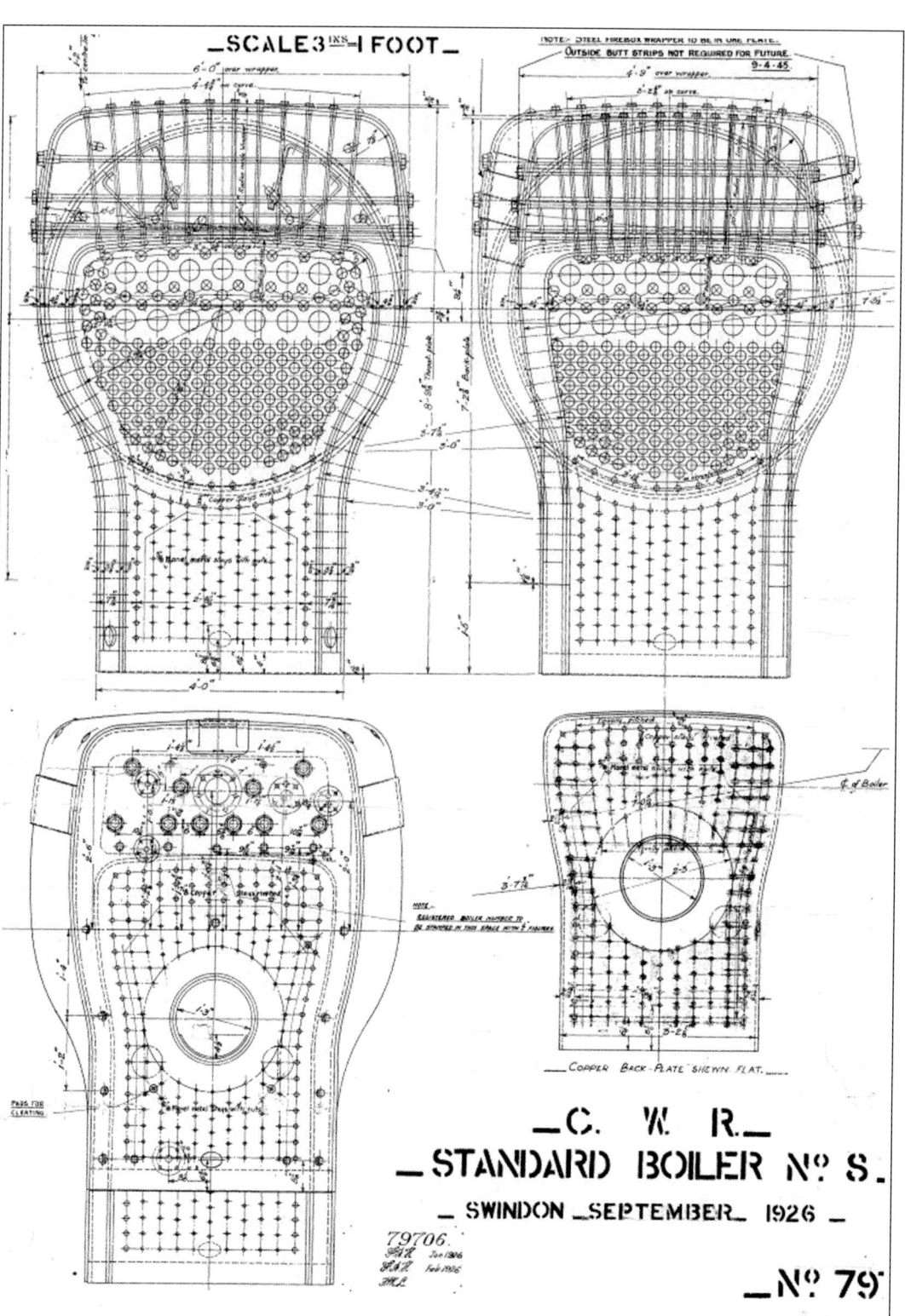

Right and opposite above: DRAWING
No. 79706 STANDARD BOILER No. 8
These drawings were made in January 1926 and show the revised version of the Number 8 boiler which had water spaces of increased width. The drawing is a very complex one which is a supreme example of the draughtsman's art with many different views of the firebox in particular. It particularly serves to demonstrate the vast number of firebox stays needed to support the loads imposed on the fireboxes by the then high pressure of 225lbs per square inch. In plan view, the No.8 boiler occupied the same footprint as the apparently bigger standard No.7 boiler, but the barrel and firebox were generally reduced in cross section to provide a boiler which was somewhat lighter than the No.7 in order to reduce engine weight to satisfy the civil engineer's weight limits. Given relaxation of those limits, it would have doubtless been possible to fit a No.7 boiler to a Castle, but such a notion was precluded by the King class in 1927.

Opposite below: ARRANGEMENT OF BOILER CLEATING
Swindon always used the word 'cleating' to describe the casing fitted not only to boilers, but cylinders and steam pipes as well. This provided the decorative casing which also had the benefit of containing the asbestos thermal insulation for the boiler. It was made from mild steel sheeting and held together by cleating bands which effectively acted as a form of belt to hold everything together. Clearances on the underside of the barrel were particularly tight and several indentations were required to provide clearance for a frame stretcher and the tops of the expansion links. This drawing dating from 1935 applies to later batches of the engines, and in particular the corners of the backplate casing panels were somewhat different in earlier engines.

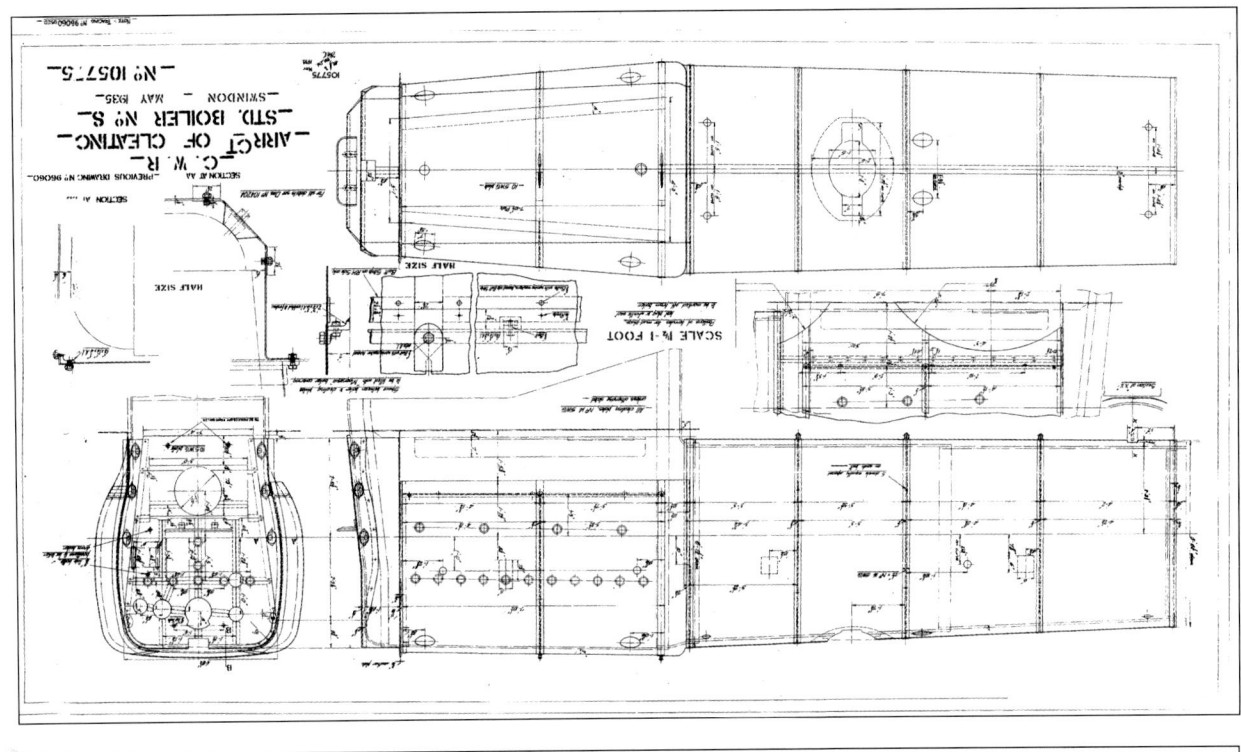
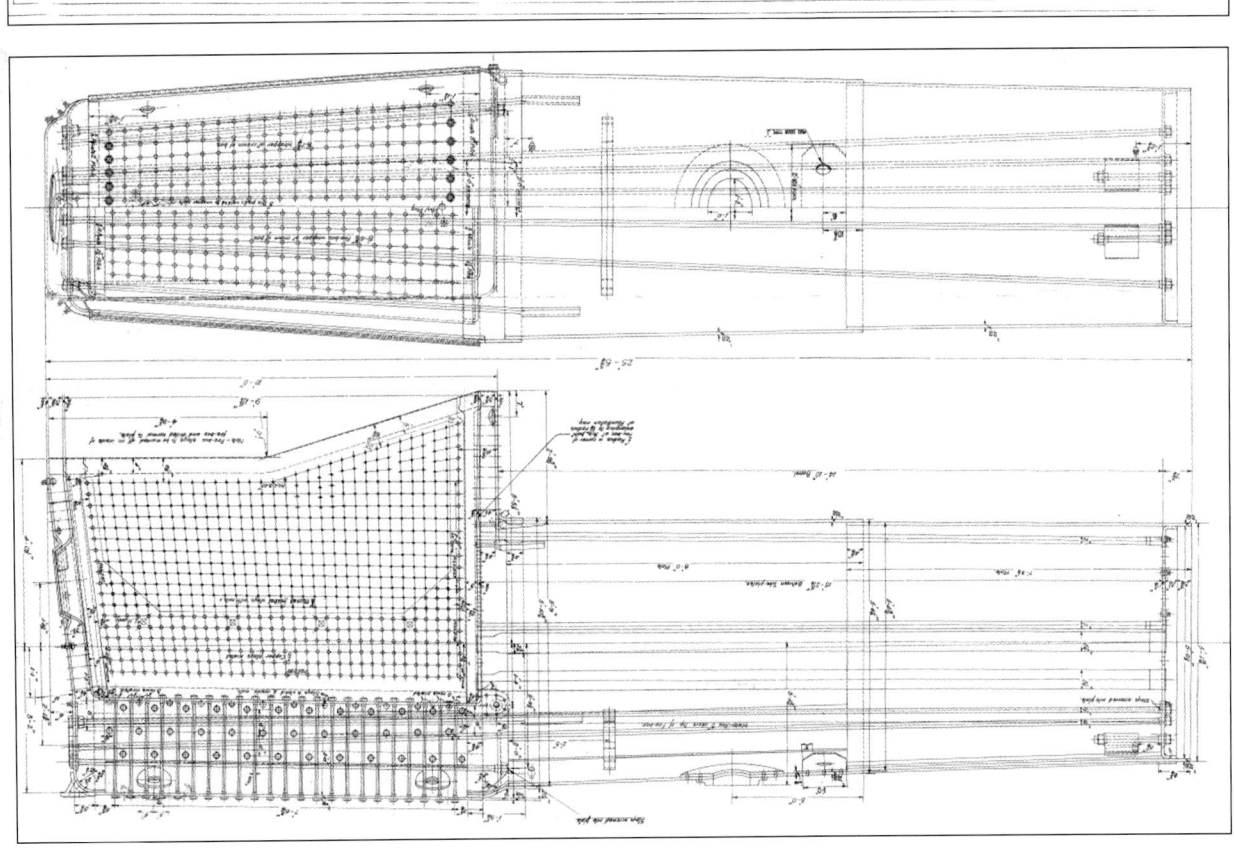

design to those used in the LMS 2-8-0s built at Swindon during the war. Despite concerns that LMS attempts at the inclusion of the regulator valves within such headers were not very successful, Hawksworth was apparently keen to retain the regulator valves within the header, and following careful consideration and design, the GWR version proved entirely satisfactory and was eventually extended to incorporate four rows of elements.

As part of this re-design the area through the regulator valves in these headers was increased to be around 50 per cent greater than the original standard regulator valve. A corresponding change was also made to increase the size of the main steam pipes within the smokebox and four were fitted to give individual feeds for each cylinder. Sadly, the diameter of the cylinder

Smokeboxes

With one exception, smokeboxes were always of the same diameter and length, but there were certain detail differences with the passage of time. Some of the differences were associated with the lubrication system, and these will be dealt with under 'Lubrication', but perhaps the inlets was never increased to take advantage of this development.

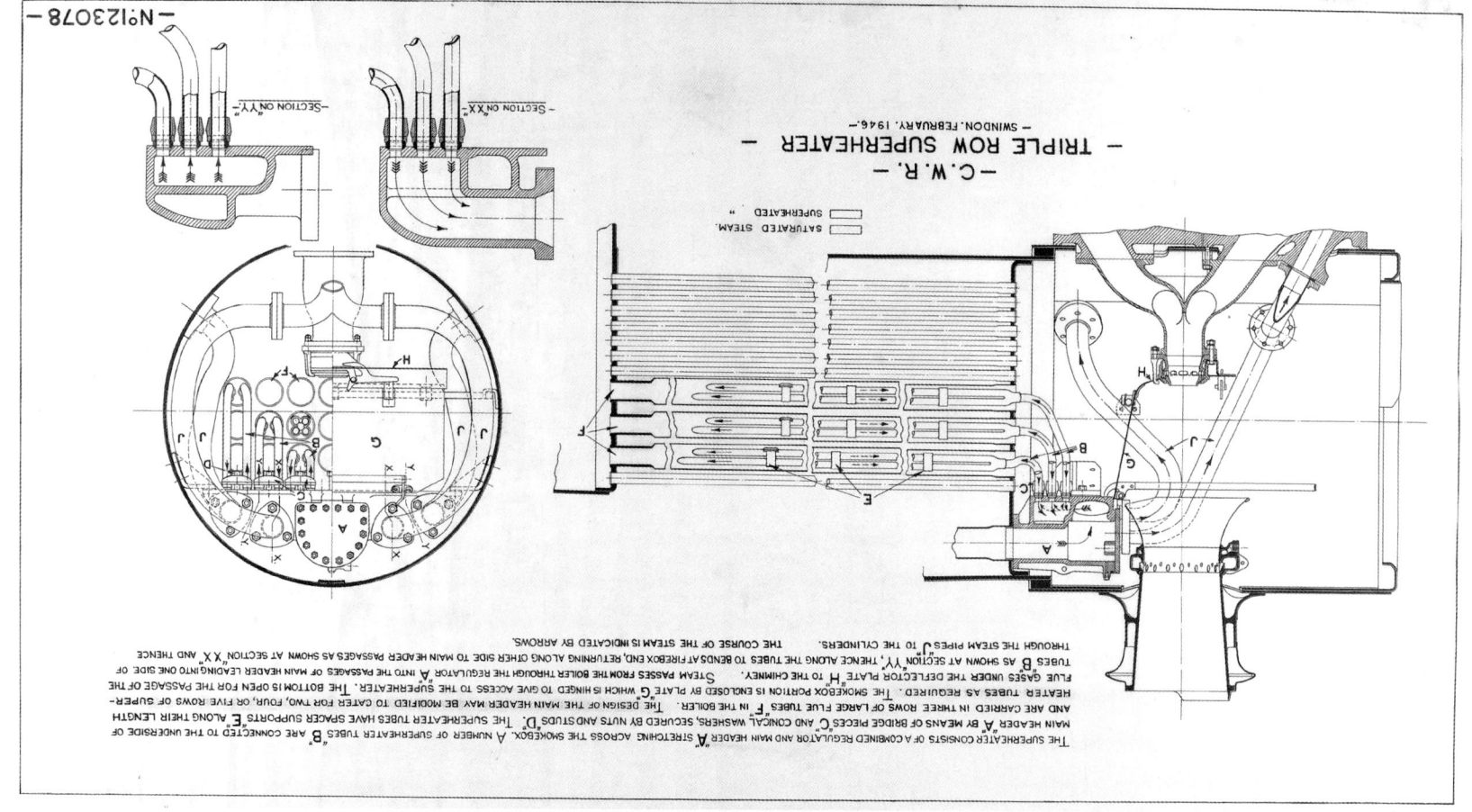

DRAWING 123078 ARRANGEMENT OF TRIPLE ROW SUPERHEATER

Beginning with engine 5098, all newly constructed Castles were fitted with the revised HB version of the No. 8 boiler, carrying a three row superheater. This drawing shows the arrangement of an HB smokebox. The standard Swindon No. 3 superheater was displaced by the use of Melesco type bifurcated elements of the type adopted by Stanier after he went to the LMS. The superheater header was of a new pattern which still incorporated the traditional header regulator valve. Hawksworth was apparently fearful that this would lead to leakage as experienced by the LMS but in the event the Swindon design succeeded in avoiding any leakage past the valves. It may be noted here that there were now four main steam pipe outlets from the header, one for each cylinder.

other most noticeable feature was the patch of rivets which appeared in later days around the centre line just behind the front of the smokebox. The existence of these rivets denoted that the smokebox was fitted with the later type of hinged door crossbar. Also, the HB and HC type boilers were fitted with removable panels in the top of the smokebox to the rear of the chimney. These were provided to enable the heavier superheater headers fitted to these boilers to be finally lifted into position with the assistance of shop cranes.

A small detail variance arose in BR days when new pattern smokebox door handles were fitted. These were furnished with knobs at the end to prevent the oily hands of staff sliding off, following a fatal accident when someone lost their grip and fell backwards off the front of an engine. Original members of the class had their top lamp bracket mounted on top of the smokebox, but from No. 5023 of 1934 the lamp bracket was mounted on the smokebox door and all earlier engines were so modified by around 1936.

Outside Main Steam Pipes

No. 4073 was the first 4-cylinder engine to feature outside main steam pipes. They closely resembled the solution applied to fitting steam pipes to the outside cylinders of the French compound engines when they were fitted with Swindon standard No.1 boilers. All engines were originally fitted with the early pattern which appeared to be straighter and more direct, but this was to prove somewhat troublesome with a number of fatigue fractures of the pipes in service, which came to a head in the 1950s. Most, if not all of the class

received modified pattern steam pipes which were noticeably more curved to improve flexibility.

Cylinders

The class was fitted with several variants of the cylinders. All members of the class were fitted with cylinders of 16 inch diameter and 26 inch stroke. The valves were 8 inch diameter of the early semi plug type with small diameter valve spindles. The initial design had the narrowed inside cylinders featured in the Star class to suit the joggled frames. The first design change was to increase the width of the inside cylinder casting to suit the straight frame plates of engines from No. 4093 onwards. With the advent of the 5013 class in 1932 further modifications to the cylinders took place, the most notable being the fitting of the revised semi plug piston valves with spindle wear sleeves of increased diameter. These ran in large bore bronze bushes inserted in the valve chest covers in order to better support the weight of the valves and increase the life of bushes and valve spindle gland packings. They also had better provision for the lubrication of the front bush of each valve which had previously been fitted with blind covers which depended on carry over of oil in the exhaust for their lubrication.

The Star class rebuilds would have been fitted with new cylinder castings of the same pattern fitted to the first twenty engines as the smokebox saddle portion of the inside cylinder casting would not have matched the greater outside radius of the No. 8 boiler's smokebox. They would also have been fitted with new outside cylinders of the larger Castle type.

Finally, during the 1950s modified inside cylinders were introduced which had additional stiffening ribs to the exhaust channels from the front exhaust ports. This also necessitated the inside cylinder casting to be fitted with a raised section in the centre to accommodate the increased height of the casting. With increasing mileage and the increased power of the engines it was found that the older members of the class tended to suffer from the outside cylinders working loose due to the racking stresses around the front end of the frames caused by alternating piston loads and a certain lack of horizontal stiffness. This resulted in steam leakage from the exhaust channel joints where they met the frame plate, producing a cloud of steam that at its worst could prevent forward vision from the cab in certain atmospheric conditions. There are numerous photos of such issues. Various measures were tried to arrest the loosening of the cylinders on the frames, including special types of locking nuts to the cylinder bolts, but eventually Swindon resorted to the method developed by the London Midland Region at Derby to deal with similar issues affecting the Princess Royal class pacifics. This basically involved welding shear strips to the frame fore and aft of the cylinders, following which fitted keys were driven into the gap between the shear strips and the cylinder to prevent fore and aft movement. This did much to alleviate the problem but was never a complete success. Standard pattern anti vacuum, or sniffing, valves were fitted to the front of each of the outside cylinders, with one only attached at the front of the common inside

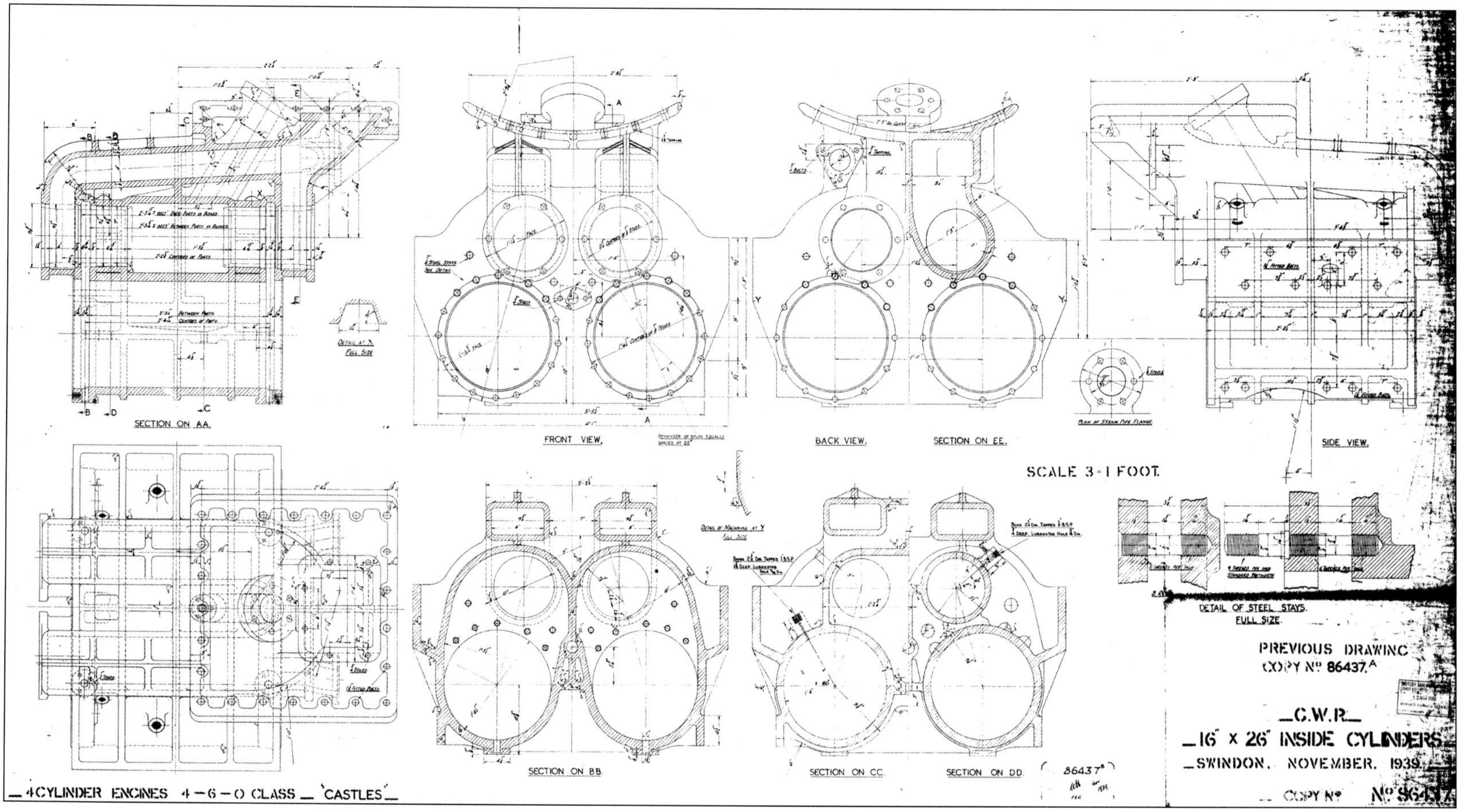

DRAWING No. 86437 INSIDE CYLINDERS

During the long history of the Castle class engines, a number of differing drawings were issued for the inside cylinders, due to a process which is often now referred to as continuous product development. This drawing was made in 1939 and shows cylinders fitted to later batches, and which would then have been used for renewals as and when earlier engines came due for new cylinders due to wear or damage. The drawing carries a number of differing sectional views which were intended to convey the complexities of the casting to the pattern makers and machine shop. It will be noted that there was only one common steam pipe connection serving the common steam chest above the two cylinders, and reference to the smokebox drawings will show that the left and right inside steam pipes were connected to it by a special branch pipe. The exhaust channels can be seen along the top of the valve chests and in later years these had strengthening ribs added which occasioned the additional raised portion of the inside cylinder cleating ahead of the smokebox.

Right: **The additional** stiffening ribs on late pattern cylinder exhaust channels which necessitated the raised portion modification to the inside cylinder cleating. (Bob Meanley)

Above: **DRAWING No. 86437 INSIDE CYLINDERS**

cylinder valve chest. These were standard throughout the life of the class. There is a common and entirely incorrect statement amongst certain commentators that the reporting number bracket fitted to 'streamlined' engine No. 5005 was a different type of snifting valve.

One minor change was that later cylinders had cylinder covers with a differing number of securing studs to the earlier pattern and from 5043 onwards the inside slidebars were attached to the rear cylinder covers, rather than being entirely supported by the centre motion plate or cradle as it was known.

Inside Cylinder Valve Chest Cleating

Varying patterns of valve chest cleating (sometimes referred to as casing) were fitted during the life of the class. The initial pattern fitted to the first twenty engines had fluted top corners. The front valve chest covers had the blind valve spindle guides associated with the early pattern of piston valve spindles projecting through. At this point there was no auxiliary oil box fitted to the cover for lubrication of the valve spindles. The rebuilt Star class engines also had this style of cleating fitted during their rebuilds.

The next twenty engines from 4093 had the wider inside cylinders due to the deletion of the frame joggle and consequently the valve chest cleating was noticeably wider although still of the same style with fluted top corners.

With the introduction of the so-called 5013 class, the inside cylinder cleating was once more modified to a more straightforward box shape. At the front the top corner was radiused and the change coincided with the introduction of modified piston valve spindles which had more prominent glands in the front covers. This led to modified cleating to the front valve chest covers having a prominent fairing over the valve spindle which extended to the front platform plates. The new gland arrangements also required an auxiliary oil box which was fitted above and between the valve chest covers.

This last pattern of casing endured thereafter to the last engine constructed, but inevitably modifications occurred over the years. The top corner radius proved to be something of a hazard to shed staff working on the front end, and to improve their footing, fabricated chequer plate angle strips were fitted over the radius to improve safety. Contrary to some commentary these were merely small additions and were not complete renewals of the cleating. Another similar additional modification often mis-stated as a complete renewal was the addition of a raised central portion to the top surface to provide additional clearance for the raised exhaust channels of the later modified inside cylinder castings. Finally, many cleatings had access panels fitted to each side to enable access to the additional valve chest oil pipe connections associated with mechanical lubrication.

Rods and Valve Motion

During development of the class, there were a number of changes made to the coupling and connecting rods, but the valve motion saw far fewer changes, and it is entirely possible to find odd pieces of valve motion stamped with the numbers 111 still in place on preserved locomotives.

Changes to the coupling rods first centred around the rod bushes which were originally pressed in and secured by set bolts. These were changed to purely pressed in brasses with the bolt holes deleted from the eye ends of the rods. Lubrication details also saw modification with trimming feeds superseded by oil regulation using felt pads inserted into the bearings. The 5013 class saw the introduction of coupling rods having somewhat larger rod eyes for increased strength.

Connecting rods went through several similar modifications. The small end bushes were lubricated by a drip feed from a crosshead mounted oil box, much in the way that those of the Dean Goods were. This was inherited from the Star class, but problems started to arise with Stars on long distance workings, whereby the oil supply became exhausted leading to seized bearings and broken rods. Consequently, a modified oil box was initially clipped to the small end of the rod, oil feed being regulated by a needle valve. From 5013, this oil box was combined with the rod forging and oil feed regulation was eventually changed to be by felt pads within the bearing.

The crossheads and their lubrication came in for modification over time. The crosshead slippers were originally bolted to the actual crosshead centre and they were lubricated by slidebar mounted oil boxes. The bottom slipper had a small oil pot incorporated into it. Later crossheads were fabricated and larger integral oil boxes were formed from fabricated steel plate. These fed the slipper bearings via integral felt pads and the slidebar oil boxes were consequently deleted.

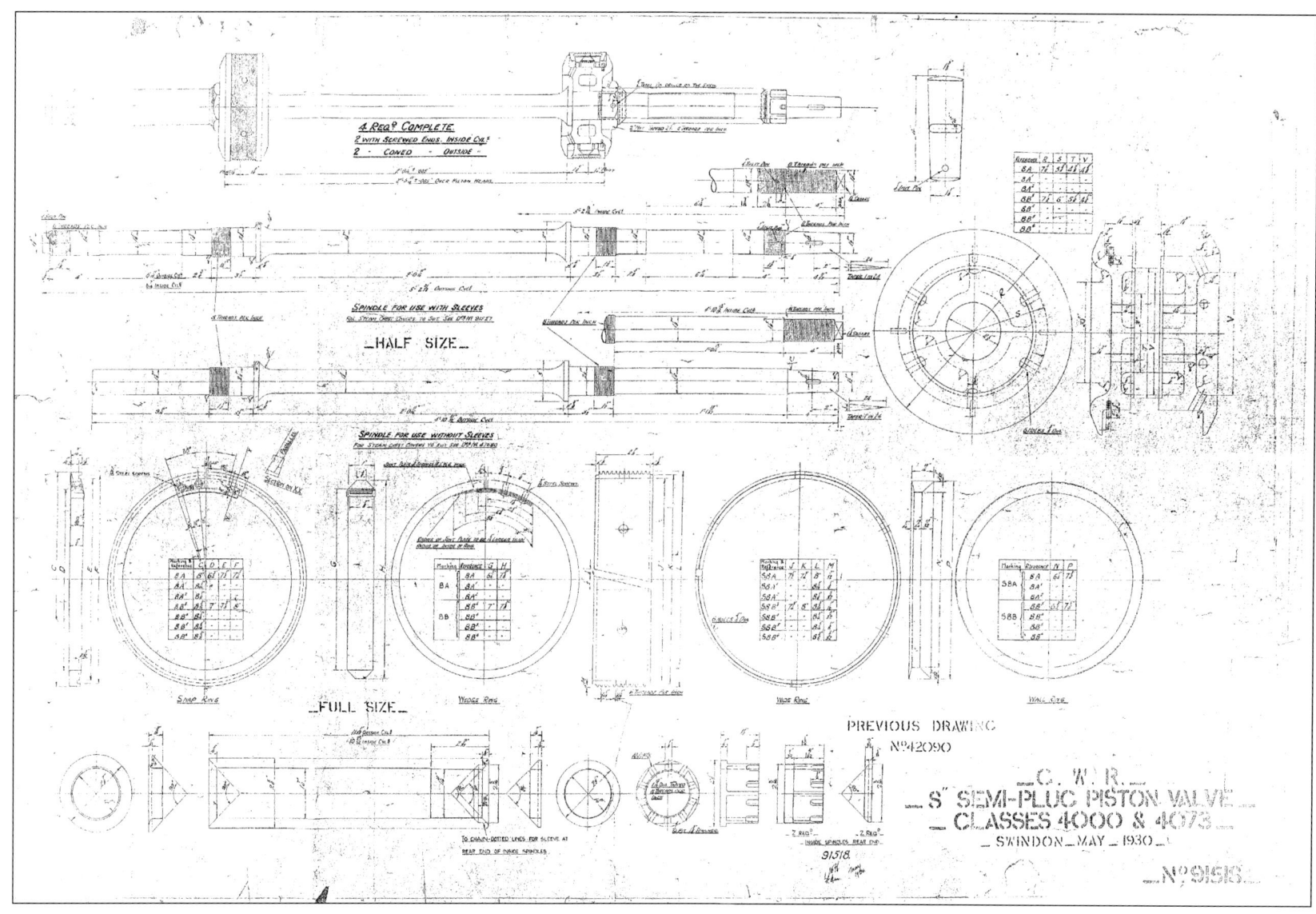

DRAWING No. 91518 8 INCH SEMI PLUG PISTON VALVES

This, sadly, slightly faint copy of drawing 91518 shows the later version of the famous semi plug piston valves developed by Churchward's team at Swindon. It conveys the complexity of these valves which required careful manufacture to enable them to function reliably. Each valve head comprised two parts locked against a shoulder on the valve spindle by a large bronze nut. Each head contained two distinct sections, two snap rings and their intervening wide ring forming the outer sealing element and then the wedge ring and wall rings which locked up the whole assembly. When steam was admitted to the valve chest, the wide ring expanded as did the wedge ring, the action of which caused the wall rings to clamp the snap rings in their expanded steam tight position hard against the valve head castings.

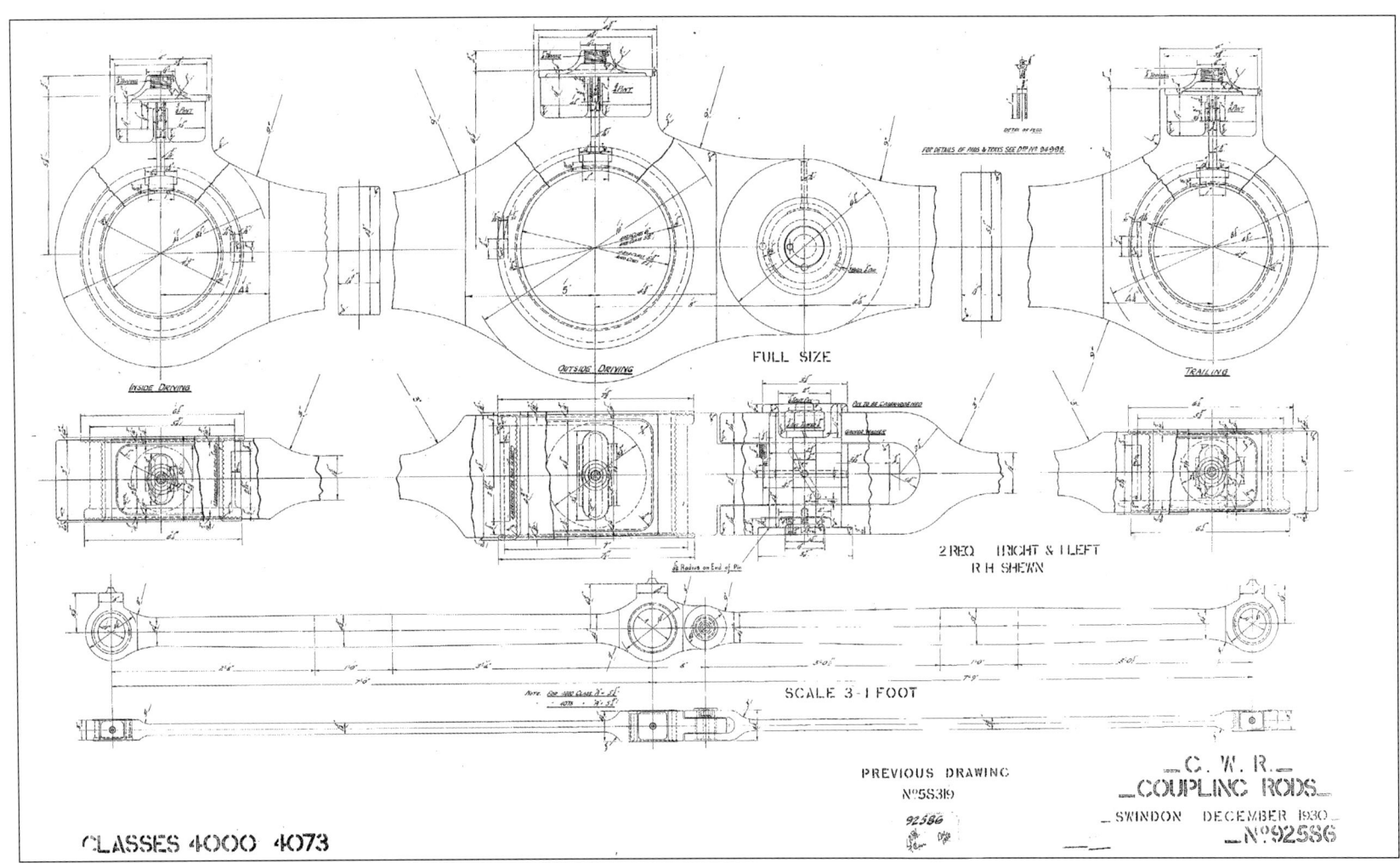

DRAWING No. 92856 COUPLING RODS
This drawing shows the later pattern of coupling rod with the knuckle joint arranged behind the outside driving crankpin rather than the position in front of that pin in earlier batches. This was a practice which has frequently been questioned but appears to be something which Churchward took from turn of the century American practice. Later rods also had somewhat enlarged rod eyes when compared with earlier lots.

Cylinder Lubricaton

During the lifetime of the class there was almost a continuous evolution of the cylinder lubrication system. When first introduced, the then standard system was employed with the old pattern three glass sight feed lubricator in the cab. This had two glasses feeding into a single supply for the cylinders and another glass feeding the regulator valve. Both pipes ran down the right hand side of the boiler to the smokebox where the cylinder feed was connected to a four way splitter box which distributed the oil to each cylinder steam pipe within the smokebox. This arrangement may be recognised by the fact that the smokebox only has an oil pipe cover on the right hand side.

By 1930, design thinking had moved on and the five glass sight feed lubricator with 10 pints capacity had come into use. This had two glasses each for left and right side, each side feeding into a single pipe onward from the combining valve. The remaining glass fed the regulator. This arrangement is recognisable by oil pipe covers being mounted on both sides of the smokebox. Whilst this was a standard arrangement throughout the 1930s, experiments were conducted with even higher capacity lubricators which had increased numbers of glasses.

During the Second World War, Swindon works became acquainted with William Stanier's standard method of mechanical cylinder lubrication, due to their construction of eighty Stanier class 8F 2-8-0s. Commencing with the 1946 construction of the 5098 batch of lot 357, the ten engines were split into five pairs, each of which had a differing system of cylinder lubrication. This was brought about due to the increase of the superheater to a 3-row variant and concerns regarding performance of the lubrication system with increased steam temperatures. Engines 5098 and 5099 had the normal standard hydrostatic system. The following four pairs introduced mechanical lubricators with varying numbers of feeds and methods of providing steam atomisation to the oil, all of which saw the fitment of the auto drifting valve developed in the 1930s and first fitted to Hall class engine No.4952. This was immediately noticeable by the large casing enclosing the valve which was fitted adjacent to the right hand side outside steam pipe. Mechanical lubricators of the 'Silvertown' pattern were fitted on the platform to the rear of the right side steam pipe. Many of the fittings including the atomisers were standard LMS fittings.

The following thirty engines built after nationalisation were all fitted with mechanical lubrication, the lubricators again being standard 14-feed Silvertown products, giving three feeds to each cylinder and valve and one feed to the regulator with the fourteenth blanked off. Three 4-feed atomisers were fitted, which were located amidst a tangle of pipes under the right front corner of the engine platform. This was not the final iteration however, because complaints were received from footplate staff that the positioning of the lubricator restricted the access for oiling parts of the inside motion and consequently a revised arrangement was designed with the lubricator mounted above the platform at the right front corner replacing the somewhat awkward nature of the original arrangement with some significant trip hazards, such are the vagaries of design! The fitting of mechanical lubrication caused the deletion of oil pipes passing into the smokebox and their associated oil pipe covers, but the advent of the HB and HD type boilers led to the steam pipe to the blower being run externally inside the boiler cleating to the smokebox and that required a somewhat larger box shaped cover being fitted to the right side of the smokebox to cover this pipe.

The final iteration was the experimental fitting of the Davies and Metcalfe 'patent valveless lubrication system'. This lubricator was of the Davies and Metcalfe 'FSA' type which was basically a licence built version of a lubricator developed by Friedmann of Austria. The arrangement was immediately notable by the 10-gallon supplementary oil reservoir which was mounted to the right hand side of the smokebox in a position which it was hoped would keep the oil warm and fluid. It was in many respects a more complicated system than the standard arrangement and doubtless whatever benefits may have accrued, it was overtaken by the modernisation plans of 1955 and subsequent dieselisation. In the event only five engines were fitted with the system, Nos. 4087, 4088, 5084, 7013 and 7014.

The Design • 45

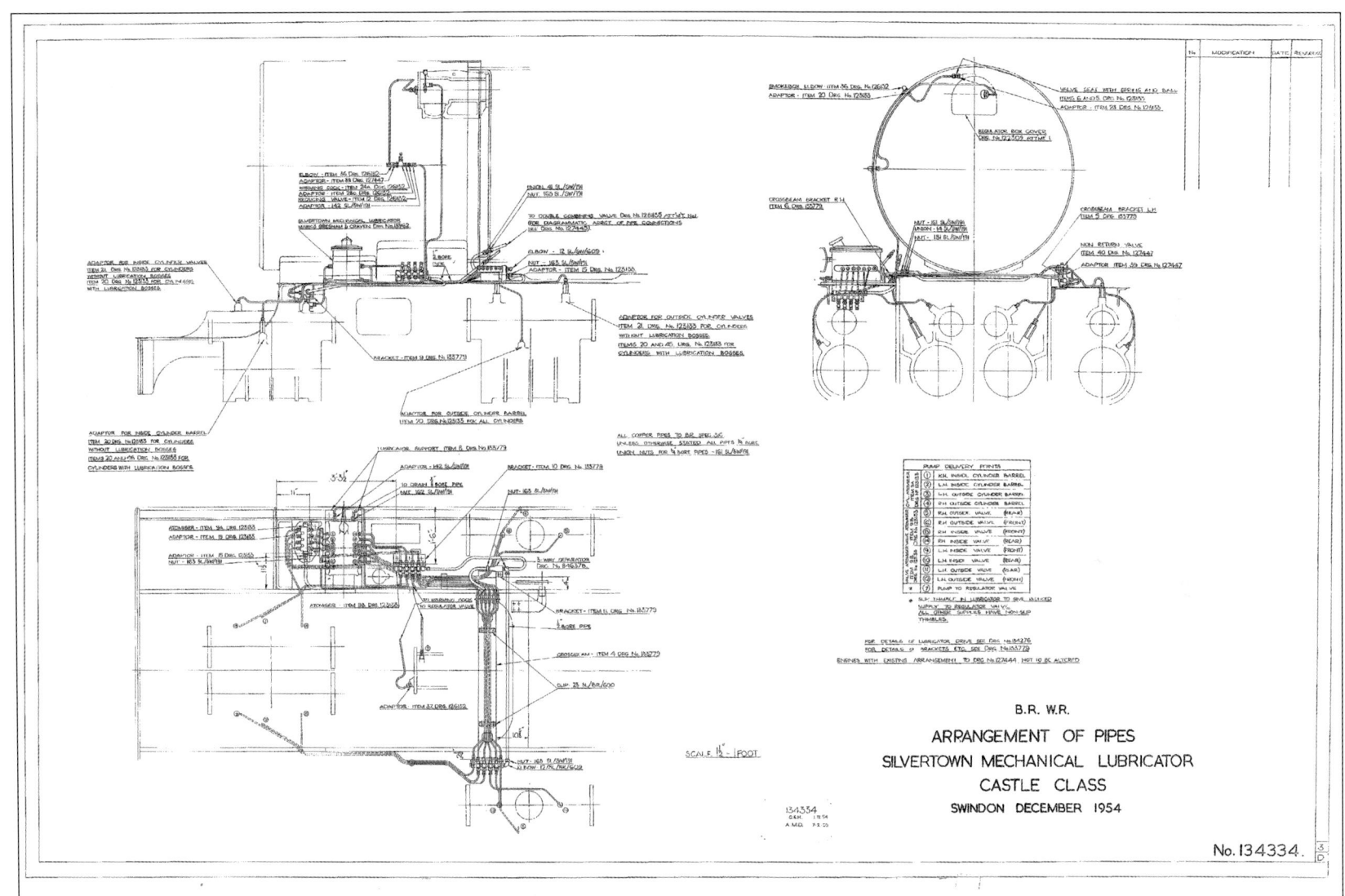

ARRANGEMENT OF SILVERTOWN MECHANICAL LUBRICATOR

The first arrangement of mechanical lubrication had the lubricator itself mounted in a somewhat inconvenient position behind the main steam pipe. In an attempt to improve access, a revised arrangement was introduced which placed the lubricator on the front corner of the left side platform and the pipe runs were amended accordingly, as shown by this drawing. A 14-feed lubricator was employed, providing 12 feeds to the four cylinders and one feed to the regulator, leaving one pump spare and unused. Each cylinder had a feed to each valve head and one feed to the actual cylinder barrel. All 12 cylinder feeds were provided with steam atomisation.

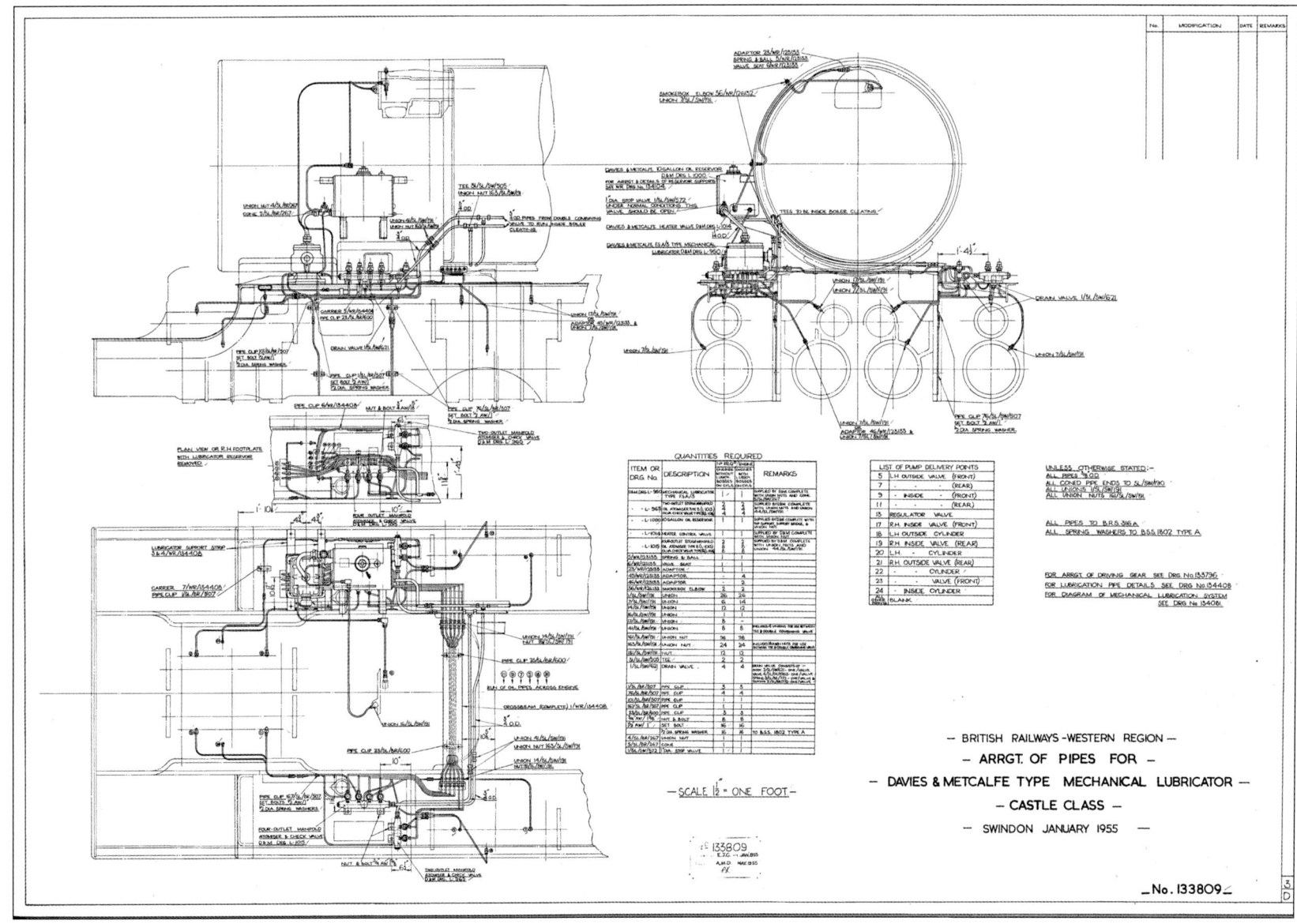

ARRANGEMENT OF DAVIES AND METCALFE PATENT LUBRICATOR

During the 1950s, the well-known firm of locomotive equipment suppliers, Davies and Metcalfe, took up the manufacture of a lubricating system which was based on equipment originally manufactured by the Austrian company of Friedmann. It was somewhat more complex in its fittings than the Silvertown version and its fitment probably resulted from commercial pressures at the BTC. The stand-out feature of the system was undoubtedly the huge 10 gallon reservoir which was mounted to the right hand side of the five engines selected for fitment.

Brake Gear

All Castles were fitted with the standard GWR vacuum brake system. However, it was inevitable that some changes were to come about. To start with, the brake ejector was the original 4-cone ejector in which all four cones worked together. This is plainly visible on early members of the class by the somewhat simpler arrangement of pipework to the ejector in front of the cab. Around 1930, the 'improved four cone ejector' was designed and put into production. This used the original steam valve portion of the brake valve to supply steam to just three of the cones in the ejector, with a separate small 'Lambert' Valve supplying steam from the top of the brake valve to the fourth ejector cone. Henceforth these valves became known as the large and small ejectors respectively. Soon after the introduction of the improved ejector, the vacuum pipe connections to it were rearranged to have the small ejector train pipe connection redirected to a point on the train pipe close to the vacuum retaining valve.

A small variation to the system was the change from the original tall brake standpipe at the front buffer beam which was soon altered to the lower, and henceforth, characteristic arrangement for stowage of the hose to the buffer beam.

As previously mentioned, brake gear was fitted to the bogies of the first ten engines but was removed during the mid-1920s.

One minor notable feature of the brake gear in early years were the small spring loaded setting bolts fitted to the engine brake blocks in order to support them so that they did not hang down under their own weight and drag on the tyres. This was later considered to be unnecessary, and they were removed. Many brake hangers on preserved engines still retain the holes for their fitment.

Sanding Gear

A feature of the Star class was that they only had sanding gear pipes to the front of the inside and outside driving coupled wheels and no facility for adequate sanding when in reverse. This was in all probability due to a perceived lack of space to include sandboxes on the Stars. This arrangement was replicated in the first forty Castles. It was perhaps recognised that the additional one foot of frame length at the rear of the Castles permitted the inclusion of trailing sandboxes and engines from 5013 had sandboxes underneath the cab floor, hidden by the cab sides, and filled from pipes projecting through the cab floor. It is apparent that many of the first forty were modified to have the type of trailing sandbox fitted to the 5013 class by the mid-1930s.

From engine No.5057, a further type of trailing sandbox came to be fitted which was mounted in a lower position, thus shortening the sand pipes and allowing the filler lid to be positioned in a location which enabled easy access from ground level, something which would have saved preparation crews the considerable amount of energy previously expended in lugging sand up on to the footplate. Many of the earlier engines were modified during the 1950s to have the final arrangement of sandbox, probably at the same time as the later type of cab floor was installed.

Buffers

From the first engine, the Castles were fitted with the newly developed GW2 or 'Dew' pattern buffers of continuous tapered shape. These buffers had stamped steel cases enclosing volute springs and worked in much the same way as the earlier cast iron GW1 or 'Matthews' patent buffers. The 'Dew' buffers were credited as being to the suggestion of Walter Dew, the Chief Erecting shop foreman. Dew buffers were fitted as standard to all Castles as built. During the 1950s, Castles began to appear from Swindon fitted with the more substantial GW3 or 'Turton' pattern of buffer and by the mid-1960s the Dew buffers had disappeared from use save for a set of specially polished examples which appear to have been retained by Old Oak Common depot for Royal Train duties. The exchange of buffers was an easy matter as all buffers had the same base size and bolt centres. Despite that, they were common up to the early 1960s, but only one pair of original Dew buffers survives fitted to the front of the preserved 4073.

Cabs

Whilst at first glance Castle cabs looked to be all the same, there were inevitably variations. The cabs were the first to be fitted with side windows and had a high cab roof featuring the same compound curves of the cab roof profile applied to the 4700 class. That class of engine had originally been fitted with the standard wooden cab roof boards of the Churchward era. When their roofs were eventually extended to provide somewhat better cover for the enginemen, the roof itself was changed to steel plate. Anecdotally, that led to a tendency for the weight of the roof to bear down and spread the top of the cab sides, and the design of the Castle cab seems to indicate that the continuous cab hand rail from platform to roof was an attempt to provide a strut to support the weight of the Castles' extended steel roof. That this was not exactly successful is borne out by further modifications to cab stiffeners over the years, but even then, the tendency for vibration was not cured and one Tyseley engineman is on record as having seen the cab roof stiffener on 7013 (ex-4082) broken through due to the vibration. One feature of the roof fitted to the first engine No.4073 were diagonal rain strips fitted at the rear corners of the roof. This was not repeated on any other engine and they were soon removed.

Front windows in the weatherboard changed too. The first twenty engines had small top windows often referred to as 'portholes' which disappeared by the late Twenties. The insides must have been almost impossible to keep clean and they must also have suffered a fairly high rate of breakage from brick particles and large pieces of rust dislodged from bridges and tunnels. The main weatherboard side windows used the standard two piece cast brass frames up to engine 5067 of Lot 303. Thereafter, a somewhat narrower version formed from 3 castings was standardised. In later years, most of these windows

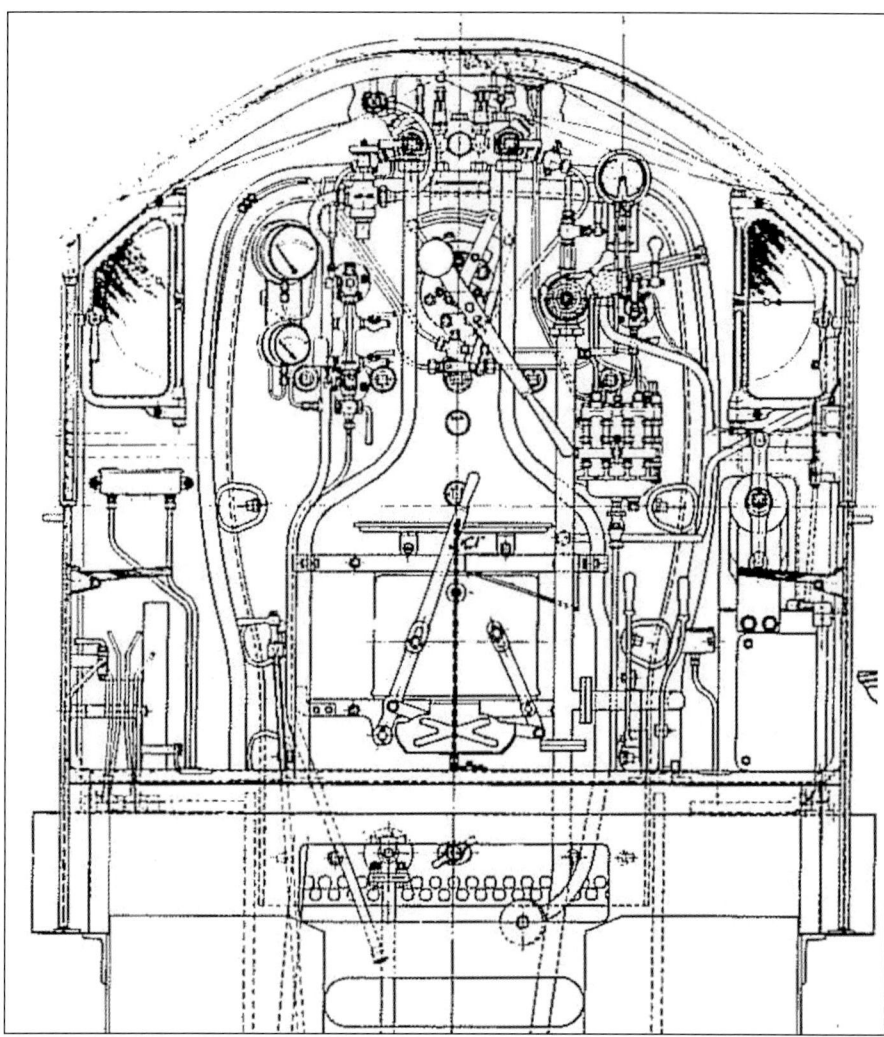

Above and opposite: **ARRANGEMENT OF BOILER MOUNTINGS**
This drawing was intended to show the disposition of the boiler mountings (often called fittings in enthusiast circles) located on the firebox backplate. It applies to the 5013 class engines as built. It is quite different to the arrangement of the 4073 class engines and would change again with time and the production of improved boiler mountings. It clearly shows all of the various components with the reverser in the right hand corner and the regulator handle mounted high in the centre of the firebox backplate. To the right of the regulator is the brake valve which incorporates not only the application disc but also the steam valves controlling the four cone ejector mounted on the side of the firebox outside the cab. The blower steam valve is mounted just to the right of the brake valve and below them is the then new 10 pint, 5 feed version of the standard GWR sight feed cylinder lubricator. Just under the cab roof is the steam fountain with valves controlling steam feed to the injectors, whistles, steam heating apparatus, and sight feed lubricator. To the left of the regulator is the single water gauge column, and to the left of that are the pressure gauges for boiler pressure and steam heat. Up in the front left corner at floor level are the handles for controlling the ashpan damper gear openings. The firedoors are at the centre above the cab floor, and to the right of that are the levers for cylinder drain cocks and sanding gear.

were fitted with hand operated windscreen wipers. It has to be borne in mind that not all motor cars were so fitted at that time!

The cab side windows were accompanied by short handrails to aid passage around the side and on to the main platform. Originally these were straight and horizontally mounted just below the side windows but from engine No.5098 they became 'L' shaped with a vertical portion in front of the side window.

Originally cab floors were supported on a timber frame resting on the platform plates which ran through the cab. Commencing with 5013, a steel framed cab floor was introduced which gave far better support and was probably more economical in its resistance to the inevitable wear and tear. A noticeable amount of chequer plating surrounded the cab sides and firebox backplate cleating, and it provided a more substantial anchorage for the intermediate fall plate. This style of floor eventually became fitted to all engines of the class.

The increasing size of fireboxes lead to a general increase in the length of fire irons particularly the heavy chisel bars used for regular lifting of the fire. This came to present a significant safety risk to enginemen, and a small number of very nasty accidents occurred whilst bars were being manoeuvred from the tender fire iron rack to the firebox and return. The provision of a suitable rack alongside the firebox was suggested and the initial experimental fitment was to engine No.4085. It was a rather ugly contrivance, being very angular and at a height which may well have been inconvenient. Consequently, a much better arrangement was fitted to engines from No.5013 onward.

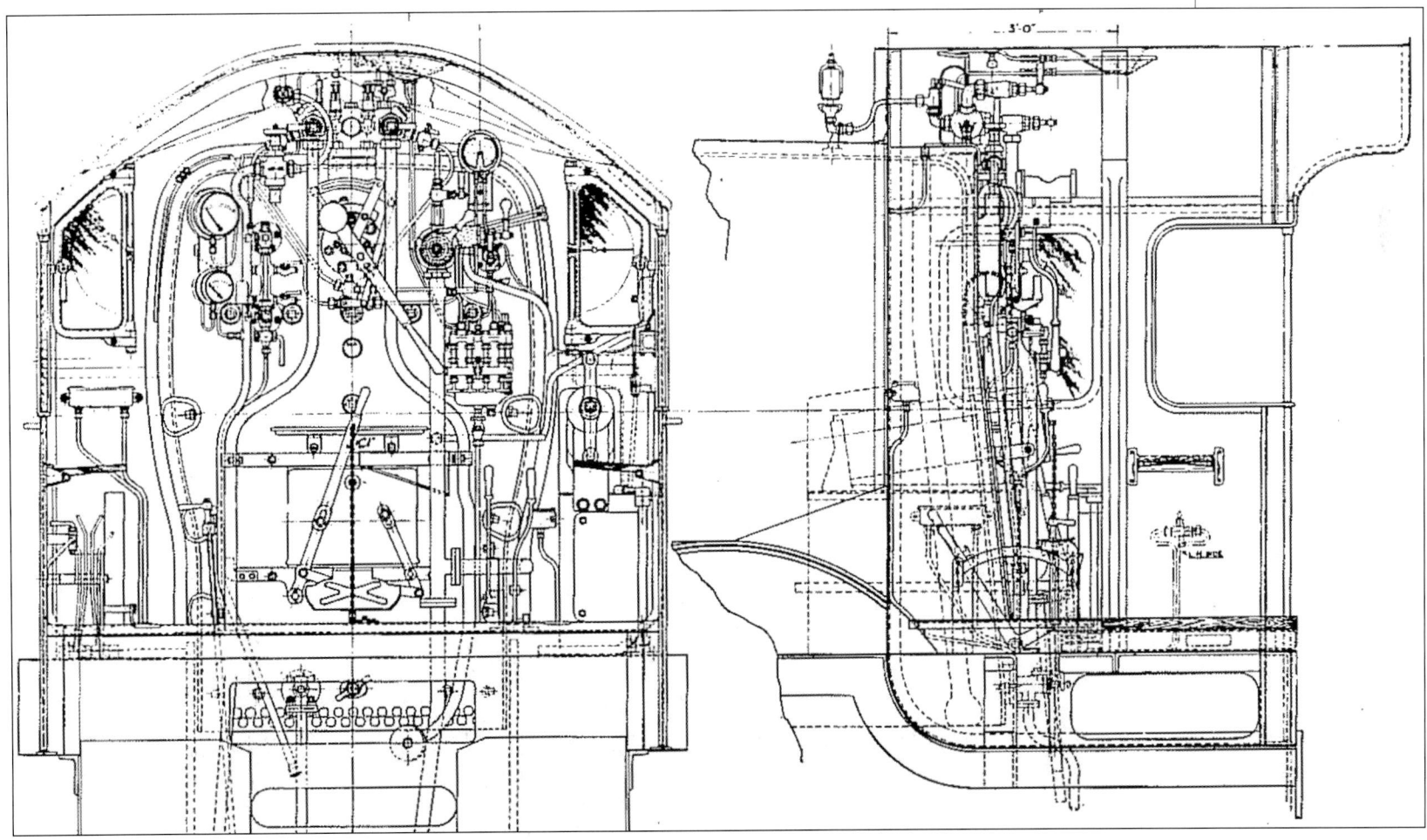

During the 1950s, the absence of these racks on the first forty engines was addressed and as part of their fitting, the entire construction of the cab weatherboard was changed, resulting in the weatherboard being flush with the front of the cab side, leaving no location for the traditional brass beading which was consequently deleted from the cabs of these engines. This feature can be clearly seen on the modified cabs of the preserved Nos. 4073 and 4079.

Inside the cab there were numerous changes to the firebox backplate and its associated boiler mountings. To start, the backplate cleating on early engines differed in detail to late ones particularly the firebox corners which became more angular and less rounded during the 1930s. The boiler mountings too were subject to considerable development with different and more robust injector and steam heat cocks, improved sight feed lubricators and additional pipework.

Speedometers made their appearance in 1933 with experimental fitments to Nos.5003 and 5008. They became standard features from engine No.5033 and were eventually fitted to all of the class. The equipment chosen was manufactured by the British Thomson Houston Company (BTH) and consisted of an alternating current (AC) generator driven by the right trailing coupled crankpin, powering a voltmeter to indicate speed irrespective of direction of running. There were shortages of equipment and spares during the Second World War but by the late

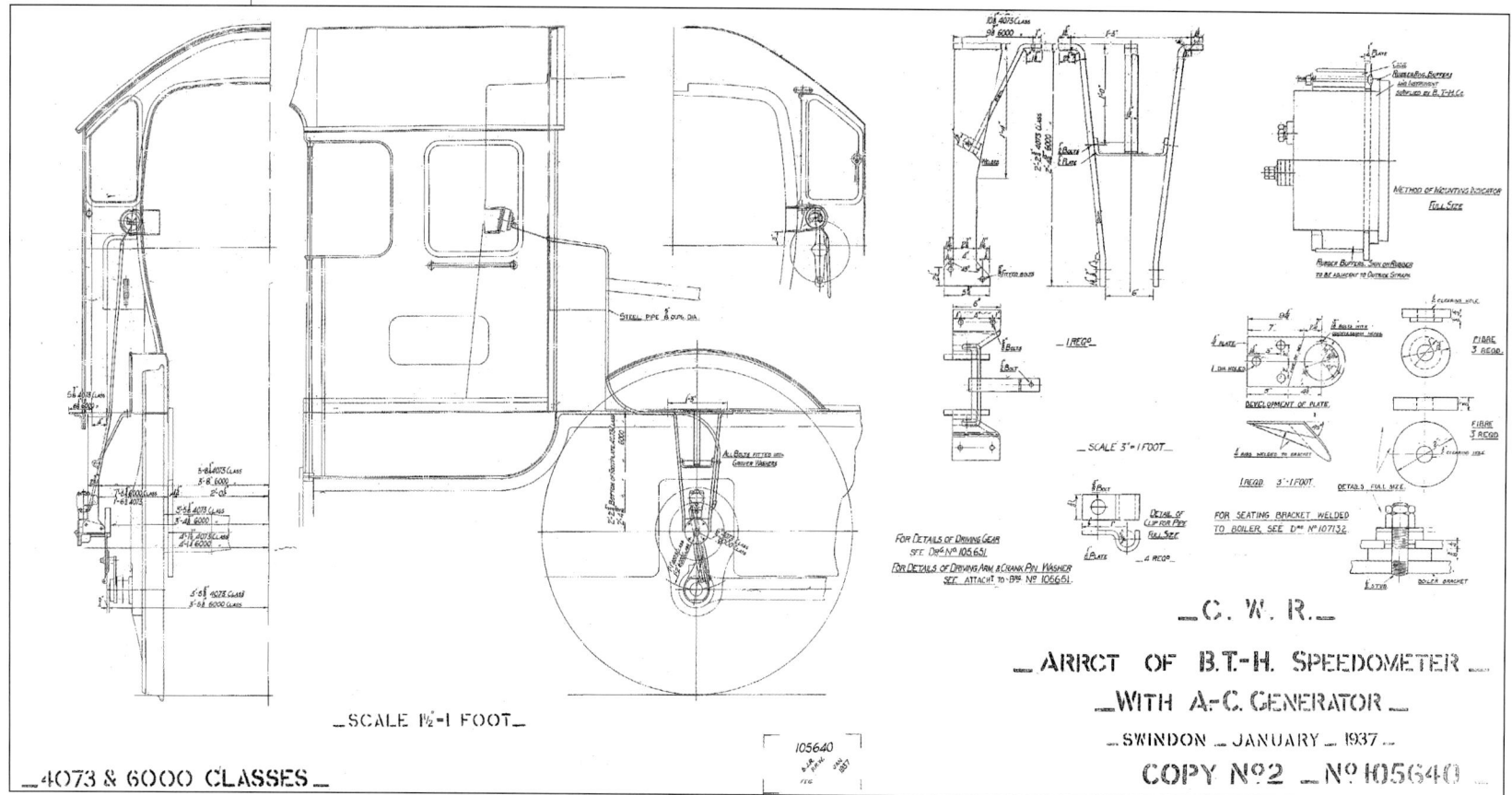

DRAWING No. 105640 ARRANGEMENT OF BTH SPEEDOMETER
Following trials, engines of the Castle and King classes were fitted with speedometers manufactured by the British Thomson Houston company. This equipment consisted of a crankpin driven gearbox which in turn drove a generator providing AC current. That was connected to a speedometer in the cab which was actually an AC voltmeter calibrated in miles per hour divisions. In service they proved durable and remarkably accurate, giving quite stable indications. A number of examples can still be seen in operation on preserved locomotives, where their reliability and freedom from need of batteries is appreciated.

1940s the situation was regularised, and the class ran to withdrawal fully equipped.

Another safety feature fitted to the class was the GWR standard Automatic Train Control system (ATC). Engine Nos.4084 to 4095 and 5003 onwards were fitted with this equipment from new in 1927, with all earlier engines so fitted soon after. Engines up to No.5022 had the ATC receiver mounted beneath the cab, but from 5023 onwards, the location of the receiver was moved to being suspended beneath the leading bogie axle, a position confirmed by the electrical conduit for this being run along the bottom of the right hand hanging bar before turning up into the cab, where the battery box was located under the reverser stand and the ATC bell unit was located in its familiar position inside of the right side cab window.

Whistles and Baffle

The two standard whistles were mounted in front of the cab on a bracket fixed to the firebox top. Drainage of condensate from them provided a constant source of corrosion for cleating and firebox alike. The issue of steam drifting from whistles somehow became a concern during the mid-1920s when Nos.4082 and 4085 were fitted with whistle baffles in an attempt to deflect drifting steam. The first new engine to be fitted was No.5000 in September 1926 and all engines in the class were so fitted by 1936.

Safety Valve Bonnets

The introduction of the Castles saw a new pattern of the traditional brass safety valve bonnet which at 14 inches high was some 4 inches shorter than the previous 'tall' type. The shape and size of the steel fairings covering the top feed clack boxes remained standard to both types. There were isolated examples of the tall bonnets being carried by Castles from time to time, engines 4009, 4088, 5029 and 5097 being so noted.

Chimneys

The original pattern of chimney fitted to the Castles was similar in appearance to those fitted to later examples of the Star class, and stood 1ft 10ins above the smokebox. No.5044 was built new in 1936 with a new pattern of chimney 2 inches shorter. This new type was finally fitted as standard to new engines from No.5058 and beginning with No.5024, they were gradually fitted to older engines of the class, although it was almost in the last years of the class before the final remaining examples disappeared.

Whilst the later pattern of chimney was clearly recognisable, there was no mistaking the next change when No.7018 was fitted with an experimental double chimney and blast pipe during 1956. At the time, this engine was considered something of a black sheep amongst the class, but following conversion, its performance was transformed even though it was only fitted with a three row superheater HB boiler. At the time of conversion, it was also fitted with a self-cleaning smokebox arrangement, similar in detail to those fitted to the King class. The decision to fit the self-cleaning gear seems to have been taken a short time before the decision was made to remove the similar gear from the Kings and consequently 7018 was the only Castle to carry the equipment until the preservation era. The second engine to be given a double chimney was 4090 and it also received a smokebox which was 4 inches longer than standard. The manufacture of this longer smokebox appears to have overlapped the decision to remove the self-cleaning gear from the Kings. The reasons for this modification have never been discovered, but the author's experience with the fitting of the self-cleaning gear to engine 5043 in the preservation era pretty clearly indicates that it was likely to have been to provide more space in front of the mesh screens to enable effective circulation of the particles of smokebox char to enable them to be broken down before ejection. The experience of the self-cleaning arrangement in the preservation era indicates that it was totally effective, and had no discernible effect on the steaming capacity of the engines fitted (5043 and 7029), but extra space in front of the screens might well be useful.

In total, sixty-six engines were eventually fitted with the double chimney and blast pipe over a relatively short period at the end of the 1950s and early 1960s. Given a propensity for throwing fire at high outputs the engines were all fitted with a basket type arrestor, which had the ability to hold back large quantities of char and did little to break it up into smaller particles unlike the self cleaner type. The size of blastpipe orifice in the double chimney engines remained constant throughout.

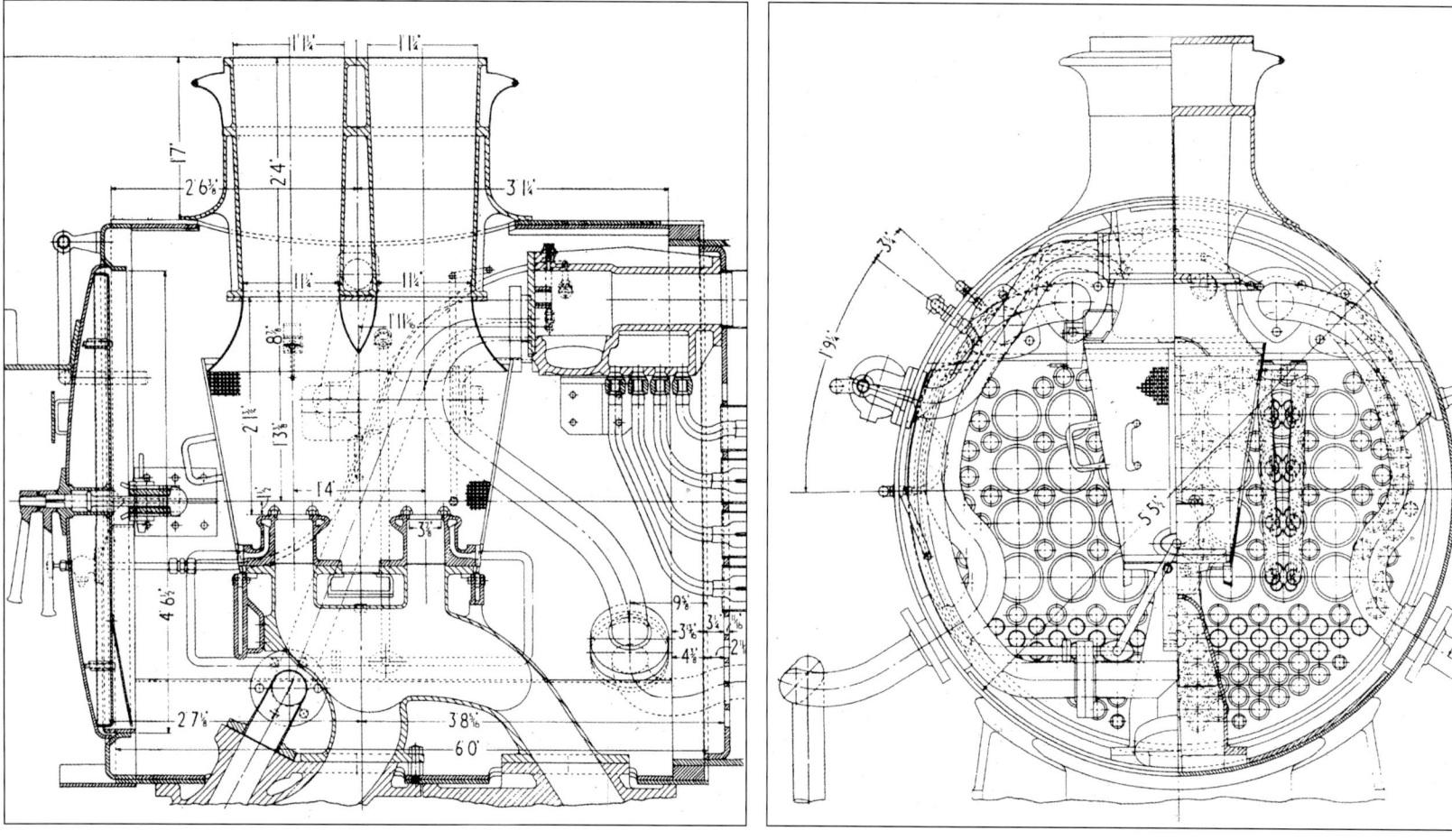

ARRANGEMENT OF FOUR ROW SUPERHEATER AND SPARK ARRESTOR
During 1956, No. 7018, a three row engine with an HC boiler and a poor reputation, was fitted with a double chimney in order to improve steaming performance. This was the only Castle fitted with a self-cleaning spark screen arrangement. With one exception, further double chimney fitment was undertaken to engines with the four row HC boiler, all of which were fitted with basket type spark arrestors, and this elevation and cross section show how this was accomplished. The enlarged superheater header necessitated the siting of the double chimney to be somewhat ahead of the position occupied by single chimneys and this can be clearly seen on the sectional elevation.

Given the deterioration of available coal supplies during the 1950s, efforts were made to improve the steaming of single chimney engines and rather like the Improved Draughting (ID) modifications carried out on many 2-cylinder 4-6-0s, the Castles began to be equipped with solid blast pipe caps rather than the standard Jumper Top type of blastpipe nozzle. This modification enabled the engines so fitted to cope with lower quality fuel supplies, during the final 1960s run down.

Oil Burning

The story of how the GWR engaged with oil burning has been stated on many occasions, but it may be worth just stating the basic facts that it was done at the exhortation of the post-war government in an attempt to free up coal supplies for export. When the project was well under way it had to be halted as the government did not possess the foreign exchange to acquire the necessary oil. Otherwise, the project proved to be technically very successful.

The conversion process was actually quite straightforward, involving a new but interchangeable ashpan known as a firepan. Fireboxes were lined with firebrick up to a certain height to prevent direct flame impingement on the copper plates. The ribbon type burner was situated at the front of the firebox and the flame directed to the back where it was deflected by firebrick to pass between the firebrick arch and the crown of the inner firebox. The burner worked by permitting a variable ribbon of oil fuel to run out of the burner orifice where it was caught and atomised by a steam jet. Much of the system and equipment, including the burner and regulating valve, appear to have been identical to the system fitted to oil fired WD/LMS 8F 2-8-0s during the recent war. The fuel itself was heavy fuel oil which needed steam heating to the tank fitted in the tender, in order to make it sufficiently fluid to flow to the burner under gravity. Control of the fuel flow and burner atomising steam was under the control of the fireman. Because of the direction of combustion, the normal firehole doors were removed and the hole was sealed by a closure plate. The cabs required some modification as during winter they were found to be surprisingly cold and in order to cut down draughts, sliding shutters were fitted to the cab side cut outs, and draught screens were fitted to the rear of the cab side sheets much as those later fitted to the cabs of BR standard classes. Some engines were also fitted with cab radiators. Confusingly, sliding cab roof ventilators were also fitted to certain engines.

Castle class engines fitted were 100A1 1/47 to 9/48; 5039 12/46 to 9/48; 5079 1/47 to 10/48; 5083 12/46 to 11/48 and 5091 10/46 to 11/48. Most engines were coupled to 4,000 gallon tenders but 5091 ran with a Churchward 3,500 gallons type for around four months when first converted in 1946. With the system in order manned by competent enginemen, the locomotives apparently were able to steam faultlessly. However, it does remain to see what the long-term effects on firebox life cycles would have been.

Tenders

Mention has previously been made of the differing types of tender fitted to the Castles during their time in traffic. The subject of standard Great Western tenders is so complex that it seems unlikely that a definitive history is ever likely to be assembled. It seems apparent that tender numbers usually stayed with the frames during heavy repairs when tanks were often removed and then refitted to different tenders. They were very much viewed as little more than six wheeled coal trucks! So it is possible to find in later years early tanks on late frames and vice versa. Nevertheless, they can be divided into some form of definite grouping.

The 4073 class were initially paired with standard 3,500 gallons tender, the 'Churchward' tender beloved of modellers, but officially designated as 'Tender 3,500 gallons capacity with well bottom'. The first ten engines appear to have been fitted with new tenders of the type but the second lot of ten engines were coupled to second hand, repaired tenders, some of which were built before the First World War. The use of these tenders continued for some time, and it was the 1930s before any regularity appeared. The tenders were in essence a complete mixture caused by constant ongoing development over the period of manufacture which ran for almost twenty-five years. In essence they were a development of Dean's standard tenders which could be found behind his famous single driver engines, and the wheels, axles and axleboxes remained standard up to the last GWR tender built at Swindon. Frame plates differed between batches as they were continually strengthened, spring gear varied as did brake gear, with drop forged brake hangers replacing the old twin hanger pattern. The tanks too came in for modification with revised arrangements of tank fillers, air vents and pick up domes, and after tender 2058 the use of flush riveting was superseded by snap head rivets giving a somewhat different external appearance.

The last 3,500 gallons tenders constructed were a small batch of ten tenders which appeared during late 1925, Lot No. A112, Nos. 2374 to 2383. These had deeper sides and longer side fenders and became referred to as the 'Intermediate' type. They are often confused by inexperienced commentators with the later 3,500 gallons flush bottom type tenders. They had a somewhat greater coal capacity than standard and a number were coupled to Castles during the late 1920s, including 100, 4016, 4032, 4037, 4074, 4084, 4085, 4088, and 4092.

Interestingly, a number of 4,000 gallon tenders built during the early Churchward period, but classified as Dean tenders, were also coupled to a number of the first forty Castles. Only ten were built and in their original state they were not easy to differentiate from the standard 3,500 gallons version.

Several were rebuilt with Collett era style continuous fenders, and again were easily confused with the flush bottom 3,500 gallons tenders of the late 1920s but the clue to their identity is that, whilst they look like the later tenders, they are flush riveted. Engines known to have had them attached include 4076, 4077, 4078, 4079, 4083, 4088, 4091, 4097, and 5001. Interestingly tender 1539 attached to No.4091 from new in 1925 was built for the first 4-6-0 No.100 in 1902, and tender 1513 was attached to 4088 as late as 1942!

Change came in 1926 with the appearance of the 4,000 gallon capacity tender 'with flush bottom' otherwise known as the Collett tender. The first version appeared in September 1926 and there is some confusion amongst the records as to which engine was first fitted with one. The first tender is shown coupled to No.5002, but anecdotal evidence suggests that the first tender was actually built with a fender which continued at full height around the rear of the tender. On release from the shops, it was found that the standard GWR water columns fouled this fender and it had to be returned for immediate modifications. This claim is supported by the fact that the original tender arrangement drawing bears traces of this fender having been included on the drawing but erased and redrawn in the shape as finally built. Happily, the erasure was not fully achieved. What is certain is that engine No.5000 was sent for trials on the LMS West Coast main line during that September coupled to one of them and it is left for debate as to which tender it actually was, although it is suspected to be 2385.

The fronts of these tenders were somewhat different to later versions with coal boards rather than the later gates, large sandboxes on the front platform and twin fillers to the rear of the tank. During the course of subsequent production, frame plates changed shape, spring gear was changed and strengthened, steel front platforms substituted for the original wooden version and filler hatches modified to a single central version. Whilst early ones were fitted with Dew pattern buffers, many later ones were turned out new with Turton pattern buffers.

Mention has been made of the Collett type of 3,500 gallons tender and instances occurred of several being attached to Castles at various times. Also, during 1931 tender No.2586 of lot A123 was turned off works with an 8-wheeled frame. It is believed that this was an experiment to determine any benefit with more even and lower loadings of axles, but it was not replicated, although the tender survived in traffic until 1963. During its service life, it was attached to quite a number of differing engines including Castles Nos. 5001, 5032, 5071, 5049, 5017, 5068, 4093, in that order. The final batch of these tenders was constructed in 1946 during Hawksworth's time as CME. Lot A186 was authorised for twenty tenders but only the first ten were built and it is considered that the first five tenders of that lot, Nos. 4010 to 4014, were constructed with experimental welded tanks to the otherwise standard 'Collett' shape. These tenders were coupled to newly built Castles Nos.5098, 5099, 7000, 7001 and 7002.

Following on from the experimental welded tanks on the five Collett type tanks, production switched to a modified version of the 4,000 gallon welded tenders which were constructed for the Hawksworth County class engines. This new batch were basically narrowed down from the County tender's 8 feet 6 inch width down to the standard 8 feet of earlier tenders. Constructional details were straightforward and followed the County tenders closely. The tender fronts were a lot more enclosed than earlier tenders and the coal doors were not particularly high. Added to these issues was the fact that small wet Welsh coal was often reluctant to use the alleged self trimming slopes of the bunker, and they had all the ingredients necessary to generate a certain dislike of them by the crews.

The final type of tender attached to the Castles came with the construction of two self weighing tenders for testing purposes. These were of basic Hawksworth pattern with somewhat cut down bodies which enabled the incorporation of a steelyard capable of weighing the contents of the bunker for coal consumption tests. Numbered 4127 and 4128, the former was painted green and the latter black and they were used in tests performed on a range of engines. 4128 was withdrawn in 1958 but 4127 was still in store at Swindon in late 1964.

LIVERIES

The subject of liveries has been debated almost to extinction. It is sufficient to say that the Castles were painted in green for the vast majority of their existence. From their introduction in 1923 until around 1956, that green was the standard GWR engine green which was usually defined as Middle Chrome Green. Under British Railways, the colour changed subtly and was defined as locomotive green, colour number 30 in the BR standard range of colours. It should be noted that it was never Brunswick Green and was never officially referred to as such. The Castles appeared just as the GWR had reverted to its pre-First World War livery details and as the newest creations they qualified for a full complement of lining, together with much brass and copper embellishment. Whilst the colour and lining details remained constant until the Second World War, the insignia changed twice. Starting with the words GREAT and WESTERN flanking the garter crest of the company, the garter crest was displaced by the company's twin coat of arms for London and Bristol in 1927, followed by all being swept away and replaced in 1934 by a rather insignificant roundel displaying the letters GWR. The lining was carried out in orange and black and buffer beams and buffers were painted in the subtle and rather unusual China Red, rather than the variety of bright red favoured by lesser concerns.

The Second World War brought severe economies including lengthy periods between repaints and the deletion of lining. Such repaints as were undertaken were carried out with heavily thinned green paint which quickly blackened and much brasswork was painted over. Further safety measures saw the cab side windows plated over. Post-war recovery was slow but 1945 saw the company reinstating the lined green livery with certain economies still in place. All lining below platform level was deleted and the tenders still just bore the letters G and W flanking the company's twin crests, much as they had done during the years of wartime plain green.

Nationalisation in January 1948 initially brought little change other than the application of the words BRITISH RAILWAYS executed on the tender sides in the old Egyptian serif letters from Chuchward's days. The following year or so brought further small changes but they were nothing to the changes which the new standard BR livery brought to other regions. The British Transport Commission decided to adopt the durable GWR livery for all normal express passenger engines of power class 7 and below. The standard GWR engine green was adopted with the same orange and black lining which had a few detail changes such as corner radii and boiler bands. On the Castles' cabside and cylinder, lining was changed somewhat but overall the style was still recognisably Great Western. The BR cycling lion emblem was affixed at the centre of the tender panel. 1956 brought the final changes when the colour was subtly changed to a slightly darker green styled by BR as 'Locomotive Green', and the tender badge was changed for the last time to the final BR steam era badge featuring a Lion rampant holding a wheel, flanked by bars proclaiming BRITISH and RAILWAYS. Buffer beams were painted in bright Signal Red.

Chapter 3
CONSTRUCTION AND OPERATION, 1923–1927

At the time of the handover from Churchward to Collett at the beginning of 1922, Lot 217 for twelve 'Stars', 4061-4072, was in the process of construction at Swindon at a total estimated cost of £90,199 or an average of £7,516 per locomotive, costs having doubled after the First World War. Collett's enlarged design was authorised under Lot 224 and 4073 *Caerphilly Castle* emerged from Swindon Works in August 1923 to great publicity, described by the GWR as 'the most powerful passenger train engine in the Kingdom', on account of its tractive effort exceeding that of Gresley's and Raven's Pacifics. 4074 followed in December and 4075-4082 were completed by April 1924. The ten cost an estimated £55,650 at an average of £5,565 per locomotive, a significant reduction in both the cost of materials and also a reduction in the Works salaries and wages attributed to the new order. The ten Castles were provided with the standard 3,500 gallon tender raising the cost to £6,841 per machine. The first ten engines were named after the most well-known castles on the GWR territory, but in alphabetical order denying the most famous of all, Windsor Castle, its rightful place as class leader.

4073 *Caerphilly Castle*
4074 *Caldicot Castle*
4075 *Cardiff Castle*
4076 *Carmarthen Castle*
4077 *Chepstow Castle*
4078 *Pembroke Castle*
4079 *Pendennis Castle*
4080 *Powderham Castle*
4081 *Warwick Castle*
4082 *Windsor Castle*

All ten were immediately allocated to Old Oak Common and, with

4073 *Caerphilly* Castle as built in 1923 in Works Grey but with the later fitted 4,000 gallon tender. The bogie brake gear and diagonal cab roof rain strip have already been removed. (MLS postcard collection)

4076 *Carmarthen Castle* as built and newly delivered to Old Oak Common, February 1924. (F. Moore/MLS Collection)

virtually no teething problems, took command of the GWR's fastest and heaviest services to the West of England. 4082, built in April 1924, headed the Royal Train with King George V and Queen Mary from Paddington to Swindon and after their visit to the Works, 4082 was driven back to the station by the king, with the queen and other company officials on the footplate. Thereafter 4082 was used whenever possible as the GW's royal engine.

4073 was displayed at Wembley in the Palace of Engineering at the British Empire Exhibition between May and October 1924, alongside the LNER's Gresley Pacific 4472 *Flying Scotsman,* and there was some scepticism about the GWR's claim to have the most powerful locomotive when compared with the obvious larger size of 4472.

A series of dynamometer tests were carried out with 4074 in March 1924 between Swindon and Plymouth and the results were published in a paper read by Collett in 1924 at a World Power Conference held in London. The paper was entitled 'Testing of Locomotives on the Great Western Railway' and, in the paper, Collett quoted the figures of coal per drawbar horsepower hour from 4074's tests which astounded the other UK railways' engineers – just 2.83lbs compared with 4.5-6lbs on most other British express engines.

4082 *Windsor Castle* as exhibit number 50 at the Darlington Centenary of the Stockton & Darlington Railway, July 1925. Note the plaque on the cabside commemorating the visit and cab ride of King George V at Swindon the previous year. (MLS postcard collection)

Dynamometer Tests March 1924
Swindon-Taunton
4074 *Caldicot Castle*
15 vehicles, 484 tons

		14.3.24		19.3.24		25.3.24		
Miles	Location	Times	Speeds	Times	Speeds	Times	Speeds	Gradient
0	Swindon	00.00		00.00		00.00		
4.9	Wootton Bassett	09.43	sigs	09.20	sigs	08.36		
9	MP 87 (Brinkworth)	15.12		13.53		12.56		1/300 F
11	MP 89 (L.Somerford)	17.07	63 ½	15.47	65	14.43	69	
16	MP 94 (Hullavington)	22.15	52	20.57	53	19.37	53	1/300 R
22	MP 100 (Badminton)	29.19	50	27.56	51½	26.36	50	1/300 summit
26.6	Chipping Sodbury	34.12	sigs	33.00	sigs	31.24	sigs	
31.9	Winterbourne	40.51	65	39.19	66	37.48	66	
38	Stapleton Road	50.26		49.06	sigs	47.08		
40.3	Pylle Hill Jcn	55.14		55.43		52.49		
44.6	MP 123 (Flax Bourton)	62.18	45	61.51	44	58.51	45	1/180 R
55.2	Puxton	72.05	75/73½	72.04	71/68	68.47	73/72	L
66.9	Highbridge	81.57	70/63	82.17	66½ /64	78.39	69/68	L
73.2	Bridgwater	87.55	62	88.03	65½	84.12	68	L
79.6	MP 158 (Durston)	94.12	55½/60	93.59	61/64½	90.03	sigs	1/300 R
84.7	Taunton	100.30		100.15			sigs	

Dynamometer Tests March 1924
Taunton-Exeter
4074 *Caldicot Castle*
11 vehicles, 385 tons
March 1924

Miles	Location	Times	Speeds	Cut-off	Regulator opening	Gradient
0	Taunton Yard	00.00		45%	Full	
1.75	MP165 (Norton Fitz)	03.23	42	30%	Full	1/369 R
2.75	Victory Sidings	04.34	50 ½	30%	Full	1/203 R
5.75	Poole Sidings	07.59	53	30%	Full	1/174 R
6.75	Wellington	09.08	52	30%	Full	1/170 R
8.75	MP 172	11.29	48½	30%	Full	1/90 R
9.75	MP 173	13.00	39½	30%	Full	1/86 R
10.75	Whiteball	14.48	33½	30%	Full	1/80 R
13.75	Sampford Peverell	18.03	56	18%	1/8	1/115 F
15.75	Tiverton Junction	19.42	73	18%	1/8	1/216 F
18.75	Cullompton	22.13	69/73	18%	1/8	1/155 F
21.75	Silverton	24.45	71	18%	Full	
25.75	Stoke Canon	28.03	75	18%	Full/Shut	1/435 F
30.75	Exeter St David's	32.59	35*	25%	Full	

The tests continued to Plymouth with 4074 hauling the maximum 292/310 tons gross, completing the 31.9 miles from passing Newton Abbot at slow speed to the Plymouth stop in 41 minutes 33 seconds (39 ¾ net). The dynamometer results published and quoted in Charles Collett's paper were:

Calorific value of coal B.Th.U	14,700
Water evaporated per lb of coal	9.95 lb
Coal per ihp hour	2.1 lb
Water per ihp hour	20.9 lb
Coal per dhp hour	2.83 lb
Water per dhp hour	28.1 lb
Thermal efficiency of boiler	79.8%
Thermal efficiency overall	8.22%
Drawbar pull sustained at 71mph	2.35 tons

The coal consumption of the first ten Castles in ordinary service was low at around 41 to 46lbs per mile including light and heavy work, light running and standing time. This was around a 10 per cent improvement on the 'Stars'.

A year later, a further batch of ten Castles was constructed, Lot 232, at an initial cost of £6,865 for 4083-4086, reducing slightly to £6,498 for 4087 onwards. 4083 was delivered in May 1925 and 4092 in August. This series was named:

4083 *Abbotsbury Castle*
4084 *Aberystwyth Castle*
4085 *Berkeley Castle*
4086 *Builth Castle*
4087 *Cardigan Castle*
4088 *Dartmouth Castle*
4089 *Donnington Castle*
4090 *Dorchester Castle*
4091 *Dudley Castle*
4092 *Dunraven Castle*

They were also supplied with 3,500 gallon tenders which they retained for around five years, though all had the Collett 4,000 gallon tenders by 1930. 4083 and 4089-4092 joined

4080 *Powderham* *Castle* departing from Paddington with the 3.30pm Paddington–Plymouth, April 1924.
(F. Hebron/Rail Archive Stephenson)

4074 *Caldicot* *Castle* at Paddington station No.1 platform at the head of a down express, 12 October 1924.
(P.J.T. Reed/F.K. Davies & John Hodge Collections)

4074 *Caldicot* Castle accelerates past Old Oak Common with a down West of England express, c1924. This engine was tested on the GWR as part of the exchange with the Gresley Pacific 4474. (A.L.P. Reavil/Rail Archive Stephenson)

the first ten at Old Oak Common but 4084-4088 were allocated to Plymouth Laira depot.

Interest in the performance of the Castles by the engineers of other companies had grown and in May 1925 an exchange was arranged between a Castle and a Gresley A1 class Pacific, with 4079 running on LNER metals and 4074 'competing' with 4474 (later named *Victor Wild*) on the Great Western. I say 'competing' deliberately although it was not seen by the engineers as such. But the GW publicity machine and the press stimulated interest and the performance of both Castles clearly outperformed the Gresley Pacifics, especially 2545 *Diamond Jubilee* on its own territory, with significant fuel economy in comparison. The table below outlines a couple of the exchange performances.

4080 *Powderham* Castle inside Old Oak Common roundhouse, its home depot, c1924. (Bernard Whicher/Rail Archive Stephenson)

King's Cross-Doncaster, May 1925
1.30pm King's Cross-Leeds
4079 *Pendennis Castle*
435/475 tons

Miles	Location	Times	Speeds		Gradients
0	King's Cross	00.00		T	
2.6	Finsbury Park	05.45	40		1/107 R
5	Wood Green	08.50	56½		1/285 F
9.2	New Barnet	13.50	49		1/200 R
12.7	Potters Bar	18.20	48		1/200 R
17.7	Hatfield	23.25	70	1½ E	1/200 F
25	Knebworth	30.45	52		1/200 R
31.9	Hitchin	37.15	65	1¾ E	1/200 F
35.7	Three Counties	40.20	77½		1/400 F
44.1	Sandy	47.40	eased		
51.7	St Neots	55.05	53		1/330 R
58.9	Huntingdon	62.35	57	1½ E	L
62	Leys Box	66.25	44		1/200 R
69.4	Holme	73.15	79		1/200 F
75	Fletton Junction	78.00	70/65		L
<u>76.4</u>	<u>Peterborough</u>	<u>80.05</u>		<u>3E</u>	
0		00.00		T	
3.1	Werrington Junction	05.55	57½		L
8.4	Tallington	11.20	65		
12.2	Essendine	15.00	60		1/264 R
15.8	Little Bytham	18.40	54		1/200 R
20.7	Corby Glen	24.30	48		1/178 R
23.7	Stoke Box	28.25	44½		1/178 summit
29.1	Grantham	33.55	60/eased		

Doncaster, after very easy running to avoid an excessive early arrival, was reached 1¾ minutes early. A return on the 3.7pm from Grantham was mostly easygoing with 4079 covering the 76.4 miles from Peterborough with a 485 ton train in 78 minutes 58 seconds (78 minutes net), although a typically vigorous start was made reaching nearly 70mph by Holme (7 miles) and a sustained 56½ on the 1 in 200 to Abbots Ripton, 77mph at Huntingdon, 43 at Stevenage and 70 at Hatfield, with a four minute early arrival. 4079 was only pressed on starting, where it outshone the East Coast Pacifics, and on the climbs northbound to Potters Bar, Leys and Stoke. On its own line to Plymouth something more enterprising was attempted and achieved. A comparison of two of the test runs as far as Exeter are shown below.

		Paddington-Exeter, May 1925						
		10.30am Paddington-Penzance *Cornish Riviera Express*						
		4474			4074 *Caldicot Castle*			
	To Westbury:	499/530 tons			498/530 tons			
	To Taunton:	427/455 tons			426/455 tons			
	To Exeter:	364/390 tons			363/390 tons			
Miles	Location	Times	Speeds		Times	Speeds	Gradients	
0	Paddington	00.00		T	00.00		T	
1.3	Westbourne Park	03.08			03.15			
5.7	Ealing Broadway	09.31			09.08			
9.1	Southall	13.15		2¼ L	12.42		1¾ L	
18.5	Slough	22.01	66½	2 L	21.26	68	1½ L	
24.2	Maidenhead	27.14	67	1 ¾ L	26.36	66 ½	1 L	
31	Twyford	33.22	67		32.49	65		
36	Reading	37.52		¾ L	37.25		½ L	
46.7	Midgham	50.17	60		48.15	62		1/440 R
53.1	Newbury	56.43	62	¾ L	54.38	58	1½ E	L
61.5	Hungerford	65.11	56		63.12	55 ½		1/264 R
66.4	Bedwyn	70.08	62	¾ L	68.17	60 ½	1¼ E	1/477 R, L
70.1	Savernake	74.25	45		72.25	46		
75.3	Pewsey	79.47	60		77.25	72		1/260 F
86.9	Lavington	90.11	72		87.00	77 ½		1/222 F
95.6	Westbury	98.30	*	1 L	94.40	*	2 ¾ E	
101.3	Frome	106.26	47		101.40	52		1/151 R
108.5	Brewham	116.06	45		110.40	51/46		1/107 R
115.3	Castle Cary	122.21	75	2¼ L	116.18	76	3¾ E	1/98 F
125.7	Somerton	132.08	60		125.28	65		
129.9	Langport	135.59	72		129.16	72		1/264 F
137.9	Cogload Junction	143.07		T	136.06		7 E	
142.9	Taunton	147.49	60	¼ E	140.30	63 ½	7½ E	
144.9	Norton Fitzwarren	149.56	58		142.22	67		L
150	Wellington	155.13	54½		147.17	58		1/174 R
153.8	Whiteball Box	160.42	34½		152.12	41		1/80 R
158.8	Tiverton Junction	165.38	75		156.46	76½		1/155 F
170.2	Stoke Canon	175.17			163.56			
173.7	Exeter St David's	178.37	* pass	¼ E	<u>169.25</u>	arr slip coach		<u>9½ E</u>

4074's hardest work was undertaken with the full load on the initial stage to Westbury. On this occasion, Driver Rowe was encouraged to make a fast time and the fireman would have been working to his limit to improve on the tight schedule to this point. It was more usual for Castles on the *Cornish Riviera Express* to drop a minute or two to Westbury as 4474 did and recover time with the reduced load and easier schedule between Westbury and Exeter. 4079 went on to run the 31.9 miles between Newton Abbot and Plymouth in 41 minutes 33 seconds, the load reduced to eight coaches, 310 tons gross, and arrival at Plymouth was fifteen minutes early on the 247 minute schedule. An equally spectacular achievement of 4074 was an up run on the *Cornish Riviera Express* on 27 April, when it ran into Paddington a similar fifteen minutes early, having run up from Exeter (173.7 miles) in 164 minutes (162 net) with 380 tons behind the tender. The long 1 in 222 from Lavington to Patney caused no further drop than 69 to 61mph and the run in from Reading to Paddington took only 31 minutes 9 seconds , averaging 74mph from Twyford to Slough and 73 from Slough to Southall. The final 1.3 miles from Westbourne Park to the Paddington bufferstops took only 2½ minutes! On the Doncaster runs the Castle averaged 49.8lbs of coal per mile and the Gresley Pacific 55.3. On the Plymouth runs the Castle averaged 41.9lbs per mile with its own Welsh steam coal. Overall, the Castle showed a 12.5 per cent advantage in fuel economy on the GW route with Welsh coal and on the LNER 6.5 per cent improvement with hard Yorkshire coal.

The operation of a Castle in order to time the *Cornish Riviera Express* with these heavy loads was described by Cecil J. Allen after he experienced a footplate run with 4079 *Pendennis Castle* in the autumn of 1924 which he wrote up in the December 1924 *Railway Magazine*. To achieve 69mph on the level with 525 tons required full regulator and 26 per cent cut-off, which, although hard working for a GW engine and crew, was almost incredible to the motive power authorities of the other companies. Between Paddington and Savernake, 4079 was being steamed at 24,000lb per hour, the coal rate being 3,000lbs per hour, the figure calculated in later BR days as the maximum that could be expected for manual firing. For most work, the crews would operate the Castles on no more than 17 or 18 per cent cut-off except on the steepest gradients. The inspector who accompanied Mr Allen calculated that the coal consumption between Paddington and Plymouth was 35lbs per mile, but between Paddington and Savernake it was as high as 50lbs. Water usage was just 30 gallons a mile. The figures published in the magazine and the subsequent calculations after the locomotive exchange caused profound interest and some scepticism.

Below left: **4079** *Pendennis* Castle makes a vigorous start from King's Cross with a stopping train to Peterborough run for route learning purposes, May 1925. (Rail Archive Stephenson)

Below right: **4079** *Pendennis* Castle makes an impressive start from King's Cross with the 1.30pm to Leeds, May 1925, passing Finsbury Park in 5¾ minutes, much less than a normal Gresley Pacific start. (F.R. Hebron/Rail Archive Stephenson)

4079 *Pendennis* Castle passing Harringay with the 1.30pm King's Cross-Leeds, May 1925. (Rail Archive Stephenson)

4079 *Pendennis* Castle working hard on the climb to Potters Bar, near Hadley Wood, with the 1.30pm King's Cross-Leeds, May 1925. (Rail Archive Stephenson)

4079 *Pendennis* Castle at Grantham station with an up Leeds–King's Cross express as part of the 1925 LNER/GWR locomotive exchange trial, May 1925.
(Rail Archive Stephenson)

Despite the acrimony aroused by the press highlighting the competitive element, the results were influential. In the previous October, Maunsell's assistant on the Southern, James Clayton, had ridden 4076 *Carmarthen Castle* on the *Cornish Riviera* and fed back to his chief a report which steered Maunsell towards the design of the Lord Nelson class. Gresley eventually learned the lesson of the long travel valve gear and modified his Pacifics accordingly. His assistant, Edward Thompson at Stratford, used to go to Paddington regularly to observe the Castles and Kings and persuaded Gresley to authorise the rebuilding of the Holden 1500 class in a similar way. Then, in 1926, James Anderson, the Locomotive Running Superintendent of the LMS, persuaded his management to test a Castle on the West Coast main line, which had the effect of challenging Fowler to proceed with a 4-6-0 (the 'Royal Scot' class) rather than pursue his outline design of a compound Pacific.

Between May and September 1926, another ten Castles were built at Swindon, numbered 4093–5002. The main difference was the design of the frame over the leading bogie wheelset, the narrow 'joggle' to make room for the bogie wheels being replaced by straight frames with a hollow dish to create the necessary clearance for the wheels. The change was apparent from the shape of the inside cylinder cleating in front of the smokebox, that for 4093 onwards being wider, between the straight main frames. 5000 also received a new type 4,000 gallon tender, as did 5002. Collett's assistants, suggested by Kenneth Cook as Stanier and Hawksworth, produced an outline drawing of a compound Castle increasing the tractive effort to around 35,000lbs and presented it to Collett in July 1926 but were rebuffed. Collett, with his Works experience, was firmly against the additional complexity and costs of a compound locomotive. 5001 ran with driving wheels temporarily turned down to the scrapping size of 6ft 6ins during December 1926 as a trial for the 'King' class, the design of which was then in preparation. The change made no apparent difference to the engine's performance, and it was subsequently re-fitted with new fullsize tyres. The new series was named:

4093 *Dunster Castle*
4094 *Dynevor Castle*
4095 *Harlech Castle*
4096 *Highclere Castle*
4097 *Kenilworth Castle*
4098 *Kidwelly Castle*
4099 *Kilgerran Castle*
5000 *Launceston Castle*
5001 *Llandovery Castle*
5002 *Ludlow Castle*

A photo of the front end frame of a Castle in the 4073-4092 series showing the 'joggle' in the frame to clear the bogie wheels. (M.W. Earley)

4073 *Caerphilly* Castle, at Taunton with a Bristol – Plymouth train, still retaining its 3,500 gallon tender in 1931. (J.G. Hubback/John Hodge Collection)

5000 *Launceston Castle* as built and in Works Grey livery, fitted with the first 4,000 gallon tender in June 1926. Note the reshaped frame front end over the leading bogie wheels. (MLS postcard collection)

The engine selected for the LMS trial in October 1926 was the brand new 5000 paired with its 4,000 gallon tender holding 6 tons of coal. The outline times (to the nearest 5 seconds) for one of the runs on the 10am Euston-Glasgow, forerunner of the *Royal Scot,* is tabled below. At this time the normal motive power would have been a pair of LMS 4P Compounds.

Crewe-Carlisle, October 1926

5000 *Launceston Castle*

400/415 tons

10am Euston-Glasgow

Miles	Location	Times	Speeds		Gradients
0	Crewe	00.00	T		
4.8	Minshull Vernon	08.20	58½		L
8.7	Winsford Junction	12.00	71½		1/300 F
14.4	Acton Bridge	16.50	72½		L
16.2	Weaver Junction	18.25	65*	½ L	
21.2	Moore	22.50	74		1/180 F, 1/567 F
24	Warrington	26.25	pws 25*	1½ E	
29.8	Golbourne Junction	33.10	50½		1/132 R, 1/156 R
33.2	Bamfurlong	36.45	64		1/417 F
35.8	Wigan	39.15	57½	1¾ E	

Crewe-Carlisle, October 1926
5000 *Launceston Castle*
400/415 tons
10am Euston-Glasgow

Miles	Location	Times	Speeds		Gradients
38	Boar's Head	41.50	46/50		1/104 R
41.6	Coppull	46.15	47½		1/119 R
45.5	Euxton Junction	49.40	71½	3¼ E	1/114 F
50.9	Preston	55.35	*	5½ E	
55.7	Barton	62.50	55½		L
60.4	Garstang	67.30	65/67	4½ E	L
71.9	Lancaster	78.10	68	5¾ E	1/98 F
75	Hest Bank	80.50	71½		L
78.2	Carnforth	83.40	65	6¼ E	
82.7	Burton & Holme	88.20	50½		1/134 R
85.5	Milnthorpe	91.00	59		L
91	Oxenholme	97.30	44	6½ E	1/111 R
94.5	Hay Fell Box	103.00	35		1/131 R
98.1	Grayrigg	110.00	26 ½		1/106 R
104.1	Tebay	116.40	66	5¼ E	L
107.1	Scout Green Box	120.20	32		1/75 R
109.6	Shap Summit	126.40	20	6¼ E	1/75 R
118.9	Clifton	135.55	79		1/125 F
123.1	Penrith	139.40	57*	7¼ E	
133.6	Southwaite	149.20	70½		1/228 F
136.1	Wreay	151.35	pws		
<u>141</u>	Carlisle	<u>157.00</u>		<u>8 E</u>	

Between May and July 1927 5003-5012 were constructed completing the first batch of forty '4073' class Castles.
These ten were named:

5003 *Lulworth Castle*
5004 *Llanstephan Castle*
5005 *Manorbier Castle*
5006 *Tregenna Castle*
5007 *Rougemont Castle*
5008 *Raglan Castle*
5009 *Shrewsbury Castle*
5010 *Restormel Castle*
5011 *Tintagel Castle*
5012 *Berry Pomeroy Castle*

5003 was also provided with a 4,000 gallon tender and 4093 acquired one, but unaccountably 5004-5012 reverted to the 3,500 gallon type probably due to production of 4,000 gallons tenders being switched to the emerging batch of new King class engines.

Around this time, several engines ran with Dean/Churchward 4,000 gallon tenders. The GW publicity department started their habit of name-changing for the Castles with this group, having initially allocated *Manorbier Castle* to 5004, *Nunney Castle* to 5006, *Oystermouth Castle* (near Swansea) to 5007, *Wallingford*, then *Whittington Castle* to 5012. Two of these, 'Oystermouth and Wallingford' were never used again, whereas 'Nunney' was used for 5029 and 'Whittington' for 5021. Most of the 1926/7 batch were allocated to Old Oak Common – 4093, 4094, 4097-5002, 5005, 5006 and 5010. Nos.4095, 4096, and 5007-5009 went to Laira, 5011 and 5012 to Newton Abbot and, strangely, 5004 to Taunton, a depot that never received more than one or two Castles throughout the shed's existence. The allocation at the end of 1927 after the full delivery of

5000 *Launceston Castle* at Euston station in October 1926 after arrival with one of the GW/LMS exchange trials from Crewe to Euston. (Rail Archive Stephenson)

4082 *Windsor Castle* at Laira depot, Plymouth, 8 August 1925. (P.J.T. Reed/ F.K. Davies & John Hodge Collections)

4085 *Berkeley* Castle heads a new Collett 8-coach articulated set on test between Badminton and Swindon, c1925. (F.K. Davies Collection/John Hodge Collection)

the first forty Castles and the first tranche of Kings was:

Old Oak Common:	4073, 4076-4079, 4081-4083, 4089-4094, 4097-5003, 5005, 5006, 5010 (24)
Newton Abbot:	4074, 4075, 5009, 5011, 5012 (5)
Plymouth Laira:	4080, 4084-4088, 4095, 4096, 5004, 5007, 5008 (11)

Taunton had lost its only representative from this series of Castles. In the meantime, Collett had taken the step of rebuilding some of the 'Stars' as 'Castles', starting somewhat controversially with 111, the GWR's only Pacific to the chagrin of the company's publicity department, the ownership of the first UK Pacific

4086 *Builth* Castle stands ready to depart from Paddington with the first portion of the *Cornish Riviera Limited*, 29 August 1925. (P.J.T. Reed/F.K. Davies & John Hodge Collections)

Newly constructed 4090 *Dorchester* Castle running in from Old Oak Common on a Paddington-Reading stopping train, near Hayes, 1925. (F.K. Davies Collection/John Hodge Collection)

4098 Kidwelly Castle departs from Paddington with an excursion train for Weymouth, 10 July 1927. (P.J.T. Reed/F.K. Davies & John Hodge Collections)

5001 Llandovery Castle built with 6ft 6in driving wheels to test Collett's concept for the 'King' class wheel dimensions, seen at Old Oak Common shortly after construction, 2 July 1927. (P.J.T. Reed/F.K. Davies & John Hodge Collections)

still having prestige even if its performance was merely adequate. 111 was rebuilt in September 1924, renamed *Viscount Churchill*, and was sent, along with Royal engine 4082, to the railway centenary celebrations at Darlington in 1925. 4009 *Shooting Star* was converted in April 1925 and 4016 *Knight of the Golden Fleece* in February 1926, all three being allocated to Old Oak Common initially, although 4009 moved to Newton Abbot and 4016 to Stafford Road before the end of 1927. 4032 *Queen Alexandra* was rebuilt in April 1926 and 4037 *Queen Philippa* in July. 4032 was allocated to Laira and 4037 to Stafford Road. 4016 and 4037 were the first Castles allocated to Stafford Road as the new Kings became available for the heaviest West of England services. A sixth engine, 4000 *North Star* itself, was rebuilt also, but not until November 1929, and it was then allocated to Swindon for a year before being transferred to Newton Abbot. It is thought that the decision to rebuild these 'Stars' was the need to renew their cylinders or boiler so the opportunity was taken, though why only these conversions were made before the later 'Abbeys' is unknown. Of course, Swindon was busy building 'Kings' between 1927 and 1930, so the Works may not have had the capacity. The later (1929) decision to rebuild 4000 may have been a reluctance to scrap such a well-known engine, after earlier Board disapproval of the virtual scrapping of *The Great Bear*. Costs of the conversions ranged from £1,545 to £2,666. The variations would undoubtedly be due to the differing work required to bring these rebuilt engines up to a satisfactory ex-works condition. Part of the costs would undoubtedly be for the new boiler, smokebox and cylinders. The Star boilers would have been repaired and placed in the spares pool for further use. All of these engines would have required the welding on of frame extensions. It is likely that other required repairs would have varied from engine to engine creating some of the variations in the charges. The cost of rebuilding 111 was much higher at £4,192. These costs compare with £5,615, that of new Castles constructed at the same time.

The GWR Pacific, 111 *The Great Bear*, at Old Oak Common, c1912. (R.W. Miller Collection/ MLS Collection)

111 The *Great Bear* passing Kensal Green with its usual duty, the 6.30pm Paddington-Bristol express, c1910. (R.W. Miller Collection/MLS Collection)

111 Viscount *Churchill*, rebuilt from *The Great Bear* in 1924, en route to the Darlington Centenary Exhibition with a set of the latest GW rolling stock at Nottingham Victoria, July 1925. A Great Central Robinson D9 4-4-0 is just visible. (T.G. Hepburn/Rail Archive Stephenson)

111 *Viscount Churchill* with 4,000 gallon tender, being serviced at Bristol Bath Road shed in the early 1930s. It would be withdrawn in July 1953 after running 1,462,356 miles as a Castle (1,989,628 over its whole career). (MLS Collection)

4009 *Shooting Star* after rebuilding as a Castle in April 1925, at Swindon. It would be renumbered and renamed 100A1 *Lloyds* in January 1936. It was the first Castle to be withdrawn in March 1950 while new Castles of the 70XX series were still under construction. It ran 1,164,297 miles as a Castle (1,974,651 in total). (MLS Collection)

4009 in Swindon Works undergoing overhaul immediately prior to renaming, 12 January 1936. Note that the numberplate just signifies 'A1'. It was amended to read 100 A1. The space previously occupied by the cab numberplate 4009 can be seen from the paintwork. It was officially named at a ceremony at Paddington by Sir Robert (later Viscount) Horne, Chairman of the GWR, in the presence of the Chairman of Lloyds. 100 A1 was withdrawn in 1950. One of the nameplates was recovered and presented to the current Chairman of Lloyds in December 1977. (B. Matthews/ MLS Collection)

The naming ceremony at Paddington on 17 February 1936 of 100 A1 by the GW Chairman with the Lloyds Chairman. The Lloyds coat of arms and flags are above the nameplate. (GW official photograph)

Construction and Operation, 1923–1927 • 77

Former 'Star' 4016 *Knight of the Golden Fleece* was rebuilt as a Castle in October 1925 and renamed *The Somerset Light Infantry (Prince Albert's)* in February 1938, seen here at Old Oak Common, April 1950. It was withdrawn in September 1951 having run 1,186,663 miles as a Castle, 1,972,559 in total service. (W. Potter/ MLS Collection)

4000 *North Star* rebuilt as a Castle in November 1929 from Churchward's prototype 4-cylinder 4-4-2 No.40 and later 4-6-0 4000. It would have a long life of 51 years being withdrawn in May 1957, having amassed 2,110,396 miles, of which 1,191,592 was as a Castle. It is seen here at Stafford Road in the early 1930s. (Real Photographs/ MLS Collection)

5012 *Berry Pomeroy Castle* powered the 11.15am Paddington-Bristol in 1928 with 11 coaches/375 tons. It was delayed by a p-way slowing at Acton and so took 15¼ minutes to clear Southall and had recovered to 68mph by Slough when it encountered a second p-way slack at Maidenhead. Accelerating to 72 by Goring, it slipped three coaches at Didcot for Oxford and stations to Swindon and with 8 coaches, after yet another p-way restriction to 30mph at Wantage Road, recovered to 69 at Shrivenham, 77mph before and 83 after Dauntsey, passing Chippenham, 94 miles in 93 minutes 30 seconds, Bath in 106½ minutes and arrived at Bristol a few seconds early in 119 minutes 50 seconds (112 minutes net).

By the end of the 1920s, the Old Oak based Castles had a few regular turns to South Wales on the 3.55pm Paddington and to Wolverhampton on the 9.10am, returning with the 2.35pm Wolverhampton. The South Wales train had a conditional stop at Badminton and 4090 *Dorchester Castle* stopped there (100 miles) in 96 minutes 20 seconds (92 ¾ net) hauling 325 tons. This required steady running in the mid-70s to Swindon with an excellent climb on the 1 in 300 to Badminton where 66-68mph was sustained. 4083 *Abbotsbury Castle* completed the 100 miles with 385 tons in 99 minutes, averaging 70mph from Maidenhead to Swindon and then unusually reached 80mph in the depths of the Severn Tunnel and arrival at Newport was within the 140 minute schedule for the 131 miles.

4016 *Knight of the Golden Fleece* had been rebuilt in February 1926 and in April it was transferred to Stafford Road and was immediately rostered to the 11.35am Wolverhampton and 6.10pm return. On the latter with 343/360 tons gross to the slip of a coach at Bicester, it took 62 minutes 50 seconds including a signal check approaching High Wycombe and a permanent way slowing at Princes Risborough. It reached 66mph at Northolt Junction, falling to 50 on the 1 in 254 to Seer Green, 74 before the High Wycombe check, 44 minimum at Saunderton, 75 before Ashendon Junction, 72 maintained beyond Brill, 53 at Ardley summit, 74½ at Aynho Junction, 70 at Banbury maintained on the 1 in 330 to Cropredy and then a full 90mph at Fosse Road. Leamington was reached in 93 minutes 40 seconds (88 net). The train was badly delayed by a bridge slowing at Hatton, but then raced for Birmingham, with 78½ at Tyseley, taking just 6 minutes 25 seconds for the last seven miles to a dead stand in Snow Hill platform! 4082 *Windsor Castle* on the 9.10am with 235 tons to Banbury and 205 tons thereafter worked hard after a p-way slowing to 15mph at Old Oak West, dropping only from 66 to 60½mph on the climb to Seer Green, stopping at High Wycombe in 33 minutes 15 seconds, a couple of minutes late. It then ascended Saunderton bank at 52mph, touched 85 at Haddenham and 80 at Brill, climbed Ardley at 61mph and with 80½ at Southam Road, passed Leamington in 58.15 minutes, having picked up 3¾ minutes from Wycombe. With 49mph at Hatton, 70 at Lapworth before a p-way slack at Knowle, and 72 at Tyseley, Birmingham Snow Hill was reached 1¼ minutes early in 84 minutes 25 seconds from High Wycombe (80 net) against the 88 minute schedule.

In 1930, 4088 *Dartmouth Castle* was based at Stafford Road, and despite the presence of Kings, was allocated for several weeks to the 11.35am Wolverhampton and 6.10pm Paddington, the hardest turn on that route. O.S. Nock travelled on the 6.10pm at Whitsun 1930 when a relief train ran and so the 6.10 did not carry slip coaches but took the whole 440/475 ton train right through to Wolverhampton. Despite a slight signal check at Old Oak West, 4088 had worked the train up to 63½mph by Denham and did not fall below 51mph on the 1 in 264 to Seer Green, keeping the hard 32 minute schedule to passing High Wycombe, at admittedly rather high a speed (50mph) than the normal 35mph slowing. 42mph minimum at Saunderton summit was followed by 83½ at Haddenham and Bicester was passed on time at a few seconds over 58 minutes for the initial 53.4 miles. The 1 in 200 to Ardley was climbed at a minimum of 52½mph and with no speed higher than 78 down the tempting gradients through Southam Road, Leamington was reached in 89 minutes 50 seconds, over a minute early. Hatton Bank was then surmounted at 32mph with this full load and Tyseley was passed at 68mph but a p-way slack before Bordesley made the train three minutes late into Birmingham, most of which was recovered by Wolverhampton. Cecil J. Allen recounted the details of two up runs in the October 1929 edition of the *Railway Magazine*, when these trains were still in the hands of Castles before the 'Kings' dominated the top Old Oak turn, the 9.10am Paddington and 3pm Birmingham return, the first below with the normal load and the second with a very heavy train.

		3pm Birmingham-Paddington, 1929				
		4082 *Windsor Castle*		4080 *Powderham Castle*		
		240/260 tons		420/445 tons		
Miles	Location	Times	Speeds	Times	Speeds	Gradients
0	Birmingham Snow Hill	00.00		00.00		
3.2	Tyseley	05.15		05.26		
7	Solihull	09.25		09.40		L
10.4	Knowle	12.50		13.14		L
12.9	Lapworth	15.05	75	15.38		1/258 F
17.1	Hatton	18.45		19.35		
21.3	Warwick	21.55	79	23.11	75	1/110 F, 1/103 F
23.3	Leamington	24.30		25.41		
0		00.00		00.00		
6.1	Southam Road	08.25	54½	10.43	41	1/187 R
11.1	Fenny Compton	13.10		16.40		1/251 R
16.2	Cropredy	17.50	76	22.14	65	1/179 F
19.8	Banbury	21.40		26.01		
0		00.00		00.00		
6.1	Aynho Junction	08.25	65	07.32		L
11.3	Ardley	12.00	57½	13.08	50	1/200 R
14.1	Bicester	15.10		16.28		1/200 F
20.1	Brill	19.40	84/67	21.06	80	1/200 F, 1/200 R
23.3	Ashendon Junction	22.40		24.20		
27.4	Haddenham	26.15	74	27.43	68	L
32.8	Princes Risborough	31.00		33.07		1/176 R, 1/200 R
36	Saunderton	34.05	60½	37.02	48/43	1/88 R, 1/100 R
38.7	West Wycombe	36.25	73	39.43	70	1/164 F
41	High Wycombe	39.00		42.14		
45.8	Beaconsfield	44.50	55½ /53	47.36	56/54½	1/225 R
50.1	Gerrards Cross	48.55		51.44		1/254 F
52.7	Denham	50.55	87	53.52	77½	1/175 F
57.2	Northolt Junction	54.15	sigs	57.30		
59.7	Greenford	57.00		59.32	75	1/264 F
62.9	Park Royal	62.05	sigs	62.17		
64.2	Old Oak Common W	63.55	sigs	64.08	sigs	
67.5	Paddington	70.35	(65½ net)	74.38	(69½ net)	

The 1924-1929 period was a high water mark for the Castles at a time when their performance and economy set the new standard for steam engines in the British Isles. The introduction of the Kings in 1927 became the focus for the heaviest services and it was on high speed running with lighter loads that the Castles maintained their high public profile in the 1930s. As a last example of a Castle on trains that were shortly afterwards taken over by 'Kings', a run on the up *Torbay Limited* heavily strengthened for Easter was published in the *Railway Magazine* in September 1930.

Newton Abbot-Paddington, April 1930

4090 *Dorchester Castle*

Old Oak Common

14 chs, 465 tons

Torbay Limited

Miles	Location	Times	Speeds		Gradients
0	Newton Abbot	00.00		T	
5.1	Teignmouth	08.40			L
7.9	Dawlish	12.40	40*		L
11.6	Starcross	17.10	53		L
15.3	Exminster	21.10	60		L
20.1	Exeter St David's	26.25	40*	1 ½ L	
27.3	Silverton	35.30	52		1/219 R
32.7	Cullompton	41.45	45		1/155 R
35	Tiverton Junction	44.55	55		1/207 F
40	Whiteball	51.25	34½		1/115 R
43.8	Wellington	55.10	77½		1/90 F
	Norton Fitzwarren	-	80½		1/203 F
50.9	Taunton	60.35		3 ½ L	
55.9	Cogload Junction	64.55	60*	3 L	L
62.8	Curry Rivell Jcn	71.45	66		L
68.1	Somerton	77.15	54		1/264 R
73.6	Keinton Mandeville	82.50	69		1/330 F
78.4	Castle Cary	87.10	61½	1¼ L	1/264 R
81.9	Bruton	90.55	49		1/98 R
85.4	Brewham summit	95.55	36		1/98 R, 1/81 R
87.2	Witham	97.55	72½		1/112 F
92.5	Frome	102.50	45*/70½		L, 1/151F

Newton Abbot-Paddington, April 1930

4090 *Dorchester Castle*

Old Oak Common

14 chs, 465 tons

Torbay Limited

Miles	Location	Times	Speeds		Gradients
98.1	Westbury	109.15	30*	¼ L	
106.9	Lavington	119.05	64½		L
112.7	Patney	125.55	49½		1/222 R
118.5	Pewsey	132.50	61		
123.7	Savernake	137.50	53		1/198 R
127.4	Bedwyn	141.20	70½	3¼ L	1/175 F
132.3	Hungerford	145.15	72½		L
135.3	Kintbury	147.50	76½		1/231 F
140.7	Newbury	152.15	74	2¼ L	1/198 F, L
144.2	Thatcham	155.15	72½		1/615 F
149	Aldermaston	159.15	75		1/440 F
152.5	Theale	162.16	70½		L
155.9	Southcote Junction	165.20	50*		
157.8	Reading	167.30	45*	½ E	
162.8	Twyford	173.00	61		L
169.6	Maidenhead	179.10	69		1/1320 F
175.3	Slough	184.25	67	½ E	L
184.7	Southall	193.20	63	¾ E	
189.5	Acton	197.55	20* sigs		
192.5	Westbourne Park	202.55	3* sigs		
<u>193.8</u>	<u>Paddington</u>	<u>208.15</u>	(203 net)	<u>3¼ L</u>	

It was not always so (apparently) easy. 5004 *Llanstephan Castle* had gone down to Exeter on the sharply timed 3.30pm Paddington on the Thursday before Easter 1930 with an even heavier load, 520 tons, and found it too much for timekeeping. A dead stand for signals at Acton did not help and the train passed Reading ten minutes late. Speed fell to 41 at Savernake, and despite 79 at Lavington, the train was nearly twenty minutes late by Westbury. However, a smart climb was made to Brewham and with 76½mph at Castle Cary and 73 at Curry Rivell some time was recovered to Taunton. The driver decided not to take a banker from Taunton and unsurprisingly fell to 21½ on the steepest section of 1 in 80 to Whiteball, though recovering to 24mph at the tunnel. Exeter was reached in 193 minutes 35 seconds (187½ net), 18½ minutes late.

Old Oak Common's 4092 *Dunraven Castle*, built in August 1925, near Iver with an up express, 21 June 1930. (G.R. Grigs/Rail Archive Stephenson)

Newton Abbot's 4099 *Kilgerran Castle*, built in August 1926, and fitted here with a Collett Intermediate 3,500 gallon tender, leaving Paddington with a West of England express, October 1932. (G.R. Grigs/Rail Archive Stephenson)

Construction and Operation, 1923–1927 • 83

The rebuilt 4009 running as A1, before the addition of number 100, and named *Lloyds*, at Patchway with an up South Wales express in the winter snows of early 1937. Note the unusual fitting of a tall safety valve bonnet. (MLS Collection)

The 100 buffer beam number and number plates have now been added as *Lloyds* departs from Bristol Temple Meads with the 10.15am Taunton-Paddington in the summer of 1937. The tall safety valve bonnet is still fitted. (MLS Collection)

Chapter 4
HIGH SPEED IN THE 1930s

In 1929 the schedule of the afternoon Cheltenham - Paddington express, *The Cheltenham Flyer*, was accelerated to cover the 77.3 miles from Swindon to Paddington in 70 minutes and O.S. Nock experienced a run with 5003 *Lulworth Castle* and 275 tons which ran at a sustained 85-86mph for fifteen miles between Didcot and Reading. The schedule was cut to 67 minutes in September 1931 and on the first three days of the new timetable the public relations spotlight was on the running with 5000 *Launceston Castle* which cut the booked time to 59½, 58½ and 58¼ minutes on successive days with 190, 230 and 195 tons respectively, averaging 78, 79.4 and 79.6mph start-to-stop, new records. The last two runs were world records, breaking the USA Reading Railroad's 78.3mph average from Camden, Philadelphia, to Atlantic City, and the third was the first time 90mph on the level had been recorded on the Swindon-Paddington run.

Accelerations on the East Coast in May 1932 prompted the GWR management to counter with something spectacular, and the stage was set for 6 June 1932. Old Oak Common's 5006 *Tregenna Castle* was selected and a record-breaking start-to-stop run for steam traction of over 80mph was made, never to be surpassed. For comparison I'm showing an even more meritorious run on 30 June 1937 (the day after the debut of the LMS *Coronation Scot* and the day of the press invitation run of the LNER *Coronation*).

		Swindon-Paddington (*Cheltenham Flyer*)					
		5006 *Tregenna Castle*			5039 *Rhuddlan Castle*		
		6 chs, 189/195 tons			7 chs, 223/235 tons		
		6.6.1932			30.6.1937		
Miles	Location	Times	Speeds		Times	Speeds	
0	Swindon	00.00		3 L	00.00		T
5.7	Shrivenham	06.15	81		06.35		
10.8	Uffington	09.51	85 ½		10.10	90	
13.4	Challow	11.42	87		11.57	92	
16.9	Wantage Road	14.05	89		14.12	93	
20.8	Steventon	16.40	90	1¼ L	16.45	95	1¾ E
24.2	Didcot	18.55	91	1 L	18.57	92	2 E
28.8	Cholsey	21.59	91		21.58	92	
32.6	Goring	24.25	92		-	85	
35.8	Pangbourne	26.33	90		26.40	86	

High Speed in the 1930s

		Swindon-Paddington (*Cheltenham Flyer*)						
		5006 *Tregenna Castle*				5039 *Rhuddlan Castle*		
		6 chs, 189/195 tons				7 chs, 223/235 tons		
		6.6.1932				30.6.1937		
Miles	Location	Times	Speeds			Times	Speeds	
38.7	Tilehurst	28.28	92			-	89	
41.3	Reading	30.11	91	¾ E		30.27	86 ½	3½ E
46.3	Twyford	33.31	89			33.50	90	
53.1	Maidenhead	38.08	87			38.17	93	
58.8	Slough	42.10	87	1¾ E		42.08	90	4¾ E
64.1	West Drayton	45.51	84			45.47	85	
68.2	Southall	48.51	81 ½	2¾ E		48.46	81/eased	5¾ E
71.6	Ealing	51.17	84 ½			51.40	70/55	
76	Westbourne Park	54.40		3¼ E		57.40		3¼ E
77.3	Paddington	56.47		5¼ E		61.07		4 E

5006 was worked with full regulator and cut-off varying from 17-18%. No details of the working of 5039 were recorded but with the extra coach, the engine must have been pushed harder. Had it continued at the same rate as 5006, a time equalling the record was likely. The driver was the famous F.W. Street of Old Oak Common. Not content with 5006's record, the GW authorities returned the timing party on the 5pm Paddington-Cheltenham, making an out of course stop at Swindon (it was normally first stop Kemble). The run was slightly harder with the gradual rise in grade and took just one second over the hour.

Paddington-Swindon, 6.6.1932
5pm Paddington-Cheltenham
5005 *Manorbier Castle*
6 chs, 199/210 tons

Miles	Location	Times	Speeds
0	Paddington	00.00	
1.3	Westbourne Park	02.34	
5.7	Ealing	06.52	74½
9.1	Southall	09.25	81
13.2	West Drayton	12.26	85½
18.5	Slough	16.03	86½
24.2	Maidenhead	20.14	82½
31	Twyford	25.17	79
36	Reading	29.01	81½

Miles	Location	Paddington-Swindon, 6.6.1932 5pm Paddington-Cheltenham 5005 *Manorbier Castle* 6 chs, 199/210 tons	
		Times	Speeds
41.5	Pangbourne	33.03	83
48.5	Cholsey	38.03	84
53.1	Didcot	41.23	85½
56.5	Steventon	43.47	83½
60.4	Wantage Road	46.35	81½
63.9	Challow	49.13	80
66.5	Uffington	51.13	78½
71.6	Shrivenham	53.05	81½
76	MP 76	56.15	83½
77.3	Swindon	60.01	

On the down run a harder effort was required with full regulator and 19-20% cut-off. The day was not yet finished. The pair of train timers (Cecil J. Allen and Humphrey Baker) were then whisked back to Paddington on the 5.15pm two-hour Bristol-Paddington express which stopped specially at Swindon to pick them up. 4091 *Dudley Castle* with a load of 280 tons finished its journey in 66½ minutes from Swindon arriving 2½ minutes early despite the extra stop, and a signal check through Reading.

The record-breaking 5006 *Tregenna Castle* after overhaul at Swindon Works, 24 April 1938. (Kidderminster Railway Museum/MLS Collection)

Although the Castles made their name initially by their economic haulage of heavy trains to the West of England, then subsequently on high speed running between London and Bristol, they were beginning to appear on heavy trains on the Wolverhampton line, especially the Old Oak 9.10am Paddington and the Stafford Road 6.10pm Paddington-Wolverhampton turns. Earlier, in 1931 the record-breaking 5006 had made another first, running a Grand National Special of 345 tons non-stop from Paddington right through to Shrewsbury, 152.9 miles in 159 minutes 12 seconds (151 net). It was heavily delayed by thick fog in the London area passing Princes Risborough over seven minutes late, then with 86mph at Haddenham, 63 minimum at Ardley, 83 at Southam Road, passed Leamington in 88 minutes 42 seconds (82½ net), Birmingham Snow Hill in 114 minutes (106 net) and after a further fling of 86mph at Shifnal arrived on time in Shrewsbury.

The economic depression hit the country between 1929 and 1931 and in order to help the recovery the GWR initiated a number of physical works to encourage employment – with station rebuilding, four-tracking the lines from Cogload Junction to Norton Fitzwarren and Lapworth to Olton plus the Berks & Hants route cut-offs bypassing Westbury and Frome. This led the way for further train schedule accelerations in the 1930s.

5001 *Llandovery* Castle at Leamington Spa with the 9.10am Paddington-Wolverhampton, October 1931. On transfer back to Old Oak Common in September it had been matched with the only GW Collett eight-wheel tender. (G.A. Coltas/MLS Collection)

The allocation of the forty Castles plus the six rebuilt 'Stars' at the beginning of 1932 was:

Old Oak Common:	111, 4000, 4037, 4073, 4076, 4082, 4083, 4089, 4093, 5000, 5001, 5003, 5006, 5009, 5012 (15)
Bristol Bath Road:	4009, 4079, 4091
Newton Abbot:	4032, 4074, 4080, 4084, 4094, 4095, 4096, 4098, 5004 (9)
Laira:	4081, 4087, 4090, 5002, 5005, 5007, 5010 (7)
Stafford Road:	4016, 4088
Cardiff Canton:	4075, 4077, 4078, 4092, 4097, 4099, 5011 (7)
Carmarthen:	4085, 4086, 5008
Total (46)	

The introduction of the 'Kings' had allowed a reduction in Castles based at Old Oak Common and Laira, with the first allocations made to Stafford Road, Canton and Carmarthen, the latter presumably to work Fishguard boat trains via the Swansea District Line avoiding Swansea High Street. It was a Fishguard boat train headed by 4085 that killed Churchward as he crossed the line from his home to Swindon Works in 1932.

In June 1932, Swindon Works restarted construction of the Castles, after delivering thirty 'Kings' and the first series of eighty 'Hall' 4-6-0 mixed traffic engines. Initially referred to as the '5013' class, 5013-5022 were constructed between June and August and had a number of design alterations. Like 4093-5012, they had the straight frame extension over the bogie wheels but the inside cylinder valve cleating in front of the smokebox saddle had a rectangular form instead of the grooved cleating of the 'Stars' and 4073-4092 or the wider grooved cleating of 4093-5012. In order to increase the water space between inner and outer firebox, the grate area was reduced from 30.3 to 29.4sqft enabling easier cleaning of the boiler during regular washouts. This did not appear to affect the steaming quality of the Castle boiler. There was also an additional compartment above the running

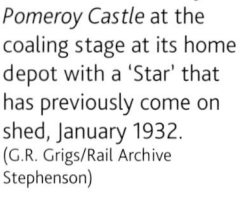

Old Oak's 5012 *Berry Pomeroy Castle* at the coaling stage at its home depot with a 'Star' that has previously come on shed, January 1932.
(G.R. Grigs/Rail Archive Stephenson)

High Speed in the 1930s • 89

Laira's 5010 *Restormel Castle* on a semi-fast train in Cornwall, c1932. (MLS Collection)

4087 Cardigan Castle was moved from Laira to Canton in July 1932 and on to Old Oak Common in July 1933. During its stint at Canton it is seen at Saltney Junction 'Chester' with a Grand National excursion train from Cardiff, 24 March 1933. (R.E. Thomas/ F.K. Davies & John Hodge Collections)

5002 *Ludlow Castle* of Cardiff Canton shed enters Paddington with an express from South Wales, July 1934. It is paired with a Collett 3,500 gallon tender.
(MLS Collection)

plate on the left hand side of the engine from the cab to behind the driving splasher to accommodate the fireirons. The earlier engines acquired this in later years as they went through works. All Castles built in the 1930s were equipped with six-wheel 4,000 gallon tenders from the start, with one exception – an eight wheel tender was constructed in September 1931 (weighing 49 tons) and initially fitted to 5001 after an initial month with 4091. This tender was acquired by 5032 (July 1935), 5071 (July 1940), 5049 (April 1942), 5017 (June 1944), 4093 (January 1946) and 5068 (April 1948 to November 1949). Subsequently it seems to have been coupled with members of the 'Hall' class, including 5957 and 6905 – it was not withdrawn until November 1963. The names of the Castles from 5013 onwards can be found in the appendix on pages 283-288.

5023-5032 were constructed at Swindon in April and May 1934 and were the first locomotives to be constructed using the Zeiss precision optical gear for lining up locomotive frames, axle-box guides and cylinders. Jigs were used for the assembly of the frame plates and cross stretchers. 5033-5042 followed between May and July 1935 and it is said that these twenty engines, built with the precision gear before the retirement of some of the most experienced fitters, had the reputation for being some of the finest examples of the class. 5023, 5025, 5032, 5035, 5037,

5001 *Llandovery* Castle at Old Oak Common with 8-wheel tender 2586, 1934. (F.K. Davies Collection/John Hodge Collection)

5038, 5039, 5040 and 5042 appeared frequently in logs of some of the best runs in the 1930s and even in later years Old Oak Common often chose 5035, 5037 and 5040 for royal train duty as well as a couple from its 1950 70XX series. The new methods and improved quality of construction led to significant increases in mileage between major overhauls. For example, 5030, built in June 1934, amassed 414,154 miles in traffic in the seven years until July 1941, before its boiler was removed from the frames in its first General Repair (after three 'Intermediate Repairs', a system introduced by Collett that extended the times between 'Heavy General' Repairs). From 5033 onwards, the Castles were fitted with speedometers. With the increase in Castle numbers and the mixed traffic 'Halls', a number of the oldest 'Stars' were withdrawn rather than incur expensive repairs or rebuilding – scrapping was part of the accountancy to offset costs of new builds of course. In the years between 1932 and 1935, ten were taken out of traffic – 4001/2/5/6/8/10/11/24/27/29.

After the spectacular running of the *Cheltenham Spa Express* in 1931 and 1932 it settled down to reliable running in the early 1930s, with the latest build of Castles allocated to Old Oak Common taking their turn on the train. Loads at the weekends could increase too but the crews made valiant attempts to maintain schedule even with nine or ten coaches instead of the seven booked. I give below three runs published by Cecil J. Allen in his regular column in the *Railway Magazine* of October 1935, one with a 1925 built Castle on the standard load, one with one of the latest build with nine coaches and a 1932 engine with ten coaches.

Swindon-Paddington, *Cheltenham Spa Express*

		4087 *Cardigan Castle* 7 chs, 218/230 tons			5042 *Winchester Castle* 9 chs, 282/300 tons			5018 *St. Mawes Castle* 10 chs, 317/340 tons		
Miles	Location	Times	Speeds		Times	Speeds		Times	Speeds	
0	Swindon	00.00		T	00.00		T	00.00		T
5.8	Shrivenham	09.15	pws 15*		07.03			07.16	71	
10.8	Uffington	13.50	78½		11.45	76½		11.19	77½	
13.4	Challow	15.52	83½		13.51	80		13.21	79	
16.9	Wantage Road	18.20	85		16.26	83½		15.58	82	
20.8	Steventon	21.03	87½	2½ L	19.22		¾ L	18.50		¼ L
24.2	Didcot	23.21	90	2¼ L	21.52	82	¾ L	21.22	80½	¼ L
28.8	Cholsey	26.33	86½		25.23	79		24.51	80	
32.6	Goring	29.08	87		28.11	77½		27.36	79½	
35.8	Pangbourne	31.25	83½		30.38	77		29.59		
38.7	Tilehurst	33.28			32.52	77½		32.09		
41.3	Reading	35.22	84½	1¾ L	34.51	77	¾ L	34.08	82	¼ L
46.3	Twyford	38.56	85		38.46	77½		37.56	76½	
53.1	Maidenhead	43.43	85½		44.05	80½		43.04		
58.8	Slough	47.48	86½	¾ L	48.33		1 L	47.22	81	¼ E
64.1	West Drayton	51.31			52.37	72½		51.24	76	
68.2	Southall	54.33	80½		55.59			54.39		
71.6	Ealing	57.05	eased		58.40	75		57.12	82	
76	Westbourne Park	61.27		½ L	62.14		1¼ L	60.41		¼ E
77.3	Paddington	64.39	(61 net)	¼ E	64.37		¼ E	63.04		2 E

In 1935, the centenary of the Great Western Railway, the company celebrated by introducing the *Bristolian* service, a lightweight seven-coach train booked over the 118 miles in 105 minutes. Although initially the service was performed by 'Kings', it was soon realised that such high speed trains were entirely suitable for Castle haulage. Also the tradition of boat trains from Plymouth Millbay Docks resumed with the French Line transatlantic liners calling there. Eight 'Super Saloons' had been built for Ocean Liner traffic in 1931 and Millbay Docks were enlarged in 1935. On 13 June 1936 Laira's 4094 *Dynevor Castle* brought up 358 passengers from the record breaking Atlantic crossing *SS Normandie* in 3 hours 38 minutes, averaging 62.4mph overall with its 247 ton train. The 13¼ miles from Bedwyn to Newbury were covered in ten minutes at an average of 80mph. There was also pressure from the GWR Board and Publicity Department to experiment with streamlining and steal a march on the LMS and LNER. However, clearly Collett was not enamoured of the idea and the partial streamlining of 5005 *Manorbier Castle* and 'King' 6014 was half-hearted. The bulbous 'bullet nose' of the two engines was particularly ugly. The more graceful cone-shaped smokebox doors of the German Bavarian and Württemberg State pacifics and the later similar adornment of the last DB class '10' pacifics showed with a little thought what could be done to make the appearance much more presentable. The streamlining caused problems of accessibility to the motion and the enclosure of the moving parts led to some overheating - a similar experience encountered by the streamlined German 01.10 and 03.10 pacifics of the Nazi era. (It is worth noting that temperatures of the valve motion inside the frames of a Castle can reach almost 70° on hot summer days without streamlining – experience in preservation: Bob Meanley.)

5005 *Manorbier Castle* in the initial streamlined form as constructed at Swindon, March 1935.
(GW Official Photograph/ F.K. Davies & John Hodge Collections)

The fully streamlined 5005 *Manorbier Castle* at Bristol Temple Meads with an express for Paddington, 1935.
(G.H. Soole/F.K. Davies & John Hodge Collection)

The semi-streamlined 5005 *Manorbier Castle* begins the descent to the Severn Tunnel through Patchway with a down South Wales express, 1936. (G.H. Soole/MLS Collection)

5005 *Manorbier Castle* at Old Oak Common, its home depot, on 7 May 1939. Most of the remaining streamlining was removed at the beginning of the war and all had been removed by 1947. (N. Fields/MLS Collection)

Old Oak Common's 4082 *Windsor Castle* with a Weston-super-Mare-Paddington express near Flax Bourton, c1935.
(G.H. Soole/MLS Collection)

Exeter's 5003 *Lulworth Castle* brings a heavy West of England-Paddington express past Somerton, c1937. Note the first Ocean Mail van.
(G.H. Soole/E. Johnson)

5007 *Rougemont* Castle with a down Bristol express on Goring troughs, c1934. (G.R. Grigs/Rail Archive Stephenson)

5029 *Nunney* Castle leaves Bristol Temple Meads with the Weston-super-Mare portion of the 9.15am from Paddington, c1935. (MLS Collection)

Old Oak Common's 5022 *Wigmore Castle* departing from Westbury with the Channel Islands boat train for Weymouth, c1937. (G.H. Soole/E. Johnson Collection)

Old Oak Common's 5044 *Beverston Castle* (renamed *Earl of Dunraven* September 1937) near Westbury with an up West of England train, c1937. This was the first engine to be built with the shorter pattern Castle chimney. (G.H. Soole/E. Johnson Collection)

Shrewsbury's one month old 5053 *Bishop's Castle* (renamed *Earl Cairns* in July 1937) at Norton Fitzwarren with the 9.10am Manchester-Paignton, June 1936. An assortment of old rolling stock has been found to strengthen the express for the holiday peak. 4073 waits in the background to back onto a Minehead-Paddington train. (J.G. Hubback/John Hodge Collection)

5047 *Compton* Castle on the 1.30pm Paddington-Kingswear passing Fairwater Yard, Taunton, probably in the summer of 1936. It was allocated to Landore but has obviously been purloined by Old Oak Common as the depot was often getting short of suitable locomotives for its West of England trains after midday. It was renamed *Earl of Dartmouth* in August 1937. (J.G. Hubback/John Hodge Collection)

The Castle allocation at the beginning of the summer timetable in 1935 (change over 1932 in brackets) was:

Old Oak Common:	111, 4009, 4037, 4073, 4075, 4078, 4082, 4087, 4099, 5005, 5008, 5018, 5022, 5023, 5025, 5027, 5029, 5037, 5038, 5039, 5040, 5042 (22, +7)
Bristol Bath Road:	4016, 4081, 4097 (no change)
Newton Abbot:	4077, 4095, 5014, 5016, 5017, 5019, 5024, 5026, 5034 (9, no change)
Laira:	4032, 4083, 4092, 4094, 5000, 5007, 5009, 5011, 5021, 5028, 5041 (11, +4)
Exeter:	4074, 4085, 4098, 5013, 5015, 5030 (6, +6)
Penzance:	4088, 4090 (+2)
Stafford Road:	4079, 4089, 5001, 5031, 5033 (5, +3)
Shrewsbury:	4000, 5032 (+2)
Cardiff Canton:	4086, 4091, 4093, 5002, 5003, 5004, 5010, 5012, 5035, 5036 (10, +3)
Landore:	4076, 4080, 4084, 4096, 5006, 5020 (6, +6)
Carmarthen:	(-3)
Total	(76, +33)

The Old Oak allocation had grown, reinforced by the latest constructions in 1935. South Wales now had seventeen and surprisingly Exeter had six including three of the latest builds. High mileage Castles from Laira tended to be allocated to Penzance for the low speed slogging on the Cornish gradients and swapped back to Laira after overhaul. I had anticipated that Bristol would have had more than three at this stage. Shrewsbury had acquired a couple including the doyenne 4000 and 5032 which was domiciled there for many years.

The GWR had invested in the Automatic Train Control system (ATC) in 1906 and had completed its application to the Paddington-Reading-Oxford route before the First World War. It was then some time before a major programme to complete the remaining routes was undertaken between 1929 and 1931. 4084-4095 and 5003 onwards were equipped with the ATC system when built and the earlier engines fitted as they next went into Swindon Works. In March 1938, ATC tests were carried out using 5055 *Earl of Eldon* on a train of 305 tons and from 69mph the train was brought to a halt in 900 yards, 450 yards before the home signal at danger. There is no doubt that the equipment gave confidence to the drivers and aided punctuality in poor weather conditions.

5043 to 5067 were constructed between March 1936 and July 1937 and I'm grateful to Tim Hillier-Graves for making available to me the GWR specification of Lot 303 for these twenty-five Castles with full breakdown of costs for both engine and tender. The detail comes from the Swindon CME's accounts office and shows that the material costs less recovered scrap were £69,165, wages for staff involved in their construction, £32,499 and establishment overheads, £21,000, making £121,222 at an average of £4,848 for each engine and £969 for the tender, a total per locomotive unit of £5,817. If 5043 cost this in 1936, it is of interest to compare the cost of its rebuilding at Tyseley in the twenty-first century, adjusted of course for the subsequent inflation of the currency. Suffice to say that the cost of that repair was estimated to have a commercial value of some £1.25 million, such is the cost of one-off engineering projects without the benefit of Swindon's vast resources! The cleating for the outside steam pipes alone cost £3,600, some three quarters of the original construction cost of the whole engine! For fuller details of the costs of the construction of this series see the Appendix (pages 293 to 294). Then the game of name-changing began. This batch were all initially allocated 'Castle' names, but in 1937, after pressure from some GWR Board members, the latest engines off Swindon Works were allocated the 'Earl' names. Unfortunately, someone with tongue in cheek (said to be Charles Collett himself) initially fixed the nameplates to the 'new' 4-4-0 double-framed 3200 class conversion of the 'Dukes' and

A pair of Landore Castles, 4080 *Powderham Castle* and newly built 5076 *Drysllwyn Castle* (renamed *Gladiator* in 1941), climb out of the Severn Tunnel between Pilning and Patchway with a heavy express just before Christmas 1938. (MLS Collection)

'Bulldogs' rebuilt for the Cambrian lines. This offended some of the dignitaries who complained to the General Manager. In order to appease these well-connected gentlemen, it was decided to transfer the names to the latest batch of Castles, thus putting the Castle nameplates back into store until used for later class members. 5071-5082, built between June 1938 and June 1939, were subsequently similarly affected when the patriotism engendered by the war saw them named after RAF aircraft that were current at the time of the Battle of Britain, consigning some of the same Castle names to the store for a second time. The initial and subsequent names of all these Castles are listed in the Appendix (page 285-286). 5069 and 5070 were named after the pioneer GW engineers, Brunel and Gooch.

The earlier decision not to rebuild any further 'Stars' but to scrap them was reviewed in 1937 and as the frames of the 1922/3 built 'Abbey' series were still in good condition it was decided that ten would be rebuilt as Castles from the Renewal Fund. Therefore, in April 1937, one of the 1922 series, 4064, was converted to Castle form and renumbered 5084, but surprisingly retaining its original *Reading Abbey* name rather than acquiring one of the discarded ones from the 5071-5082 series. 4063/5083 *Bath Abbey* was rebuilt in June 1937 and 4066 *Malvern Abbey* in December, this one receiving number 5086 and the name of *Viscount Horne*, Chairman of the GWR from 1934. The other 'Abbeys' were rebuilt

Laira's 4097 *Kenilworth Castle* approaches Patchway with a 15-coach Manchester-Penzance through train, c1938. (G.H. Soole/MLS Collection)

Landore's 4089 *Donnington Castle* climbing from Pilning to Patchway with an up South Wales express, c1938. (G.H. Soole/E. Johnson Collection)

102 • GREAT WESTERN CASTLE CLASS 4-6-0 LOCOMOTIVES – 1923–1959

Canton's 5001 *Llandovery Castle* on a down Paddington-South Wales express passing Patchway, c1937. (G.H. Soole/E. Johnson Collection)

Canton's 5002 *Ludlow Castle* with a leaking inside piston gland, working the 11.10am Milford Haven-Paddington 15-coach train passing Patchway station, c1937. (G.H. Soole/E. Johnson Collection)

Shrewsbury's 5032 *Usk Castle* at Patchway station on a Liverpool/Manchester-Plymouth express, c1937. (G.H. Soole/E. Johnson Collection)

Old Oak Common's 5043 *Barbury Castle* (later *Earl of Mount Edgcumbe*) on an up Swansea-Paddington express, passes a down freight near Patchway, c1937. (G.H. Soole/E. Johnson Collection)

Landore's 5083 *Bath Abbey*, rebuilt from 4063 in June 1937, starts the descent from Patchway to the Severn Tunnel with the 10.55am Paddington-Pembroke Dock, c1938. (G.H. Soole/E. Johnson Collection)

Newton Abbot's 5058 *Earl of Clancarty* eases away from Bristol Temple Meads with a train from the North West for Kingswear and Plymouth, c1938. (G.R. Grigs/Rail Archive Stephenson)

Old Oak Common's 5039 *Rhuddlan Castle* entering Bristol Temple Meads with a Penzance-Paddington via Bristol express, Easter Tuesday, 30 March 1937. (G.H. Soole/E. Johnson)

Old Oak Common's 5040 *Stokesay Castle* making light of the climb out of the Severn Tunnel with an up South Wales express near Pilning, c1938. (G.H.Soole/E.Johnson Collection)

Laira's 5028 *Llantilio Castle* on the 1.10pm Plymouth-Crewe North & West service at Stapleton Road, c1937. (G.H. Soole/E. Johnson Collection)

Newton Abbot's 5064 *Bishop's Castle* passing Filton Junction with a Kingswear/Plymouth-Manchester train, c1937. (G.H. Soole/E. Johnson Collection)

Old Oak Common's 4099 *Kilgerran Castle* accelerates from Filton Junction through Westerleigh with an up express, c1936. (G.H. Soole/E. Johnson Collection)

Newton Abbot's 4098 *Kidwelly Castle* passing Long Ashton near Flax Bourton with a train from Manchester to Newton Abbot and Plymouth/Kingswear, c1937. (G.H. Soole/E. Johnson Collection)

Stafford Road's 4079 *Pendennis Castle* sweeps round the curve at Yate with a Wolverhampton-Penzance express, c1934. (G.H. Soole/E. Johnson Collection)

Canton's 4079 *Pendennis Castle* rounds the curve from Filton Junction at Stoke Gifford with an up South Wales express, c1936. (MLS Collection)

Above left: 4079 *Pendennis* Castle leaves Barry with an up South Wales express for Paddington, diverted via the Vale of Glamorgan during Sunday engineering works, 1937. (J.G. Hubback/John Hodge Collection)

Above right: 5012 *Berry* Pomeroy Castle approaches Cogan tunnel with a 13-coach South Wales-Paddington express diverted via the Vale of Glamorgan route because of Sunday engineering work on the main line between Bridgend and Cardiff. (J.G. Hubback/John Hodge Collection)

Left: Old Oak Common's 5029 *Nunney Castle*, built in April 1934, climbing towards Cattybrook Tunnel and Pilning with an up South Wales express, c1936. (MLS Collection)

110 • GREAT WESTERN CASTLE CLASS 4-6-0 LOCOMOTIVES – 1923–1959

5053 *Bishop's* Castle at Bath Road shed, Bristol, in 1937 before being renamed *Earl Cairns* in August 1937. (MLS Collection)

5056 *Ogmore* Castle, built in June 1936, after running in from Swindon shed. It was renamed *Earl of Powis* in September 1937. (Rail Archive Stephenson)

Newly built 5070 *Sir Daniel Gooch* at Swindon, July 1938. (MLS Collection)

'Star' 4063 *Bath Abbey*, built in 1922, at its home depot, Exeter, shortly after a general repair at Swindon, July 1931. It was rebuilt as Castle 5083 in June 1937 having run 821,148 miles before conversion. (Kidderminster Railway Museum/ MLS Collection)

as Castles between 1938 and 1940. 4069, built as *Margam Abbey* in 1923, was renamed *Westminster Abbey* when still a 'Star' and retained that name as 5089. Only 4061 and 4062 of that series remained as 'Stars'. The rebuilt 'Abbeys' could be recognised as they approached by the shape of the inside cylinder cleating – not dished like the 'Stars' and early Castles, but a narrow rectangular casing as the frames were still 'joggled' to clear the bogie wheels.

The initial runs of the 1935 *Bristolian* were entrusted to 'Kings' and then shortly afterwards to engines of the 5023-5042 series of Castles, but the Old Oak allocated engines in the 5043-5062 series soon participated fully and engines 5043 and 5056 were particularly well-known engines on the express, still named *Barbury Castle* and *Ogmore Castle* respectively. The renowned Old Oak driver, F.W. Street, worked the train both ways in the spring of 1936. Brand new 5044, still named *Beverston Castle*, passed Slough in 17 minutes 50 seconds (18.5 miles), Reading in 30 minutes 45 seconds (36 miles) and Didcot in 43 minutes 24 seconds (53.1 miles) with 80-83mph sustained from West Drayton to Steventon. Speed dropped to 76 at Shrivenham and there was a slight signal check to 60mph at Swindon passed in 62 minutes 7 seconds (61 net), then speed was piled on again with 82 at Wootton Bassett, 96 at Dauntsey, 86 still at Box before the Bath slowing (84 minutes 58 seconds) now 6½ minutes early. Driver Street then eased to avoid too early an arrival in Bristol. Overall time was 99 minutes 26 seconds (98 net) and the average of 80mph+ was maintained for over 100 miles. He returned with the same engine in 102 minutes 55 seconds but eased right down from West Drayton – if he'd kept going at normal speed a net time of 98 minutes was easily achievable. Highlights were 61mph at Badminton, 91 at Little Somerford and 82-86mph sustained from Swindon to West Drayton.

O.S.Nock was a regular traveller between Bristol, Bath and London and recorded a number of runs on the up *Bristolian* between 1937 and 1939. These were 'normal' runs with no special encouragement of the driver and I show the outline timings of five runs below.

Above left: Stafford Road's 'Star' 4065 *Evesham Abbey* at Shrewsbury with the Chester-Wolverhampton leg of a Paddington express, c1937. It was built in December 1922 and rebuilt as Castle 5085 in July 1939. It ran 810,737 miles as a 'Star' and in its Castle form was not withdrawn until February 1964, being one of the few WR steam engines that exceeded two million miles in traffic. (Real Photographs/MLS Collection)

Above right: 5088 *Llanthony Abbey* in the course of conversion from 'Star' 4068 at Swindon, 26 February 1939. To the front of the engine is a 'motion cradle' probably awaiting assembly to the set of joggled frames standing on the right of the picture. (F.K. Davies Collection/John Hodge Collection)

Miles		5038/225t	5066/225t	5019/245t	5080/245t	5040/305t	Sch
0	Bristol	00.00	00.00 sigs	00.00	00.00	00.00	0
17.6	Badminton	22.36	24.54	22.07	23.44 sigs	23.28	23½
40.3	Swindon	41.54	45.05 sigs	40.40	42.39	42.01	42½
64.5	Didcot	60.47	64.53	59.35	60.33	59.30	61
81.6	Reading	74.01	77.46	73.08	73.48	71.54	74
108.5	Southall	94.53	97.50 sigs	94.18	94.52	94.38	94½
117.6	Paddington	104.54	108.25	103.29	105.14 sigs	104.22	105
	(Net time)		(103½)		(102½)		
Speeds (mph)							
Little Somerford		84	90	86 ½	80	91	
Uffington		84	85	86	86	89	
Maidenhead		81	82	79	78	72 easy	

I have unearthed three logs of Driver F.W. Street's running on the *Cheltenham Flyer* in 1937 and 1938 from the Railway Performance Society archives.

Swindon-Paddington, *Cheltenham Spa Express*
3.45pm Swindon-Paddington

		5037 *Monmouth Castle*			5067 *St Fagans Castle*			5056 *Earl of Powis*		
		8 chs, 251/265 tons			7 chs, 220/235 tons			7 chs, 222/235 tons		
		24.5.1937			15.12.1937			1.6.1938		
Miles	Location	Times	Speeds		Times	Speeds		Times	Speeds	
0	Swindon	00.00		2½ L	00.00		T	00.00		½ L
5.8	Shrivenham	06.35	69		07.17	73		06.50	74	
10.8	Uffington	10.22	79		11.02	82½		10.38	82	
13.4	Challow	12.10	83 ½		-	86		12.26	85	
16.9	Wantage Road	14.37	85 ½		15.16	90½		14.54	86	
20.8	Steventon	17.24	86	1¼ L	17.56	87	½ E	17.41	85/87	¼ E
24.2	Didcot	19.40	86	1 L	20.12	92	¾ E	19.57	87	½ E
28.8	Cholsey	23.01	85		23.24	87		23.16	86	
32.6	Goring	25.40	84		26.02	85		25.56	84	
35.8	Pangbourne	28.03	83		28.20	82/84		28.17	82	
38.7	Tilehurst	30.00	84 ½		30.25	83½		30.17	84	
41.3	Reading	31.56	85 ½	½ L	32.19	83	1¾ E	32.16	83	1¼ E
46.3	Twyford	35.27	85		35.59	81/84		35.53	82/84	

Swindon-Paddington, *Cheltenham Spa Express*
3.45pm Swindon-Paddington

		5037 *Monmouth Castle* 8 chs, 251/265 tons 24.5.1937			5067 *St Fagans Castle* 7 chs, 220/235 tons 15.12.1937			5056 *Earl of Powis* 7 chs, 222/235 tons 1.6.1938		
Miles	Location	Times	Speeds		Times	Speeds		Times	Speeds	
53.1	Maidenhead	40.10	86/90		40.44	87/90		40.39	87/88	
58.8	Slough	44.05	87	1 E	44.45	87	2¾ E	44.39	86	1½ E
64.1	West Drayton	47.48	86		48.27	85		48.22	84	
68.2	Southall	50.38	83	1½ E	51.47	sigs 45*		51.13	85	2¾ E
71.6	Ealing	-	pws 30*/65		54.44	76/sigs 15*		53.42	85	
76	Westbourne Park	58.23		T	60.18		¾ E	57.32		3 E
77.3	Paddington	61.07		1½ E	63.18		1¾ E	60.27		4 E
		(59 net)			(59½ net)					

Although the normal load for the *Cheltenham Flyer* was just six or seven coaches, at peak times it could significantly increase. The excellent run with 5037 above was with eight coaches and 5015 *Kingswear Castle* is recorded with a load of ten coaches, 340 tons gross, arriving 2 minutes early in a few seconds over 63 minutes. The tour de force was with 5023 *Brecon Castle* on a huge load of thirteen coaches, 435 tons, which very nearly kept time, although signal checks before Slough and at Acton made the train 7½ minutes late. The net time was only 66 minutes. The maximum speed was 79mph, with an average of just under 77mph from Uffington to Maidenhead. Who was the driver? F.W. Street of course! However, just to show that the performance was not entirely reliant on one man, an unknown recorder had thirteen runs on the 'Flyer' between 1935 and 1938, and logged the following overall actual times:

1935	14/7:	5037- 61m. 25s
1936	19/11:	5049- 65.26 (sigs app Paddington)
	10/12:	5056- 64.25 (sigs app Paddington)
1937	10/2:	5004- 65.19 (p-way slowing)
	24/3:	5004- 62.54
	18/6:	5038- 60.02
	24/8:	5067- 60.23
	21/10:	5038- 66.13 (sigs app Paddington)
1938	31/12:	5067- 62.58
	25/4:	5044- 63.02
	6/7:	5043- 62.33
	19/9:	5077- 65.26
	10/10:	5069- 66.13 (sigs app Paddington)

It is interesting that 5067, which was reputed to be a sluggish engine with valves not set as accurately as the earlier series, not only achieved two of the best times above, but featured a very high speed run in the earlier table of runs by F.W. Street.

Enthusiast train performance recorders were obviously most attracted to the heaviest and fastest services, the *Cornish Riviera Express*, the *Bristolian* and the *Cheltenham Flyer*, and it may be thought that all GW expresses in the 1930s performed in this scintillating way. However, apart from a couple of heavy expresses on the Wolverhampton route, the majority of GW expresses were more slackly timed or were semi-fast in nature and not so often under the scrutiny of the stopwatch. O.S. Nock was a regular traveller between Bath and London and recorded many runs on trains like the 8.20am Weston-super-Mare and the 4.15pm or 5.5pm Paddington back and time could be kept with speeds on the level usually in the 65-70mph range, the Castles working economically on 17-18 per cent cut-off and first port of the regulator. A 'typical' run, steady, punctual, but no fireworks, was a two-hour Paddington-Bristol train in 1934.

Old Oak's 5022 *Wigmore Castle* passing Stapleton Road with the up *Bristolian,* passing a Churchward 45XX with the 4.29pm Laurence Hill-Filton workman's train, c1937. (G.H. Soole/MLS Collection)

Newly constructed 5043 *Barbury Castle* at speed with the up *Cheltenham Flyer* near Steventon, 1936. (MLS Collection)

5056 *Ogmore Castle* (renamed *Earl of Powis* in 1937) picking up water on Goring troughs with the up *Bristolian*, October 1936. (Real Photographs/MLS Collection)

5056 *Ogmore Castle*, with cylinder cocks open to clear water from its cylinders, accelerates hard past Stapleton Road with the up *Bristolian*, c1936. (G.H. Soole/E. Johnson Collection)

High Speed in the 1930s • 117

5070 *Sir* Daniel Gooch, built in July 1938, tears over Goring troughs with the up *Bristolian*, September 1938.
(M.W. Earley postcard/ MLS Collection)

5063 *Earl* Baldwin on a Paddington-Worcester express near Iver, c1938.
(R.E. Batten/Rail Archive Stephenson)

Old Oak Common's 5035 *Coity Castle* climbing strongly to Saunderton summit with a Paddington-Wolverhampton express, c1937. The recent change from red to white painted headlamps may be noted. (H.K. Harmon/Rail Archive Stephenson)

4076 *Carmarthen Castle* left Paddington on the 11.15am with a full 375 ton train and dropped a minute and a half to Reading (37½ minutes) with nothing over 67mph, and improved slightly to Didcot, sustaining just over 70mph at Cholsey. Three coaches were slipped at Didcot – 52 minutes 49 seconds for 53.1 miles, 1¾ minutes late – but with recovery time and load reduced to 280 tons the train was a minute inside schedule at Swindon having sustained 67-68 all the way from Steventon to Shrivenham. Almost 80mph at Dauntsey and 75 at Box saw the train comfortably into Bath in 100 minutes 22 seconds, 102 minute schedule for the 106.9 miles. I found another run in the Railway Performance Society archives recorded by a passenger in the slip coach on the 11.15am Paddington-Bristol hauled by 4082 and it shows a good competent run without the spectacular running of the named trains:

Paddington-Didcot (slip coach)

4082 *Windsor Castle* – Bristol Bath Road

11.15am Paddington-Bristol

10 chs, 309/330 tons

Miles	Location	Times	Speeds	
0	Paddington	00.00		½ L
1.3	Westbourne Park	03.15		
5.7	Ealing Broadway	08.54	56½	
9.1	Southall	12.25	60½	1 L
13.2	West Drayton	16.18	66½	
18.5	Slough	20.49	72	¼ L
24.2	Maidenhead	25.34	73/70	T
31	Twyford	31.25	69	T
36	Reading	35.39	72	¼ E
38.6	Tilehurst	37.46	74	
41.5	Pangbourne	40.08	72	
44.7	Goring	42.46	74	
48.5	Cholsey	45.50	75	
53.1	Didcot	50.01		1½ E

In the 1937 and 1938 statistical surveys reported in the *Railway Gazette*, costs of the Great Western locomotives compared well with those of other companies.

1937:	Costs for coal per train mile:	GWR 6.34d, LNER 7.44d, LMSR 7.55d, SR 8.19d
	Costs of coal per locomotive:	GWR £ 494, LNER £ 563, LMSR £ 635, SR £ 672
1938:	Costs for coal per train mile :	GWR 6.65d, LNER 7.64d, LMSR 7.7d, SR 8.78d
	Costs of coal per locomotive:	GWR £ 507, LNER £ 581, LMSR £ 639, SR £ 675
	Working expenses per train mile:	GWR 19.89d, LMSR 20.76d, LNER 21.23d, SR 21.82d
	Working expenses per locomotive:	GWR £ 1,517, LNER £ 1,614, SR £ 1,677, LMSR £ 1,724

A route on which Castles were increasingly used as the numbers increased was the North & West line from Bristol to Shrewsbury via Pontypool Road and Hereford. Before the war, express services on this route were infrequent but heavy and most originated in the West Country with engines being changed at Bristol. 4000 *North Star* was allocated to Shrewsbury between 1934 and 1937 and was logged on a northbound run from Hereford whilst 5032, also Shrewsbury based, was recorded in the other direction. Accounts of both runs were published in the *Railway Magazine* in March 1935.

		Hereford-Shrewsbury and Shrewsbury-Hereford							
		4000 *North Star*			**5032** *Usk Castle*				Northbound
		304/320 tons			366/385 tons				
Miles	Location	Times	Speeds		Miles	Times	Speeds		Gradients
0	Hereford	00.00		T	51	66.09	sigs stand	1 ¼ L (63 ½ net)	
4.2	Moreton-on-Lugg	06.35	60½		46.8	58.05	66		L
7.5	Dinmore	09.55	51½		43.5	55.05	55	T	1/100 R
10.2	Ford Bridge	13.00			40.8	52.09	64		1/264 F
12.6	Leominster	15.20	62½	¾ E	38.4	49.52	64	¾ L	L
15.8	Berrington	18.30			35.2	46.49	60		1/154 R
18.9	Woofferton Junction	21.40	60	1¼ E	32.1	43.41	72	1¾ L	1/115 F
23.5	Ludlow	26.40	55/60	1¼ E	27.5	39.26	60*	2½ L	1/112, 1/134 R
25.7	Bromfield	28.55	58		25.3	37.28	67		1/160 R
28.1	Onibury	31.20	58/ sigs		22.9	35.31	74		1/286 R, 1/112 R
31.1	Craven Arm	36.05	sig stand	1 E	19.9	33.11	80½	4¼ L	
34.3	Marsh Farm Junction	41.55	43½		16.7	30.39	67		1/105 R, 1/112 R
37.5	MP 13 ½	46.05	33½			-			1/112 R
38.2	Church Stretton	47.05		1 E	12.8	26.06		5 L	
41.7	Leebotwood	50.30	62		9.3	18.36	24½		1/100 F
44.6	Dorrington	52.50	73		7.4	13.03	28		1/90 F
46.7	Condover	54.40			5.3	09.50	26½/31		1/134 F
50.2	Sutton Bridge Junction	58.10		3¾ E	1.8	02.59			1/127 F
51	Shrewsbury	60.35	(56½ net)	4½ E	0	00.00		T	

4000 started from Hereford vigorously and then worked economically as time was well in hand until the signal stand just before Craven Arms. It then worked hard having to commence the climb to Church Stretton without the usual impetus. 5032 for some unknown reason climbed poorly to Church Stretton and then ran at an unusually brisk pace for this route and would have been slightly early into Hereford without a momentary signal stop at Barrs Court Junction.

The first authenticated GW 100mph was not until 31 July 1939, although O.S. Nock recorded that a friend of his, Harold Eldred, had earlier logged a maximum of around 105mph descending Wellington Bank behind a Castle driven by F.W. Street. The train now concerned was the 12.45pm Paddington-Worcester and it left on time behind 4086 *Builth Castle* with a load of nine coaches, 306 tons. It passed Oxford in 64 minutes 45 seconds and stopped at Kingham (84¾ miles) in 87 minutes 50 seconds, where two coaches were detached. The log then read:

High Speed in the 1930s • 121

Kingham-Worcester, 31.7.1939
4086 Builth Castle
7 chs, 242 tons

Miles	Location	Times	Speeds	Gradient
0	Kingham	00.00		
2.75	Adlestrop	05.20		L
7	Moreton-in-Marsh	10.06	56	1/355 R, 1/294 R
10.25	Blockley	13.12	69	1/151 F
12.25	Campden	10.58	66½	1/154 R, L
13.75	Campden Tunnel	16.15	77/82	1/100 F
14.25	MP 99	16.37	85	1/100 F (Mickleton Halt)
15.25	MP 100	17.19	92	1/100 F
15.75	MP 100½	-	96	1/100 F (Honeybourne S. Junction)
16.25	MP 101	17.58	100	1/100 F
16.75	MP 101½	-	99	1/100 F, L (Honeybourne)
17.25	MP 102	18.34	97½	1/126 F
17.75	MP 102½	-	96	1/126 F
18.25	MP 103	19.11	94½	L
19.25	MP 104	19.49	94½	1/314 F
19.75	MP 104½	-	braked	1/314 F (Littleton & Badsey)
20.25	MP 105	20.27	70*	
22	Evesham	22.02	easy	
25	Fladbury	-	65	1/235 F
28	Pershore	27.53	55	1/198 R
32.5	Norton Junction	32.57	60/72	1/269 R, 1/347 F
36.75	Worcester	37.06		

The recorder took stopwatch readings every quarter mile between MP 99 and MP 103 with several at 9.1 seconds and one at 9.0 at MP 101½ just before the level quarter mile through Honeybourne station.

Another 100mph, though less well authenticated, was on a strange run on the 1.55pm Paddington-West Wales in March 1937, described by Cecil J. Allen in his regular article in *Trains Illustrated* in March 1953. The engine quoted is *Radnor Castle* (no number given) which is probably a confusion of 5052's name which in March 1937 was *Eastnor Castle*, becoming *Earl of Radnor* in July 1937. The train was a heavy 13-coach 450 ton load and it passed Stoke Gifford 14 minutes late at 44mph. It then accelerated very rapidly past Patchway, down the 1 in 68 through Cattybrook Tunnel, passing Pilning at 80mph and entering the Severn Tunnel at high speed. It continued to accelerate hard down the two miles of 1 in 100 inside the tunnel and was timed at exactly 100mph at MP 120 in the middle and exited at Severn Tunnel West after 2¼ miles of 1 in 90 up at 66½mph, the 4.4 miles of the tunnel passage taking just 3 minutes 6 seconds, an average of 85.2mph. Another somewhat similar run on the same route in the 1930s was described by Mr Allen in February the previous year. This time it was the 11.55am Paddington with 415 gross tons which suffered three bad permanent way restrictions between Reading and Swindon, passing the latter station 10½ minutes late. Unfortunately, the engine was not identified, though it was a Castle. It passed Badminton summit 9 minutes late, accelerated to 80½ at Coalpit Heath, careered round the Stoke Gifford curve at 60mph, touched 80 at Cattybrook and entered the Severn Tunnel at 85mph. The tunnel was threaded in 3 minutes 24 seconds, with a maximum speed of 90mph at the foot of the tunnel and Severn Tunnel West portal was passed at 56mph. Newport was reached in 143 minute 49 seconds, just 2¾ minutes late!

The Castles continued beyond Cardiff and the line to Swansea was not easy with the substantial London trains. 4089 *Donnington Castle*, a Swansea Landore engine in 1937, worked the 5.55pm Paddington with 330 tons gross non-stop from Cardiff to Neath, 37.9 miles in 41 minutes 28 seconds (schedule 44 minutes) accelerating to 61mph on gently rising gradients to Peterston, holding 44 on the 1 in 106 to Llanharan and touching 68 down the 1 in 138/157 before braking to 53 through Bridgend station. It climbed the three miles to Stormy Sidings summit (1 in 132/163) with a minimum of 46mph and sped past Margam Moors on the descent to Port Talbot at 75. After the Neath stop it was faced with two and a half miles of 1 in 99/88 to Skewen which was passed at 30mph, the 7.9 miles to Swansea High Street taking 14¼ minutes with a gentle descent into the bleak Swansea Valley and restricted curve past Landore shed.

The September 1938 *Railway Magazine* published some runs on the non-stop 5.30pm Swansea-Cardiff (Paddington) that took place between 1933 and 1937. The key times are shown in the table below.

Swansea-Cardiff

Miles	Location	4097 *Kenilworth Castle* Canton 297/315 tons c1933			5014 *Goodrich Castle* Old Oak Common 311/340 tons c1937			4079 *Pendennis Castle* Canton 379/405 tons c1937			Gradients
		Times	Speeds		Times	Speeds		Times	Speeds		
0	Swansea High St	00.00		T	00.00		T	00.00		T	
1.3	Landore	04.07	21	T	03.50	18	¼ E	04.12	20	¼ L	
	Swansea Valley Jcn	-	46		-	45		-	48		1/109 F
5.9	Skewen	11.31	27/58		11.20	36		10.35	37/58		1/91 R
7.9	Neath	13.58	34*	T	13.51	27*	¼ E	13.06	33*	1 E	
13.5	Port Talbot	20.44		¼ E	20.54		T	19.46		1¼ E	L
16.1	Margam Moors	24.29	60		24.32	68		23.23	63		L
20.1	Pyle	28.03		T	27.27		½ E	26.50		1¼ E	1/139 R
21.5	Stormy Sidings	30.18	33½		29.06	47		29.09	31		1/93 R
25.6	Bridgend	35.03	61/50*	T	34.50	easy	¼ E	34.06	58/42*	1 E	1/132 F
29.4	Pencoed	39.00	60½		39.20			38.20	60		L
32.2	Llanharan	42.46	35		42.34	48		41.45	45		1/138 R
34.7	Llantrisant	45.46	68		45.07	66		44.18	64		1/106 F
43.4	Ely	53.40	66		53.15	64/sigs		53.10	58/sigs		
45.8	Cardiff General	56.40		1¼ E	57.16		¾ E	63.51 sig stand		5¾ L (56¼ net)	

Photographer J.G. Hubback was a prolific and high quality railway photographer in the 1930s and spent time at Norton Fitzwarren and Whiteball at the high summer peak, in the Ely Valley between St Fagan's and Miskin and on the Vale of Glamorgan line through Barry and a selection of his photos now in the collection of John Hodge follow. The trains quoted are as noted by Mr Hubback, though it doesn't always tie with the listed GW train reporting number:

Landore's 4095 *Harlech Castle* drifts past Miskin with a West Wales-Paddington express, c1939. Engine cleaning has clearly deteriorated in the period just before the Second World War. (J.G. Hubback/John Hodge Collection)

Rebuilt 'Star' 5083 *Bath Abbey* of Landore at Miskin with a Bristol-Swansea stopping train, 1939. (J.G. Hubback/John Hodge Collection)

4073 *Caerphilly* Castle stands ready to take over the 2.20pm Minehead-Paddington from 'Dean Goods' 2301 and a 45XX 'Small Prairie' at Norton Fitzwarren, 1934.
(J.G. Hubback/John Hodge Collection)

4073 sets off from Norton Fitzwarren with the 2.20pm Minehead-Paddington, 1934.
(J.G. Hubback/John Hodge Collection)

Old Oak Common's 4075 *Cardiff Castle* at speed on a morning Paddington-Plymouth express near Norton Fitzwarren, 1934. (J.G. Hubback/John Hodge Collection)

Laira's 5028 *Llantilio Castle* unusually heads the down *Cornish Riviera Express* in place of the diagrammed 'King', passing Whiteball Box and beginning the descent to Exeter, 28 July 1934. (J.G. Hubback/John Hodge Collection)

Exeter's 5030 *Shirburn Castle* drops down from Whiteball Tunnel with a morning Paddington-Newquay express, 28 July 1934. (J.G. Hubback/John Hodge Collection)

Canton's 5004 *Llanstephan Castle* leaving Whiteball Tunnel with the 11.10am Paignton-Swansea, 13 July 1935. Note the motley collection of rolling stock on this peak holiday train. (J.G. Hubback/John Hodge Collection)

Above: 5014 *Goodrich Castle* of Newton Abbot with the down *Torbay Express*, 12noon Paddington-Kingswear, speeding through Norton Fitzwarren, 1935. (J.G. Hubback/John Hodge Collection)

Right: **Newton Abbot's** 5016 *Montgomery Castle* climbs the last few yards to Whiteball Tunnel with a very heavy 14 or 15 coach train banked at the rear. It is the 12.03pm Paddington-Paignton relief to the *Torbay Express,* 13 July 1935. (J.G. Hubback/John Hodge Collection)

Below: **Old Oak** Common's 5022 *Wigmore Castle* near Whiteball summit with a morning Paddington-Newquay express, 13 July 1935. (J.G. Hubback/John Hodge Collection)

5021 *Whittington* Castle alongside 5903 *Keele Hall* and an unidentified 'King' undergoing heavy overhaul in Swindon Works, c1935. (J.G. Hubback/John Hodge Collection)

Having mentioned the Worcester route earlier, there was one train booked to come up from Oxford to Paddington, 63.4 miles, in the even hour. However, the loads were more substantial than those carried post-war on the 5.35 Oxford which was similarly timed. This schedule required *Cheltenham Flyer* or *Bristolian* style running east of Didcot to keep time. A *Railway Magazine* article in February 1940 analysed a number of runs in the late 1930s and listed the following times achieved:

	Oxford – Paddington, 1937-1939			
Loco		Load	Actual Time	Net Time
4086	*Builth Castle*	290 tons	56.39	
5004	*Llanstephan Castle*	220 tons	60.36	55.15
5050	*Earl of St. Germans*	300 tons	61.09	
5042	*Winchester Castle*	330 tons	59.41	
5050	*Earl of St. Germans*	360 tons	59.03	
5049	*Earl of Plymouth*	375 tons	59.27	

The Castle allocation in the summer timetable of 1939 immediately before the changes caused by the Second World War were (changes from 1935 in brackets):

Old Oak Common: 100A1, 111, 4037, 4073, 4075, 4082, 4091, 5000, 5004, 5005, 5008, 5018, 5019, 5022, 5023, 5027, 5029, 5036, 5037, 5038, 5039, 5040, 5043, 5044, 5045, 5055, 5056, 5066, 5067, 5069, 5079, 5080, 5085, 5093 (34, +12)
Reading: 4085 (+1)
Bristol Bath Road: 4016, 4081, 4084, 4096, 5006, 5014, 5025, 5068, 5070, 5074, 5076, 5082, 5084, 5091, 5096 (15, +12)
Swindon: 4089 (+1)
Newton Abbot: 4076, 5028, 5034, 5058, 5062, 5071, 5072, 5094 (8, -1)
Taunton: 5026, 5077 (+2)
Exeter: 4099, 5003, 5011, 5012, 5050, 5059 (6, no change)
Laira: 4032, 4088, 4090, 4093, 4098, 5009, 5024, 5041, 5057, 5078, 5090, 5095 (12, +1)
Truro: 4087, 4097 (+2)
Penzance: 4077, 5013 (no change)
Stafford Road: 4000, 5031, 5033, 5035, 5053, 5060, 5075, 5081 (8, +3)
Shrewsbury: 5015, 5021, 5032, 5061, 5064, 5073, 5086, 5088, 5097 (9, +7)
Worcester: 4086, 4092, 5017, 5063 (+4)
Gloucester: 5042, 5092 (+2)
Cardiff Canton: 4074, 4079, 4083, 4094, 5001, 5010, 5020, 5030, 5046, 5047, 5049, 5052, 5054, 5065 (14, +4)
Landore: 4078, 4080, 4095, 5002, 5007, 5016, 5048, 5051, 5083 (9, + 3)

Total (129, + 54)

It will be noted that 5087 and 5089 are missing from this allocation list. In the summer of 1939, they were still unrebuilt 'Stars'. The 1936-39 build of Castles had augmented the allocations at Old Oak Common, Bristol Bath Road, Stafford Road, Shrewsbury and Cardiff Canton in particular. Exeter still had a group and small allocations are noted at Taunton, Truro and Penzance. Swindon had acquired one as had Reading and 4085 was resident at Reading for many years leading some to think that there was some problem with this locomotive.

In the 1930s, seaside holiday traffic was growing to the resorts of Weston-super-Mare and Barry Island as well as to the Devon and Cornwall resorts. As Weston and Barry were easier to access, the GWR developed substantial excursion traffic from London and also Swindon Works outings for their own staff's annual holiday shutdown. The photographer J.G. Hubback lived in Barry and took a number of photographs of these excursions and John Hodge, who now owns his collection, has been happy to share a selection of these previously unpublished images. But war was looming which would end such 'inessential' traffic and the high tide of GW performance would be over for virtually fifteen years until the resurgence in the mid-1950s.

Old Oak Common's 4009 *Shooting Star* (renumbered and renamed 100A1 *Lloyds* in 1936) passing Barry Docks with an excursion from Paddington, 1935. '180' was the train identification initially allocated to these London excursions. (J.G. Hubback/John Hodge Collection)

Old Oak Common's rebuilt 'Star' 4037 *Queen Philippa* crossing the isthmus between Barry Town and Barry Island with a Paddington excursion, 1936. (J.G. Hubback/John Hodge Collection)

Old Oak Common's 4084 *Aberystwyth Castle* departing from Barry Island with a returning London excursion in the late 1930s. (J.G. Hubback/John Hodge Collection)

High Speed in the 1930s • 131

Canton's 5052 *Earl of Radnor* passing the sidings holding coal awaiting shipment from Barry Docks, with a return excursion for Paddington, 1938. Old Oak engines usually worked these excursions but on this occasion it looks as though Canton has had to find a replacement for the return trip. The train reporting number for London excursions has now been changed to '010'. (J.G. Hubback/John Hodge Collection)

4099 *Kilgerran Castle* and another member of the class with stock for special trains to London in connection with the Coronation of King George VI in 1937. (J.G. Hubback/John Hodge Collection)

4099 *Kilgerran* Castle underway with the Coronation excursion at Dinas Powis, 1937.
(J.G. Hubback/John Hodge Collection)

The Great Western ran a number of holiday express excursions to popularise resorts such as Weston-super-Mare and Barry Island. Old Oak Common's 5045 *Earl of Dudley* heads a 'Holiday Haunts Express' as part of this programme to Barry Island near Dinas Powis, in the late 1930s.
(J.G. Hubback/John Hodge Collection)

Swindon Works management sponsored a number of special trains for the workers' day trips during the Works August closure fortnight. 5044, still named *Beverston Castle* before being renamed *Earl of Dunraven* in September 1937, with excursion No. 45 passing a Taff Vale 'A' tank on a Cardiff bound local train at Barry Docks, August 1937. (J.G. Hubback/John Hodge Collection)

Chapter 5
THE SECOND WORLD WAR AND ITS AFTERMATH

With the immediate slowing down and cancellation of some passenger services and the increase in wartime freight, one might have expected a reallocation of engines to meet new traffic flows. In fact, no initial significant changes occurred. Engines from Laira and Newton Abbot had occasional moves into Cornwall, Bristol engines to the Weston super-Mare sub-depot and Cardiff and Landore engines to Carmarthen as their mileage grew before Swindon overhauls, but these moves were usually short-lived. By mid-1940, Laira, Landore and Stafford Road had gained one or two each, Canton being the main loser. By mid-1944, there had still been no major redistribution though 26 of the 131 Castles then existing had moved sheds, but the net change was small – Stafford Road had gained four and Canton had regained its full fleet. The only shed to have a significant proportional loss was Exeter. It is perhaps of note that few of the smaller depots now had Castles – none in Cornwall, none at Weymouth or Weston-super-Mare or Carmarthen or Oxford or Chester, all depots that had had small numbers of Castles at different periods. Earlier 'Saints' and 'Stars' that might have been withdrawn as more Castles were constructed could cover those depots' needs – in fact the tenth 'Star' of the 'Abbey' series, 4067, was rebuilt as Castle 5087 as late as November 1940. The actual allocation at the beginning of 1944 was:

Old Oak Common:	100A1, 4037, 4073, 4075, 4076, 4091, 5000, 5004, 5005, 5008, 5014, 5018, 5022, 5023, 5027, 5029, 5035, 5036, 5037, 5038, 5039, 5040, 5043, 5044, 5045, 5055, 5056, 5066, 5069, 5085, 5087 (31, -3)
Reading:	4085 (no change)
Bristol Bath Road:	4080, 4081, 4084, 4089, 4093, 4096, 5019, 5024, 5025, 5048, 5074, 5076, 5082, 5084, 5091, 5096 (16, +1)
Swindon:	5067, 5068 (+1)
Newton Abbot:	4016, 4077, 4097, 4099, 5011, 5028, 5034, 5047, 5058, 5062, 5071, 5072, 5094 (13, +5)
Taunton:	5003, 5077 (no change)
Exeter:	5012, 5026, 5050, 5059 (4, -2)
Laira:	111, 4032, 4087, 4088, 4090, 4098, 5009, 5041, 5057, 5060, 5078, 5090, 5095 (13, +1)
Truro:	(-2)
Penzance:	(-2)
Stafford Road:	4000, 5021, 5031, 5033, 5053, 5070,

	5075, 5081, 5088 (9, +1)
Shrewsbury:	5015, 5032, 5061, 5064, 5073, 5086, 5097 (7, -2)
Worcester:	4086, 4092, 5017, 5063, 5092 (5, +1)
Gloucester:	4079, 4082, 5042 (3, +1)
Cardiff Canton:	4083, 4094, 5001, 5007, 5010, 5020, 5030, 5046, 5049, 5052, 5054, 5065, 5080 (13, -1)
Swansea Landore:	4074, 4078, 4095, 5002, 5006, 5013, 5016, 5051, 5079, 5083, 5089, 5093 (12, +3)
Total (131, +2, i.e. 5087 & 5089)	

The main change seems to have been the gathering of the small allocations at Penzance, Truro and Exeter back to the main depots at Newton Abbot and Laira, to cope with the military and naval activity around Plymouth.

After an initial drop in passenger traffic in 1940, when troop movements were heavy, but the public was discouraged from travel ('Is your journey really necessary?'), passenger miles grew and as the number of passenger trains was reduced from pre-war levels, train loads increased very significantly. Instead of high speed exploits with six-nine coaches, Castles found themselves facing twelve, thirteen, fourteen coaches especially on routes over which military traffic was heavy – for instance, the Berks & Hants and North & West routes to the naval base in Plymouth, or deep into Wales for armed forces' training camps. Passenger journeys increased during the war from 129 million to 190 million journeys a year. Passengers per train mile on the Great Western were up by 92 per cent, a massive increase and much greater than on the other railway companies (which ranged from 40-60 per cent). A total of 538,559 special trains were run during the war, mainly for the military. Freight, measured in 'net ton miles', increased over the whole country by 50 per cent.

The only visual change to the Castles during the war was the replacement of glass in the cab side windows with a steel plate to reduce the visibility of the glare from the fire during blackout and the use of blackout sheets from cab roof to tender for the same reason though this was soon abandoned as it made conditions on the footplate unacceptable due to excessive heat. Livery was amended from the standard passenger lined green to unlined green with just GW and crest on the tender. Cleanliness suffered as the war progressed with the shortage of young men available for cleaning duties.

Performance was affected by the slowing of schedules, the imposition of line speed limits, the use of lower grade coal and the increasing maintenance problems as the war was prolonged and periods between overhaul were extended and the disruption caused by enemy action caused engines to miss planned boiler washouts and other maintenance carried out at home depots. Because of traffic pressures and delays, engines were frequently sent out inadequately prepared or with blocked tubes. The 9.50pm Paddington-Plymouth via Bristol is said to have required five different locomotives one night following successive failures.

The GW Castles were fortunate to escape the war without any becoming air raid victims, despite their significant presence in London, Bristol, Newton Abbot and Plymouth which all suffered extensive bombing. Just one, 4091 *Dudley Castle*, was involved in a fatal accident on 2 July 1941 whilst hauling an overnight Plymouth-London via Bristol train which collided head-on with an LMS 8F 2-8-0 on loan to the GWR. The 8F, 8293, on an unfitted heavy freight from Old Oak Common, overran signals on the down relief line and collided with 4091 which was crossing from the up main to up relief line at Dolphin Junction, Slough. The 8F was not fitted with the GW ATC safety system which might have prevented the accident. Although receiving damage to the front end, 4091 was repaired and back in traffic at Old Oak Common by November. Engines received damage from strafing attacks or derailments after track had been damaged by bombing, although the main victims on the GW seemed to be members of the 'Hall' class, one of which (4911) was destroyed during a raid at Keyham, Plymouth, in April 1941. The only known damage to a Castle was the strafing by a lone enemy plane of 5005 *Manorbier Castle* near Newton Abbot when the cab and tender were damaged by bullets and the crew injured.

Old Oak Common's 5043 *Earl of Mount Edgcumbe* with a lightweight up express at Dolphin Junction, Slough, 5 May 1940. The cab window plate to avoid the fire glare alerting enemy aircraft is clearly visible. (W.S. Garth/Rail Archive Stephenson)

5010 *Restormel Castle* of Canton is diverted via the Vale of Glamorgan with a Paddington–Swansea express, c1941. (J.G. Hubback/John Hodge Collection)

The Second World War and its Aftermath • 137

5010 *Restormel* Castle at Miskin between Cardiff and Bridgend with a down Paddington-Swansea express in the early war years, before neglect and lack of cleaning set in, c1941. (J.G. Hubback/John Hodge Collection)

5080 *Defiant* with the 11.55am Paddington - West Wales express at Miskin, summer 1947. (J.G. Hubback/John Hodge Collection)

A very rundown 5008 *Raglan Castle* hurries a westbound train through Southall, steam leaking from every pore, 26 December 1946. (MLS Collection)

A 60mph line speed restriction was implemented on all lines in the initial stages of the war and therefore the only performances of interest would be on routes with significant gradients to overcome or where exceptional loads were hauled. One of the routes that received some attention during the war was the North & West route between Shrewsbury and Bristol. In September 1940 O.S. Nock had a footplate pass on a Newton Abbot Castle working the double-home Liverpool-Plymouth express that alternated daily between Shrewsbury and Newton Abbot engines and crews. 5072, then named *Compton Castle* but renamed *Hurricane* just two months later, had a load of 414 tons, 445 gross, and made an excellent climb to Church Stretton in 21 minutes 50

5052 *Earl of Radnor* in somewhat better condition with an express from South Wales at Southall on Boxing Day 1946. (MLS Collection)

Stafford Road's 5015 *Kingswear Castle* passes Warwick Goods Yard with an express for Wolverhampton in the summer of 1946. (G.A. Coltas/MLS Collection)

seconds for the first 12.8 uphill miles, reaching 41mph on the initial 1 in 127/134 to Condover, 50mph in the slight dip before Dorrington, 37mph on the 1 in 100 past Leebotwood and 32 at the summit of the 1 in 100 at All Stretton Halt. After that it was a matter of restraining the engine to avoid exceeding the line speed limit, a maximum of 63mph being recorded to Hereford, around 65 minutes net, 69½ actual (schedule 72 minutes) for the 51 miles. The climb to Llanvihangel, culminating in three miles of 1 in 100 from Pandy to Llanvihangel, pulled 5072 and its train down from 62 at Pontrilas, 46 past Pandy to 34mph at the summit. The 33.4 miles from Hereford to Pontypool took 44½ minutes, well inside the schedule. 63mph was attained in the middle of the Severn Tunnel and 5072 made an excellent climb out, with 36mph on the 1 in 100 to Pilning and 34 on the nasty 1 in 68 through Cattybrook Tunnel to Patchway.

Later, the 60mph limit was eased to 75 and I table below three runs between Hereford and Shrewsbury typical of the loads and best running on that route. The schedule was 72 minutes.

The collision at Dolphin Junction, Slough, between 4091 *Dudley Castle* on the 6.20pm Plymouth and LMS 8F 8293 on loan and working the 1.30am Old Oak Common-Severn Tunnel unfitted freight, 2 July 1941. (R.C. Riley Collection)

Hereford-Shrewsbury

Miles	Location	5032 *Usk Castle* Shrewsbury 416/450 tons 7.30pm Bristol Mail 1940		5060 *Earl of Berkeley* Laira 426/470 tons 8.45am Plymouth 1941		5086 *Viscount Horne* Shrewsbury 392/420 tons 8.45am Plymouth 1942		Gradients
		Times	Speeds	Times	Speeds	Times	Speeds	
0	Hereford	00.00		00.00		00.00		
4.2	Moreton-on-Lugg	07.35		08.01		07.50		L
7.5	Dinmore	11.25	52 ave	11.50	52 ave	11.37	53 ave	1/100 R
10.2	Ford Bridge	14.55	47 ave	15.23	46 ave	14.45	52 ave	1/264 F
12.6	Leominster	17.20	62½	18.02	pws	17.05	64	L
15.7	Berrington	20.25		21.58		20.26		
18.9	Woofferton	23.40	65	25.37	60	23.48	66	
23.5	Ludlow	28.50		30.44		28.42		
28.1	Onibury	34.10	37	36.25	sigs	33.57	39	1/160 R, 1/112 R
31.1	Craven Arms	38.05	50	40.59		37.47	50½	
35.6	Marsh Brook	44.55		47.40		43.46		1/105 R, 1/112 R
38.2	Church Stretton	49.45	27	52.17	28	47.54	37	1/112 R
41.7	Leebotwood	53.35		56.17		51.36		1/100 F
44.6	Dorrington	-	65	58.40	78	53.53	82	1/90 F
46.7	Condover	58.15		60.27		55.35		
	Sutton Bridge Jcn	-		-	sigs	-	sig stop	
51	Shrewsbury	63.40		68.00	(64½ net)	64.55	(61 net)	

The 11.15am Swansea-Manchester with 435 tons did even better. 5080 *Defiant* of Canton averaged 30mph on the 5½ mile 1 in 106/95 climb from Ponthir to Pontypool Road, then a similar speed on the 1 in 82/95 climb to Llanvihangel, although the train was badly checked on to Hereford. A splendid run was made from Hereford to Shrewsbury in 64 minutes 53 seconds, only 59 net, averaging 40mph on the 7.1 mile climb from Craven Arms to Church Stretton, with a minimum of 37mph at the summit of the 1 in 112.

Old Oak Common's 4073 *Caerphilly Castle* has been borrowed by Shrewsbury shed to work the 8.20am Crewe-Bristol, seen climbing to Church Stretton at Leebotwood, 10 July 1948. (J.D. Darby/MLS Collection)

Canton's 5001 *Llandovery Castle* with a Shrewsbury-Hereford stopping train at Leebotwood, 10 July 1948. (J.D. Darby/MLS Collection)

Shrewsbury's rebuilt 'Star' 5086 *Viscount Horne* (ex-4066 *Malvern Abbey*) working the 11.12am from Shrewsbury to Bristol at All Stretton with a heavy 14-coach load, 21 May 1949. 5086 was a regular on the North & West during the war years. (J.D. Darby/MLS Collection)

Stafford Road's 4000 *North Star* off course at Bristol Temple Meads with the 11.45am express for Paddington, 1949. (G.A. Coltas/MLS Collection)

Other areas where good performance could still be recorded in the war years were in Devon and Cornwall and north of Wolverhampton. The London-Birmingham route could also show some vigorous hill climbing but the heaviest loads were normally in the hands of 'Kings'. Stafford Road's 5033 *Broughton Castle* and Old Oak Common's 111 *Viscount Churchill* were both timed with 500+ ton loads between Banbury and Leamington with speeds in the low 40s on the 1 in 179 to Cropredy and 70-72 on the descent to Leamington at Fosse Road. 5022 *Wigmore Castle* with 450 tons ran from Wolverhampton to Wellington (19.6 miles) in 22½ minutes with 77½mph at Cosford and an excellent 43½ minimum on the five miles of 1 in 150 to Hollinswood. The eighteen miles from Gobowen to Shrewsbury were tightly timed even in the wartime years and 5061 *Earl of Birkenhead* with 275 tons touched 77½mph below Leaton and 5066 *Wardour Castle* with 330 tons 73, 5061 completing the start to stop run in nineteen minutes exactly and 5066 in 19¾ net. O.S. Nock had a footplate trip on 4000 in July 1950 between Wolverhampton and Shrewsbury on the 11.10am from Paddington with a substantial load of 460 tons gross working through to Chester. After a 20mph p-way slack at Oxley 4000 managed to accelerate to 60, falling to 55 on the 1 in 183 after Codsall, then running down the 1 in 100/137 past Albrighton to 77½mph at Cosford. 34mph was then sustained on the five miles of 1 in 150 to Hollinswood and Wellington was reached in 23½ minutes net for the 19.6 miles. 71 at Walcot and 63½ minimum at Upton Magna was enough to bring the train into Shrewsbury in 13 minutes net for the 10.2 miles well on time. The engine was in good nick, described by Nock as a 'real beauty'!

At the end of the war, the GW locomotive stock (like the engines of other companies) was in poor shape, maintenance having been neglected to give priority to munitions supply work and emergency repairs to track and stock. Somewhat unfairly, in the argument for nationalisation of the railways in 1946, the Labour Chancellor of the Exchequer, Hugh Dalton, described the railways

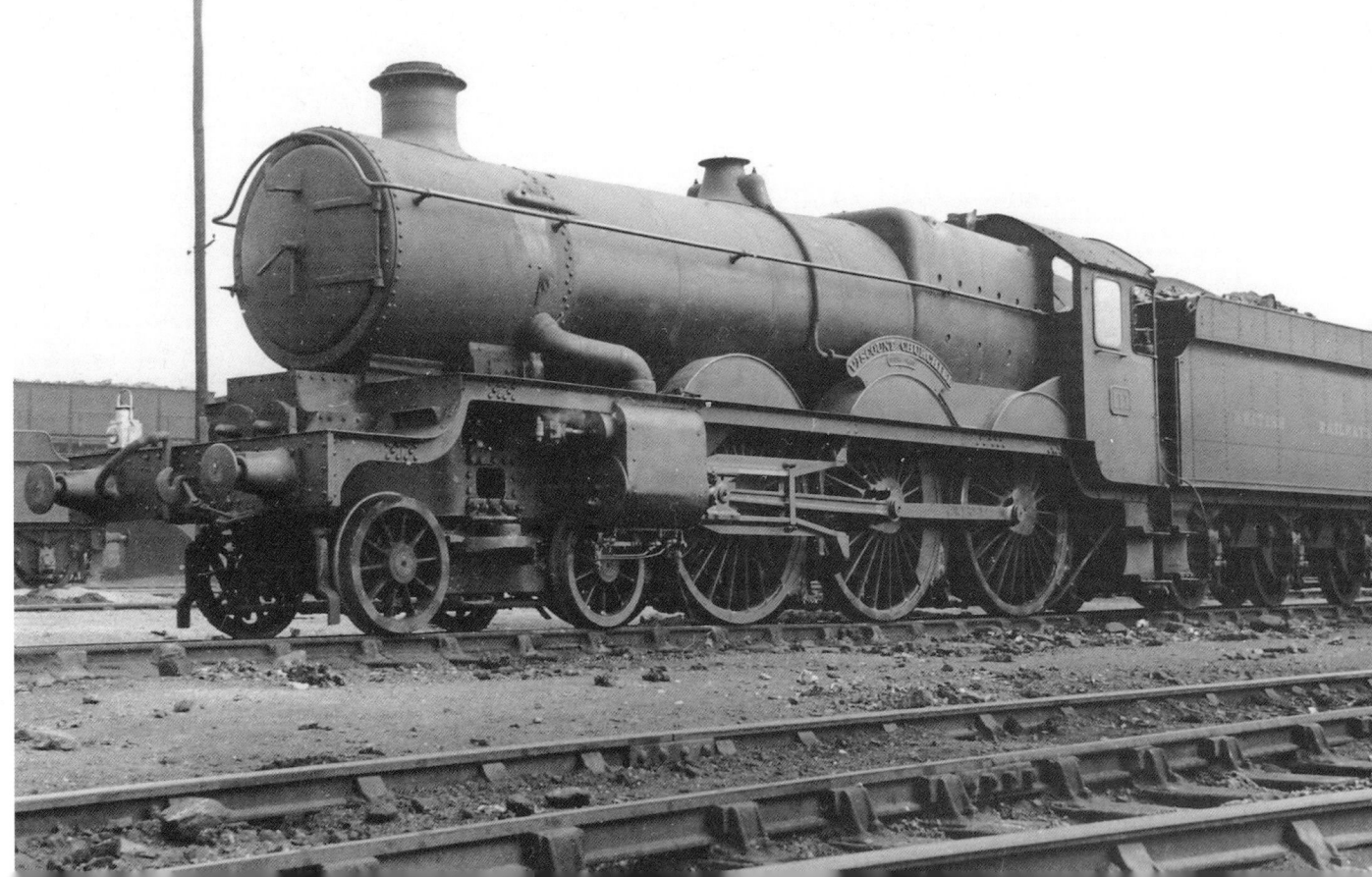

111 *Viscount Churchill* looking a bit drab in early BR livery at its home depot, Old Oak Common, in 1948. It was transferred to Laira in May 1950 and withdrawn from there in July 1953. (Rail Archive Stephenson)

Canton's 5001 *Llandovery Castle* with a trainload of parcels vans eastbound at St Fagan's, June 1949. (Transport Treasury/MLS Collections)

during a debate on a new Transport Bill as 'a very poor bag of assets … the rolling stock is in a state of dilapidation … the railways are a disgrace to the country …' This was in contrast to Winston Churchill's letter to the railways' General Managers' Conference, including words such as … 'Thanks for the highly efficient manner in which they have met every demand … the railways were subjected to intensive attacks, … yet the results of the damage were overcome very speedily … traffic kept moving … gratitude to every railwayman who participated in this great transport effort which is contributing so largely towards final victory.' But there is no doubt – the GW locomotives as well as their crews were exhausted at the end of the war.

As I have written previously in the Pen & Sword books on both the 'Counties' and the 'Kings', some of Collett's Swindon team were exploring the steam engine design developments by André Chapelon in the late 1930s, but the war had prevented experimentation with any of these. However, after the war, in February 1946, one of that team, S.O. Ell, had produced a paper on boiler design and high superheat, comparing the theoretical effect of using 2-, 3- or 4-row superheater units, concluding that a 4-row superheater of 369sqft would give the best results. Despite the building of Hawksworth 'Counties' from 1945, the Castles were still the most economical of the GW passenger engines and the building of more of the 1923 design was authorised by the GW Board in 1946. Hawksworth had already concluded higher superheat was necessary to counter post-war conditions, especially the lack of availability of best quality steam coal, and ten new Castles with 3-row superheaters, numbered 5098 to 7007, were delivered between May and July 1946.

The engines were named:

5098 *Clifford Castle* (was allocated *Sudeley Castle* but never carried)

5099 *Compton Castle* (was allocated *Tenby Castle* but never carried)

7000 *Viscount Portal* (was allocated both *Thornbury Castle* & *Cranbrook Castle* but never carried)

7001 *Sir James Milne* (was allocated *Chester Castle* but never carried)

7002 *Devizes Castle* (was allocated *Hereford Castle* but never carried)

7003 *Elmley Castle* (was allocated *Drysllwyn Castle* but never carried)

7004 *Eastnor Castle*

7005 *Lamphey Castle* (renamed *Sir Edward Elgar* in August 1957)

7006 *Lydford Castle*

7007 *Ogmore Castle* (renamed *Great Western* in January 1948)

The allocation of names of the Great Western hierarchy was decided as nationalisation loomed. 7007 was both the last Castle and last passenger engine built by the GWR.

The shortage of coal in 1946 prompted the GWR to test an oil-firing scheme which was seized on by the government to encourage the adoption of oil-firing country-wide, and a large number of locomotives of all companies were converted between 1946 and 1948 before the government halted the scheme through the shortage of foreign currency to purchase the oil. The intention was to convert twenty-five Castles and oil facilities on the GWR to be concentrated west of Newton Abbot, but the locomotives converted included only five Castles – 100A1, 5039, 5079, 5083 and 5091. All had the 1,950 gallon oil tank on the 4,000 gallon tender apart from 5091 which had its tank mounted on a 3,500 gallon tender. Despite the intention to use the engines in the West Country, the Castles concerned were initially based at Swindon for test and observation purposes, though 100A1 and 5039 soon reverted to their Old Oak Common base, 5083 and 5091 were at Bristol and 5079 was the only one actually allocated to Laira. O.S. Nock experienced three of them running between London and Bristol including a competent performance with 5039 *Rhuddlan Castle* on the 9.5am Paddington with 375 tons to Bath.

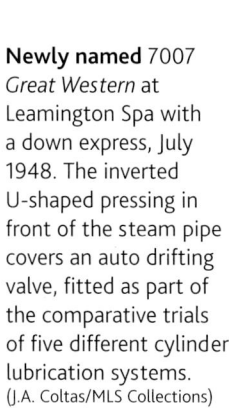

Newly named 7007 *Great Western* at Leamington Spa with a down express, July 1948. The inverted U-shaped pressing in front of the steam pipe covers an auto drifting valve, fitted as part of the comparative trials of five different cylinder lubrication systems. (J.A. Coltas/MLS Collections)

7001 *Sir James Milne* and 5000 *Launceston Castle* at Stratford-upon-Avon prepared for the royal train, 20 April 1950. (T.E. Williams/F.K. Davies & John Hodge Collections)

67½mph was the maximum speed before a p-way slack at Ruscombe and then after the Reading stop 64 at Goring before a succession of signal checks between Challow and Wootton Bassett clearly following the heavy 8.55am Paddington-South Wales. 5039 then accelerated to 76 at Dauntsey and the three Bath coaches were slipped punctually in 76 minutes from Reading (70.9 miles) and Bristol was reached on time. Harder work was exhibited by 5079 *Lysander* west of Plymouth. Throughout 1947 it was achieving 320 miles daily with two return trips from Plymouth to Penzance including the up and down *Cornish Riviera Express* as well as an early morning down parcels train and an evening stopping train. O.S. Nock had a run on 5079 on the down *Cornish Riviera* with 365 tons to Truro and 325 on to Penzance when time was kept but 5079 had to be worked hard on the steepest gradients. 22½mph was sustained on the 1 in 68 after St Germans and 34 on the 1 in 74 after Menheniot and 28 on the 1 in 74/58 towards Doublebois. The 34.7 miles to Par took the 52 minutes scheduled. The 29 minute schedule from Par to Truro over the 19 miles, including the initial seven miles of heavy climbing straight from Par station to St Austell mostly around 1 in 60, was rarely kept and 5079 dropped three minutes with only 19mph on the steepest gradient and 61 maximum on the descent from Grampound Road. However, time was recovered on the next section to Gwinear Road despite a p-way slowing before Redruth and Penzance was reached on time. It is interesting that the oil per train mile consumed varied from 2.88 gallons on the London-Bristol run to 4.78 in Cornwall.

5098 was extensively tested on the Swindon test plant and on the road in 1948 and 1949 at varying speeds and loads with coal consumption varying from 2.95dhp/hour on level track at 65mph to 3.6 depending on the load. When 5098 was steamed at its maximum rate of 24,000lb of steam per hour, coal consumption

5091 Cleeve Abbey as rebuilt for oil-burning, the sole example to have the equipment on a Churchward 3,500 gallon tender, 1946. (GW Official photograph/ F.K. Davies & John Hodge Collections)

Oil-burning 100A1 *Lloyds* at Old Oak Common, 21 May 1948. (W. Potter/F.K. Davies & John Hodge Collections)

per dhp/hour ranged from 3.1 with a test plant load of 544 tons at 69½mph to 4.3 at 86.5mph with 254 tons. 5098 was used on Ocean Liner specials from Plymouth Millbay Docks in August and September 1949 and completed the runs with 303 and 348 tons in 243 (239 net) and 247 minutes respectively, the latter time including three minutes to detach the pilot engine used over the Devon gradients. Exeter to Paddington was completed in under even time on both occasions. Mr Nock travelled on the footplate with 5098 and a Shrewsbury crew throughout from Newton Abbot to Shrewsbury on the 9.45am Newton

Oil-burning 5039 *Rhuddlan Castle* at Warwick with the 11.10am Paddington-Birkenhead, August 1947. (H.W. Robinson/F.K. Davies & John Hodge Collections)

Abbot (8.45 Plymouth double-home turn) in September 1949. The load was 13 coaches, 421/460 tons and the climb to Whiteball was excellent with a minimum of 48½mph before a p-way slack at the tunnel. With 84mph after Wellington, Taunton was reached a minute early in 37 minutes 8 seconds for the 30.8 miles. The train ran via Weston-super-Mare with a maximum of 64½mph on the level before Uphill Junction and Bristol was reached on time. Five minutes were dropped to Pontypool Road as a result of two severe p-way slacks at Magor and Llantarnam, but a couple of minutes were recovered on to Hereford with 22mph at Llanvihangel summit and 74 through Pandy. Signal checks at Bromfield and before Shrewsbury and two more p-way slacks at Leominster and Church Stretton plagued the last section, and arrival was three minutes late. Despite starting the climb to Church Stretton at only 49mph following the checks, the minimum was 38½mph at the top of the 1 in 112 before the Church Stretton restriction. Average coal consumption was 40-42lb per mile.

The tests with 5098 were compared with 2-row standard superheated engine 5087 *Tintern Abbey* and the latest experiment with 5049 *Earl of Plymouth* which had been fitted with a 4-row superheater unit. 5049's superheater had been enlarged to 393sqft. 5098 was, like 5099, fitted with the GW standard hydrostatic lubricator, though the other eight engines of that batch, 7000-7007, were fitted with four different variants of a mechanical lubrication system. (5098 was subsequently fitted with a mechanical lubricator situated behind the outside steam pipe on the right hand running plate.) Runs between Swindon and Paddington with it showed very economical working with coal consumption ranging from 24½lbs to 34lbs per mile, but although a decision was made to convert all the 'Kings' to 4-row superheat, the decision to convert any more Castles did not take place until 1957. 5049, based at Canton since 1939, was reputed to remain a strong engine despite the decision not to replicate it at the time.

Mr Nock recorded 138 runs of more than 70 miles non-stop between 1946 and 1950, mostly between Bath and London, at an average speed of 54.4mph, on which just nine had time booked

5053 *Earl Cairns* with a Paddington-Wolverhampton via Oxford train on Goring troughs, 1947. (Colling Turner/Rail Archive Stephenson)

Old Oak Common's rebuilt 'Star' 5089 *Westminster Abbey* on a West of England train between Reading West and Southcote Junction, in the summer of 1948. (M.W. Earley/MLS postcard collection)

against the engine (48 minutes in total). 342 minutes of lost time through checks were regained. The average load was 420 tons. The net average speed was 56.2mph and 48 different engines were encountered. He had 55 runs with shorter journeys at a net average speed of 50.4mph with 34 different engines with 159 minutes gained and 46 lost (one on oil-burning 100A1 accounting for 21 minutes of that). The average load was 447 tons. Performance at this time was not ideal for the Castles. Coal was poor, engines were still suffering from delayed maintenance and the average loads were heavy and not in the range for which the Castles excelled. However, occasionally a crew with a good engine would show some semblance of pre-war sparkle. 5038 *Morlais Castle* worked the 7.45am Weston-super-Mare with 460 tons to Didcot before slipping a coach, and after just holding the schedule to Swindon maintained over 70mph between Uffington and a p-way slack at Reading with a top speed of 74 through Didcot. Net time to Paddington for the 94 miles from Chippenham was 92¾ minutes, a gain of 11¼ minutes on the schedule. Newly built 7019 *Fowey Castle* left Chippenham seven minutes late with the 445 ton 5.25pm Bristol-Paddington, attained 71 at Uffington before a p-way slowing at Challow and then got up to 75mph by Cholsey and maintained that speed until past Tilehurst. 7019 had regained four minutes of lost time to Swindon and had improved on the scheduled 46 minutes from Swindon to Reading by 6¼ minutes.

The rest was easy and Paddington was reached on time. 7036 *Taunton Castle* on a 'King' diagram brought up 15 coaches, 535 tons gross, from Exeter, topped Whiteball at 37½mph, and with 82 before Norton Fitzwarren, cut the Exeter-Taunton 38 minute schedule by a minute. It then chopped 3½ minutes from the 55 minute Taunton-Westbury schedule with a minimum of 53mph at Somerton, 34½ at Brewham and a maximum of 72 before Westbury. A high speed ATC test was carried out in October 1947 with 5056 *Earl of Powis* and a lightweight train of 141 tons. The test started from Reading and 82mph was achieved by Twyford (5 miles) with a maximum of 96.8mph a mile before Maidenhead station when a successful test ATC brake application was made.

Canton's 4094 *Dynevor Castle* at Cheltenham Malvern Road with the 9.35am Swansea-Birmingham train, 21 May 1948. (K.D. Rhodes/F.K. Davies & John Hodge Collections)

Bristol's 5025 *Chirk Castle* at Saltford with the 11.20 Bristol Temple Meads-Salisbury, 2 October 1949. (J.D. Darby/MLS Collection)

The building of Castles recommenced in May 1948 with 7008 *Swansea Castle* and continued through to August 1950 with the completion of 7037 which was named *Swindon* in a ceremony at the Works. All of these were coupled with Hawksworth flush-sided tenders similar to the ones with which the 'Counties' were equipped. 7017 was named *G.J. Churchward* and a lot of Castle names were reused, some for the third or even fourth time (e.g. *Ogmore Castle* was used on 5056, 5080, 7007 and finally 7035). Some Castle names were allocated and never used and others reused once, replaced and never used again. The names identified but rejected were:

Exeter Castle (*Powderham Castle* was used instead)

Hatherop Castle (intended for 5053)

Liddington Castle

Oystermouth Castle (intended for 5007)

Picton Castle (intended for 5058 and 7023)

Wallingford Castle (intended for 5012)

Wilton Castle (intended for 5067)

Castle names that were used, then replaced and never used again, included *St Donat's Castle* (ex-5017), *Wardour Castle* (ex-5066) and *Lamphey Castle* (ex-7005).

Nationalisation occurred in January 1948 and although 'Rebuilt Royal Scots' were included in the Exchange trials that year, the Castles were overlooked even though they were still under construction. Their limited route accessibility because of their larger loading gauge width would have told against them. Various passenger liveries were tried out before the GW 'middle chrome green' was chosen and 4089, 4091, 5010, 5021, 5023 and 7010-7013 appeared in a light green with red and grey lining not unlike the LNER apple green livery.

7017 has worked up from Bristol on the 7am from Weston-super-Mare and will be turned and placed in Paddington station to be named *G.J. Churchward* at a ceremony on 2 October 1948. (P.J.T. Reed/F.K. Davies & John Hodge Collections)

7011 *Banbury Castle* in the experimental BR light green livery at the head of an express to Bristol, in early 1949. A 50XX Castle is at the head of another express on the adjacent platform. (MLS Collection)

5021 *Whittington* Castle in the experimental BR light green livery at Par station in Cornwall with the down *Cornish Riviera Express*, 25 August 1948. (K.D. Rhodes/F.K. Davies & John Hodge Collections)

7032 *Denbigh* Castle temporarily renumbered 7037 and named *Swindon* for a special occasion at Swindon Works, 21 June 1951. (C.J. Alcock/F.K. Davies & John Hodge Collections)

7014 *Caerhays Castle* at Westbourne Park with a Paddington-Bristol express, August 1948. 7014 was built the previous month and would be withdrawn from Tyseley in February 1965. (Colling Turner/Rail Archive Stephenson)

The allocation of Castles in 1950 once all had been delivered was as follows (change from 1944 shown):

Old Oak Common: 4016, 4037, 5004, 5014, 5029, 5034, 5035, 5038, 5039, 5040, 5043, 5044, 5055, 5056, 5065, 5066, 5069, 5081, 5085, 5087, 7001, 7004, 7013, 7024, 7025, 7030, 7032, 7033, 7036 (29, -2)

Reading: 4085, 5036 (+1)

Oxford: 5026, 7008, 7010 (+3)

Bristol Bath Road: 4073, 4075, 4084, 4091, 4096, 5000, 5019, 5025, 5037, 5048, 5064, 5067, 5074, 5076, 5082, 5094, 5096, 7011, 7014, 7019, 7034, (21, +5)

Swindon: 100A1 (withdrawn 3/50), 5009, 5018, 5068, 5083, 5084, 5091, 7015, 7037 (9, +7)

Weymouth: 4080 (+1)

Newton Abbot: 4077, 4098, 4099, 5011, 5024, 5028, 5041, 5047, 5071, 5078, 5079, 7000, 7029 (13, no change)

Taunton: 4032, 5003 (no change)

Exeter: 5059, 5062 (-2)

Plymouth Laira: 111, 4088, 4089, 4097, 5012, 5021, 5023, 5057, 5058, 5060, 5090, 5095, 5098, 7027, 7031 (15, +2)

Penzance: 4087, 4090 (+2)

Stafford Road: 4000, 4083, 4092, 5008, 5010, 5015, 5022, 5031, 5045,

	5053, 5061, 5070, 5088, 7026 (14, +5)
Shrewsbury:	5032, 5050, 5073, 5097, 7035 (5, -2)
Chester:	4076, 5027, 5033, 5075 (+4)
Worcester:	4082, 4086, 4093, 5017, 5063, 5086, 5092, 7005, 7007 (9, +4)
Gloucester:	4079, 5042, 7006 (no change)
Cardiff Canton:	4094, 5001, 5005, 5006, 5007, 5020, 5030, 5046, 5049, 5052, 5054, 5077, 5080, 5089, 5099, 7016, 7017, 7020, 7022, 7023 (20, +7)
Swansea Landore:	4074, 4078, 4081, 4095, 5002, 5013, 5016, 5051, 5072, 5093, 7002, 7003, 7009, 7012, 7018, 7028 (16, +4)
Carmarthen:	7021 (+1)
Total:	(171, +40)

Thirty of the forty new Hawksworth Castles were allocated to the key depots of Old Oak Common, Bristol Bath Road, Stafford Road, Cardiff Canton and Swansea Landore. They were nearly all additions to those depots' stock of Castles, apart from Old Oak Common, where the allocation of nine of the new engines displaced a similar number of older locomotives. The most curious increase was at Swindon which had gained seven Castles. At this time there was a backlog of work at Swindon and a number of Castles were in store awaiting Works attention. Did they include some of those 'temporarily' allocated to Swindon? Or had Swindon gained a number of Castle turns on the combined Bristol/Gloucester services that join at Swindon, or on the Swindon-Banbury route? They worked the 1.25am Paddington-Swansea sleeper via Gloucester to Cardiff and were also regularly seen on the milk traffic to and from West Wales.

7014 *Caerhays* Castle, now somewhat more travel-stained, heads the 4.15pm Paddington-Bristol-Plymouth express in Sonning Cutting, 23 July 1949. (A.C. Gilbert/MLS Collection)

The Second World War and its Aftermath • 157

Old Oak Common's 7025 *Sudeley Castle* just days after entering service, with a down mid-morning Paddington-Bristol express in Sonning Cutting, 15 August 1949. (MLS Collection)

7007 *Great* Western threads past High Wycombe station with the 4.10pm Paddington-Wolverhampton train, August 1948. (H.K. Harmon/Rail Archive Stephenson)

The last Hawksworth Castle, 7037, built in August 1950 and named *Swindon* by Princess Elizabeth during a visit to the Works, is seen here at its home depot Swindon in the early 1950s being cherished by the depot's cleaners, where it remained until transferred to Old Oak Common in September 1960. It was constructed with a Hawksworth tender but exchanged it for a Collett tender at a Works visit – tender types were exchanged indiscriminately between any of the Castles after 1950. (Rail Archive Stephenson)

Chapter 6
RESURGENCE IN THE 1950s

British Railways came and at first little changed after the flurry of livery experiments and the excitement of the Locomotive Exchanges. The country became more prosperous and the annual fortnight holiday became an institution. The Great Western serviced a huge influx of holiday makers from London, the West Midlands and the North West to Devon and Cornwall every summer Friday night and Saturday. I can remember the excitement of my family venturing in 1952 to Paignton after a few seasons of 'boring' holidays in Brighton and Bognor and Margate. We went from Surbiton via the South Western main line but somehow the holiday really seemed to start at Exeter St David's awaiting the crowded train from Cardiff or Birmingham and hanging in the corridor (on the sea side of course) and flinging the toplight window wide to smell the ozone and hear the sharp bark of a Great Western locomotive. In 1952, it was *Shotton Hall* but we went again in 1953 and our train to Newton Abbot was headed by Bristol Bath Road's 5069 *Isambard Kingdom Brunel*. I can't remember too much about the short journey other than peering out of the open window and getting a smut in my eye. In 1953 we stayed in Newton Abbot, and I remember being allowed to leave my family sitting on the beach in Torquay while I ventured to Dawlish and amid all the GW engines, was confronted by 'Britannia' 70021 *Morning Star* with the 11am from London. I was thrilled to find my return to Newton Abbot was to be behind Shrewsbury's 5097 *Sarum Castle* on the 9.5am Liverpool-Plymouth, the daily through double-home diagram between Shrewsbury and Newton Abbot whose engines and crew alternated. The previous year it had been Shrewsbury's 5050 *Earl of St Germans* and Newton Abbot's ex-works 4077 *Chepstow Castle*. In 1953 Newton Abbot's 7000 *Viscount Portal* alternated with 5097. A couple of times we went to spend the day on Goodrington Sands and our train back on each occasion was with the Newton Abbot Castle off the down *Torbay Express*, 5028 *Llantilio Castle* and 5047 *Earl of Dartmouth*, both in pristine external condition. The 'Britannias' did not make a very impressive introduction to the Western Region. *Trains Illustrated's* 'Motive Power Miscellany' Western Region column was full of reported failures in the Spring and Summer 1953 magazines. A more successful competitor to the Castles at this time was the Metrovick Gas Turbine 18100, which on test hauled eighteen coaches, 609 tons, up the 1 in 42 of Hemerdon bank (18mph at the summit) from a standing start at Plympton and became a regular performer on the down *Merchant Venturer* and up *Bristolian*. The Brown Boveri 18000 nicknamed *Kerosene Castle* was not so successful, and a number of failures were reported on Bristol-Paddington trains in the early 1950s.

5097 *Sarum Castle* of Shrewsbury depot on arrival at Newton Abbot with the 9.5am from Liverpool, 17 August 1953. (David Maidment)

Exeter's 5021 *Whittington Castle* above the beach huts at Goodrington Sands with an Exeter-Kingswear stopping train, 8 June 1954. (F.A. Blencowe)

The rebuilt *Great Bear*, 111 *Viscount Churchill*, was seen in the Newton Abbot area in its final years, here approaching that town with a down express, c1952. (J.D. Mills/ Rail Archive Stephenson)

Newton Abbot's 5012 *Berry Pomeroy Castle* departs from Exeter St David's with the down *Torbay Express*, 14 August 1952. (R.O. Tuck/Rail Archive Stephenson)

5028 *Llantilio Castle* of Newton Abbot with flush-sided tender of a 70XX at its home station ready to depart with the northbound *Devonian*, 26 July 1951. (MLS Collection)

Newton Abbot's 5024 *Carew Castle* at Goodrington Sands Halt with a train for Kingswear, 7 August 1951. (T. Lewis/MLS Collection)

5034 *Corfe* Castle departs from Newton Abbot with a stopping train for Kingswear, 1 August 1952. (T. Lewis/MLS Collection)

Penzance's 4090 *Dorchester Castle* comes off the Royal Albert Bridge at Saltash with an express for Penzance, 28 July 1951. (A.C. Gilbert/MLS Collection)

5074 *Hampden* with a down Paddington-West of England express at Norton Fitzwarren, 12 August 1951. Note that 5074 has the Castle tall chimney. (P. Hutchinson/MLS Collection)

The holiday lines were so congested that locomotive performance was regulated by the signalman. I remember in later years when based at Old Oak Common that we had 43 Summer Saturday diagrams for Castles and had only 33 of the class allocated to the depot. Most of the holiday extras therefore found themselves with Old Oak's 'Modified Halls' (ironically nicknamed 'Old Oak Castles') or 'Halls' acquired from London Division sheds – Southall, Reading and Didcot – while relief trains from the Midlands or North West had 'Halls' or 'Granges' from the freight depots of St Philip's Marsh, Pontypool Road or Oxley, often with excessive loads and causing a procession of faster services to dawdle behind them. Sometimes power was so short that engines were turned round at Paddington (Ranelagh Bridge Sidings) without the fire being properly cleaned which would lead to trouble later. 4093 *Dunster Castle,* a Worcester engine, arrived from Wolverhampton at 11.10am on a 1952 summer Saturday and was already back on the 11.55am to South Wales. 5052, coming up from South Wales on the same day, was turned back extremely quickly on a train as important as the 1.30pm to Plymouth.

In the early 1950s, the punctuality of Britain's railways was still not very good and *Trains Illustrated* used to quote the published annual figures where the Western and London Midland regions used to compete for bottom place, with 'right time' around 40-50 per cent only. Many of the WR logs at this time not only showed signs of locomotive performance still not recovered to pre-war levels, but operating standards seemed to have slipped with high numbers of permanent way slacks as the Civil Engineer rebuilt the railway from the war ravages, but also signal checks approaching junctions and termini became all too frequent. There was clearly a backlog of maintenance and many of the Castle records show engines stored at, or awaiting, Swindon Works in 1950. There was at this time an industrial dispute over piecework prices and as a result a lack of availability of some critical parts. However, Swindon overhauls were thorough and to a high standard and in the 1950s the Castles were averaging 87,500 miles between major overhauls, superior to other

4076 *Carmarthen* *Castle* of Chester rounds the curve south of Shrewsbury station with a heavy express for Chester and Birkenhead, 12 May 1951. (T. Lewis/MLS Collection)

Resurgence in the 1950s • 165

4079 *Pendennis* Castle stops at Marshfield with a Gloucester-Cardiff passenger train, 12 May 1951. One of the newly built Hawksworth flush-sided tenders (4120) has briefly been attached to a 1924 built Castle. (R.O. Tuck/Rail Archive Stephenson)

4000 *North* Star runs through Shrewsbury station ready to drop back onto a stopping train to Chester, 11 June 1953. 4977 *Watcombe Hall* is taking water before proceeding with the Chester portion of a London train. (R.O. Tuck/Rail Archive Stephenson)

Region's engines in the same power classification (Lord Nelsons 81,600, V2s 78,000, Bulleid light pacifics 74,500 and Royal Scots 70,500).

In February 1952 King George VI died and after his body was brought back to London from Sandringham to lie in state, the funeral train and a number of specials for the invited guests ran from Paddington to Windsor. Unfortunately, the GW royal engine 4082 *Windsor Castle* had been admitted to Swindon Works for heavy repairs only two days before the king's death. The last Castle through the Works, 7013 *Bristol Castle,* was selected for the honour and exchanged number and nameplates with 4082 and the exchange remained permanent – in fact the 1924 built engine now

4079 *Pendennis* Castle, recently transferred from Gloucester to Stafford Road, runs into Shrewsbury with a Chester-Wolverhampton stopping train, 16 July 1953. (R.O. Tuck/Rail Archive Stephenson)

5089 *Westminster Abbey* at Cardiff General with the 3-coach Cardiff portion to add to the 11.50am Swansea-Manchester, 2 December 1952. This rebuilt 'Star' still retains the 'joggled' frame front end section. This train later was photographed by R.J. Doran climbing Llanvihangel bank, the winning image in *Trains Illustrated* 1952/3 photographic competition. (R.O. Tuck/Rail Archive Stephenson)

numbered 7013 outlived the 1948 built engine, now 4082, by several months. The 'Processional Train' conveying the royal mourners and international guests was hauled by 7004 *Eastnor Castle* and four other specials for invited guests left Paddington at ten minute intervals between 10.50 and 11.20 behind 4091 *Dudley Castle*, 4097 *Kenilworth Castle*, 5039 *Rhuddlan Castle* and 5065 *Newport Castle*, all Old Oak Common engines. They were all allowed 30 minutes for the 21 mile journey. The Processional train left Paddington at 12.25 and was allowed 33 minutes. 4082 left with the funeral train at 12.30 and was due at Windsor at 1.10pm – it arrived two minutes early. The Processional train and the four

4082 *Windsor Castle* (the renamed 7013 *Bristol Castle*) heads the funeral train of King George VI out of Paddington station, 15 February 1952. (GW Trust)

4082 *Windsor Castle* passing Southall station with the funeral train of King George VI, 15 February 1952. (R.E. Vincent)

Above left: **4082** *Windsor* Castle with the royal funeral train on the Windsor branch, 15 February 1952. (M.W. Earley)

Above right: **7004** *Eastnor* Castle heads the 'Processional Train' on the Windsor branch, conveying the invited royal guests and other VIPs to King George VI's funeral at Windsor Castle, 15 February 1952. (M.W. Earley)

4082 *Windsor* Castle renumbered and named 7013 *Bristol Castle* after it was found not fit to work the royal funeral train. It is at Swindon Works a few days later awaiting entry to the Works for heavy overhaul, 24 February 1952. (MLS Collection)

specials returned to Paddington between 3 and 3.45pm, and as the royal party returned by road, 4082 and the WR officials returned under ordinary express headcode. A special train carrying officers and men of the Royal Marines returning to Plymouth left Paddington at 3.20pm, hauled by 7029 *Clun Castle*.

There were standby Castles at Southall and Slough but all booked engines performed perfectly and no standby was needed.

Some logs found their way into the *Railway Magazine* or *Trains Illustrated* in the early 1950s – giving their recorders a glimmer of hope that better times were coming. The wartime speed limit of 75mph was still in force apart from relaxation to 85 between Pewsey and Lavington, Keinton Mandeville and Athelney, and Whiteball and Cullompton, all of which 4098's driver took advantage on the down *Torbay Express* in October 1951.

Paddington-Exeter *Torbay Express*
4098 *Kidwelly Castle*
Newton Abbot
7 chs, 230/245 tons

Miles	Location	Times	Speeds	Gradients
0	Paddington	00.00		
1.3	Westbourne Park	03.21		¼ L
5.7	Ealing Broadway	09.05	55	
9.1	Southall	12.49	58/pws 37*	
18.5	Slough	24.16	56	2¼ L
24.3	Maidenhead	30.11	63	2¼ L
31	Twyford	37.30	sigs 25*	
36	Reading	45.00	sigs 15*	5 L
37.8	Southcote Junction	48.03		
44.8	Aldermaston	54.57	64	
53.1	Newbury	63.08	61/66½	5½ L
61.5	Hungerford	71.06	62	
66.4	Bedwyn	75.46	64	¾ L
70.1	Savernake	79.41	50	2 L
75.3	Pewsey	84.37	69	
81.1	Patney	90.21	55/65	2¼ L
86.9	Lavington	95.03	82	
94.6	Heywood Road Jcn	101.34	pws 47*	1½ L
97	Fairwood Road Jcn	104.37	52	2½ L
106.4	Witham	114.24	64/61	
108.3	Brewham	116.13	55½	
111.7	Bruton	119.24	74	
115.1	Castle Cary	122.23	66	1¼ L

Paddington-Exeter *Torbay Express*

4098 *Kidwelly Castle*

Newton Abbot

7 chs, 230/245 tons

Miles	Location	Times	Speeds	Gradients
120	Keinton Mandeville	128.15	pws 15*	
125.5	Somerton	138.30	72/69	
130.8	Curry Rivell Jcn	137.43	82	
134.7	Athelney	140.46	75	
140.3	Cogload Jcn	145.36	60	T
142.7	Taunton	149.25	pws 15*	1 L
149.8	Wellington	157.50	59/56	
153.6	Whiteball	162.15	45	¼ L
158.6	Tiverton Jcn	166.46	80½	
165.1	Hele	172.05	76/72	
170	Stoke Canon	176.17	74/69	
172.2	Cowley Bridge Jn	178.27		¼ E
173.5	Exeter St David's	180.25	(168 net)	1½ E

The load was light but 4098 and crew were delayed by the 11.55am Paddington as far as Reading and encountered four permanent way checks typical of most WR main lines at this time. Cecil J. Allen experienced a run to Cardiff and back in 1951 and went down on the 8.40am summer relief to the heavy 8.55. 5057 *Earl Waldegrave* had a light train of seven coaches, 230/240 tons and ran non-stop through Newport reaching Cardiff in 160 minutes 13 seconds (145.1 miles in 150 minutes net). After a 50mph check at Slough speeds were 68 at Maidenhead, 74 at Reading, 72 at Cholsey, pws 10* at Steventon, another pws after Shrivenham, 68 at Wootton Bassett, 54 minimum at Badminton passed in 103 minutes 48 seconds. The return was with a much heavier train, 5069 *Isambard Kingdom Brunel* having a 12 coach load of 420 tons gross. The schedule, however, was absurdly easy, 169 minutes for the 133.4 miles from Newport to Paddington. With little effort the train was nearly three minutes early at Severn Tunnel Junction where it was checked to 20mph losing impetus for the tunnel so that the climb out was started at only 65mph. Speed fell to 25, recovered to 32 on the short stretch of level after Pilning and the train was then stopped dead for two minutes at Cattybrook in the middle of the 1 in 100. Acceleration up the grade and into the single bore tunnel was painful and Patchway was passed five minutes late, but 5069 gradually accelerated the train to 49mph at Badminton and no more than 68mph thereafter got the train into Paddington five minutes early despite a signal check at Reading and p-way slowing at Slough.

Some accelerations took place in the summer timetable of 1952, but times were still well below those of the 1930s – for example the up *Merchant Venturer* from Bristol was accelerated to 110 minutes for the 94 miles from Chippenham, hardly demanding but a fifteen minute improvement over the 1951 timing. The WR still had ten daily slip coach services. Tests coordinated by the Swindon design team led by S.O. Ell on both draughting and coal consumption were taking place in 1952/3 – 7015 *Carn Brea Castle* was paired with one of the new self-weighing tenders on the 9.15am and 1.18pm Paddington-Weston-super-Mare in May 1952 and with 5009 *Shrewsbury Castle* on the 1.18pm Paddington from 28 July to 4 August.

Newton Abbot's 4080 *Powderham Castle* leaving Teignmouth with the up *Devonian* as seen from the sea wall, July 1953. (J. Davenport/MLS Collection)

5024 *Carew* Castle of Newton Abbot drops down from Rattery to Brent with the down *Cornishman*, 1953. (Real Photographs/MLS Collection)

5047 *Earl* of *Dartmouth* of Newton Abbot shed runs the 10.35am Torquay-Paddington beside the sea wall at Teignmouth, 27 June 1953. (MLS Collection)

Old Oak Common's 4089 *Donnington Castle* works a westbound Paddington-Bristol train between Didcot and Swindon, in the summer of 1951. (MLS Collection)

5017 *St Donat's Castle* of Worcester with a Hereford-Worcester-Paddington express at Wolvercote Junction, during the summer of 1951. Note that 5017 has a tall chimney and is seen long before the 1957 renaming. (H.H. Duck/MLS Collection)

Gloucester's 5018 *St. Mawes Castle* with a down Paddington-Worcester train at Wolvercote Junction during the summer of 1951. 5018, like 5017, also has a tall chimney. (H.H. Duck/MLS Collection)

Bristol Bath Road's 5048 *Earl of Devon* with a northbound North & West express at Pontrilas, 1952. (G.M. Shoults/MLS Collection)

7018 *Drysllwyn Castle* at Marshfield with a Newcastle-Swansea cross-country train, 4 July 1953. This was said to be one of Landore's Castles with a poor reputation – it was chosen for double-chimney experiments a couple of years later. (R.O. Tuck/Rail Archive Stephenson)

The SO 7.30am Penzance-Wolverhampton departing from Taunton and passing Creech St Michael Halt hauled by Swindon's 7037 *Swindon*, c1953. (R.H.G. Simpson/MLS Collection)

Tests were carried out altering exhaust system dimensions on the test plant and in road tests. Included in the trials was Bath Road's 5025 *Chirk Castle*, always a strong engine but better than ever after draughting modification was the reports of her crews. 'ID' (Improved draughting) was stencilled on the front platform angles just behind the buffer beam.

The results of the various tests, the increased superheat and improvement in the draughting of Kings and Castles, not to mention the completion of the backlog of permanent way repairs and renewals, meant that the WR management authorised substantial accelerations for the 1954 summer timetable. The 105 minute *Bristolian* was restored, the 1.15pm Paddington to Bristol was timed for the 106.9 miles to Bath in 97 minutes and the *Pembroke Coast Express* was given a mile-a-minute timing to Newport. The *Cornish Riviera Express* was restored to a four-hour timing to Plymouth, though that was of course diagrammed for a redraughted 'King', as was initially the *Bristolian*. Other trains on the Paddington-Bristol main line were accelerated. In the first week of the new timetable O.S. Nock in his travels experienced five 60+mph runs behind Castles, with 5063 *Earl Baldwin* on the 5.25pm Bristol-Paddington and the 5.5pm Paddington-Bristol, 5096 *Bridgwater Castle* on the 9am Bristol-Paddington and 1.15pm return and 5085 *Evesham Abbey* on the 7.45 pm Paddington-Bristol.

Bath Road's 5025 *Chirk Castle*, the first with improved draughting, at Bristol Temple Meads, 20 July 1957. The engine has also been fitted with the later mechanical lubrication arrangement, an HC boiler, modified outside cylinder steam pipes and GW3 type 'Turton' buffers. (John Hodge)

Just before the acceleration but in the immediate preceding months 7034 *Ince Castle* accomplished the 106.9 miles to Bath on the 1.15pm Paddington in 99 minutes net with a train of 350 tons, top speed 90mph at Dauntsey. A few days later with 380 tons 7034 achieved a net time of 97 ½ minutes with 92 at Dauntsey. The new timetable demanded a schedule of 97 minutes with this train but with a much lighter load. One of the 1924 built Castles, Landore's 4078 *Pembroke Castle*, brought the 10-coach 355 ton up *Pembroke Coast Express* in to Paddington five minutes early in 132 minutes 11 seconds despite signal checks to 35mph at Magor and 20mph at Pilning. 86mph was the top speed at Hullavington and 4078 sustained 70-75 from Shrivenham to Tilehurst and a further 75 at Slough.

Cecil J. Allen reported on a footplate run in September 1955 on the down *Pembroke Coast Express* with Landore's 5074 *Hampden* and eight coaches, 258/270 tons. Time was kept without undue exertion as far as the outskirts of Newport, with speeds in the 68-70mph range for most of the way to Swindon, minimum of 57 at Badminton and easy afterwards but signals at Maindee East Junction from a Birmingham-Cardiff train ahead caused the train to be 5 minutes late at Newport. He also reported on a much faster run behind the same engine with 275 tons, which started exceptionally quickly clearing Southall in 11 minutes and despite a p-way check at 15mph through Reading, with speeds in the mid-70s thereafter, passed Swindon in 73 minutes (67 net). Then 77mph at Little Somerford was followed by 67mph minimum at Badminton and 83 after, before a major delay caused by a failed freight in the Severn Tunnel. Pilning (113.1 miles) had been passed in 109½ minutes (101½ net). Actual time to Newport for the 133.4 miles was 141½ minutes (120 minutes net) and with energy afterwards Swansea was reached virtually on time.

The allocation of Castles at the beginning of the 1954 summer timetable was (change on 1950 in brackets):

Old Oak Common: 4037, 4082 (ex-7013), 4097, 5004, 5006, 5014, 5029, 5034, 5035, 5038, 5040, 5044, 5055, 5056, 5060, 5065, 5066, 5081, 5082, 5087, 5093, 5095, 7001, 7004, 7010, 7017, 7024, 7025, 7027, 7030, 7032, 7033, 7036 (33, +4)

Reading:	4085, 5036 (no change)		5088, 7026 (16, +2)		5080, 5099, 7020, 7022, 7023 (15, -5)	
Oxford:	5012, 5026, 7008 (no change)	Shrewsbury:	5050, 5073, 5091, 5097 (4, -1)	Swansea Landore:	4074, 4078, 4081, 4093, 4095, 5002, 5013, 5016, 5051, 5072, 5089, 7002, 7003, 7009, 7012, 7018, 7021, 7028 (18, +2)	
Bristol Bath Road:	4073, 4075, 4084, 4091, 4094, 4096, 5000, 5019, 5025, 5027, 5048, 5057, 5063, 5064, 5067, 5076, 5077, 5085, 5094, 5096, 7011, 7014, 7019, 7034 (24, +3)	Chester:	4076, 5033, 5061, 5075 (no change)			
		Worcester;	5037, 5086, 5090, 5092, 7005, 7007, 7013 (ex-4082) (7, -2)			
		Gloucester:	5017, 5018, 5042, 7006, 7035 (5, +2)	Carmarthen:	5039, 5043 (+1)	
Swindon:	5009, 5062, 5068, 5083, 5084, 7015, 7016, 7037 (8, -1)	Cardiff Canton:	5001, 5005, 5007, 5020, 5030, 5046, 5049, 5052, 5054, 5074,	Total (167, -4)		
Weymouth:	(-1)					
Newton Abbot:	4077, 4080, 4088, 4098, 4099, 5011, 5024, 5028, 5041, 5047, 5059, 5071, 5078, 5079, 7000, 7029 (16, +3)					
Exeter:	5003, 5021 (no change)					
Plymouth Laira:	4086, 4089, 5058, 5069, 5098, 7031 (6, -9)					
Penzance:	4087, 5023 (no change)					
Stafford Road:	4000, 4079, 4083, 4090, 4092, 5008, 5010, 5015, 5022, 5031, 5032, 5045, 5053, 5070,					

The accelerated services in the 1954 timetable were mainly on the Paddington-Bristol and Paddington-Cardiff routes and

Old Oak Common's 7001 *Sir James Milne* with plenty of steam to spare hauls one of the accelerated Paddington-Bristol trains between Reading and Didcot, Summer 1954. (MLS Collection)

the Castle transfers were mainly to bolster the numbers at Old Oak Common, Bristol Bath Road and Landore. Five Canton Castles had been replaced by the depot's first allocation of Britannias (70025-29). The most significant loss was at Laira. Newton Abbot gained three, but otherwise the size of the reduction was only partially explained by the allocation of four Britannias (70016/19/21/24) to Laira and 70022 to Newton Abbot. Old Oak's allocation of class 7 power was considerably increased not just by four Castles, but also by four Britannias (70017/18/20/23).

The accelerated services put some stress on the frames of the older engines and although the Castles did not suffer the severe problems encountered by the 'Kings' in 1955/6, some of the older Castles were developing cracks in the frames at the weak point of the frame 'joggle' behind the bogie. It was cheaper to replace the front end section of the frame with straight frames as fitted to 4093 onwards and the visible inside cylinder cleating changed to the rectangular shape associated with engines from 5013 onwards. 4037 *The South Wales Borderers*, 4087 *Cardigan Castle* and 4097 *Kenilworth Castle* had been repaired with new front ends by 1950 and eventually the following additional engines are known to have had this partial frame renewal:

4076, 4078, 4080, 4088, 4089, 4090, 4093, 4094, 4095, 5000, 5001, 5002, 5004, 5006, 5007, 5008, 5012 and 7013 (the former 4082).

One unfortunate practice of the WR authorities was to revise timings of the fastest services in the daily working timetable amendments when a train was strengthened beyond the set limit without altering the public timetable, in effect condoning unpunctuality. An example of this was on the 9am Bristol–Paddington, booked off Bath at 9.19 and due Paddington at 11.20, an easy enough schedule without being further extended. The normal formation of the train was 10 coaches but on 4 August 1955, 4091 *Dudley Castle* had a 13-coach load weighing 485 tons gross and consequently the schedule was extended by several minutes.

A shed scene at Cardiff Canton, 20 April 1954. In the foreground is Old Oak Common's 7004 *Eastnor Castle* along with 'Star' 4053 *Princess Alexandra* of Stafford Road, its own 5077 *Fairey Battle* and 0-6-2T 6634. (John Hodge)

Bristol Bath Road's 5019 *Treago Castle* which was one of the Castles seen frequently on the accelerated Bristol-London services in the 1954 summer timetable. It is on Bath Road shed, 1954. (J. Davenport/MLS Collection)

5076 *Gladiator* on the accelerated 1.15pm Paddington-Bristol near Chippenham, 1955. (Kenneth Leech/B. Hayward Collection)

7027 *Thornbury Castle* emerges from Box Tunnel with a Paddington-Bristol express, 27 May 1956. (D.M.C. Hepburne-Scott/Rail Archive Stephenson)

5074 *Hampden* departing from Paddington with the 8.50am South Wales Pullman, 1955. (Kenneth Leech/B. Hayward Collection)

Resurgence in the 1950s • 181

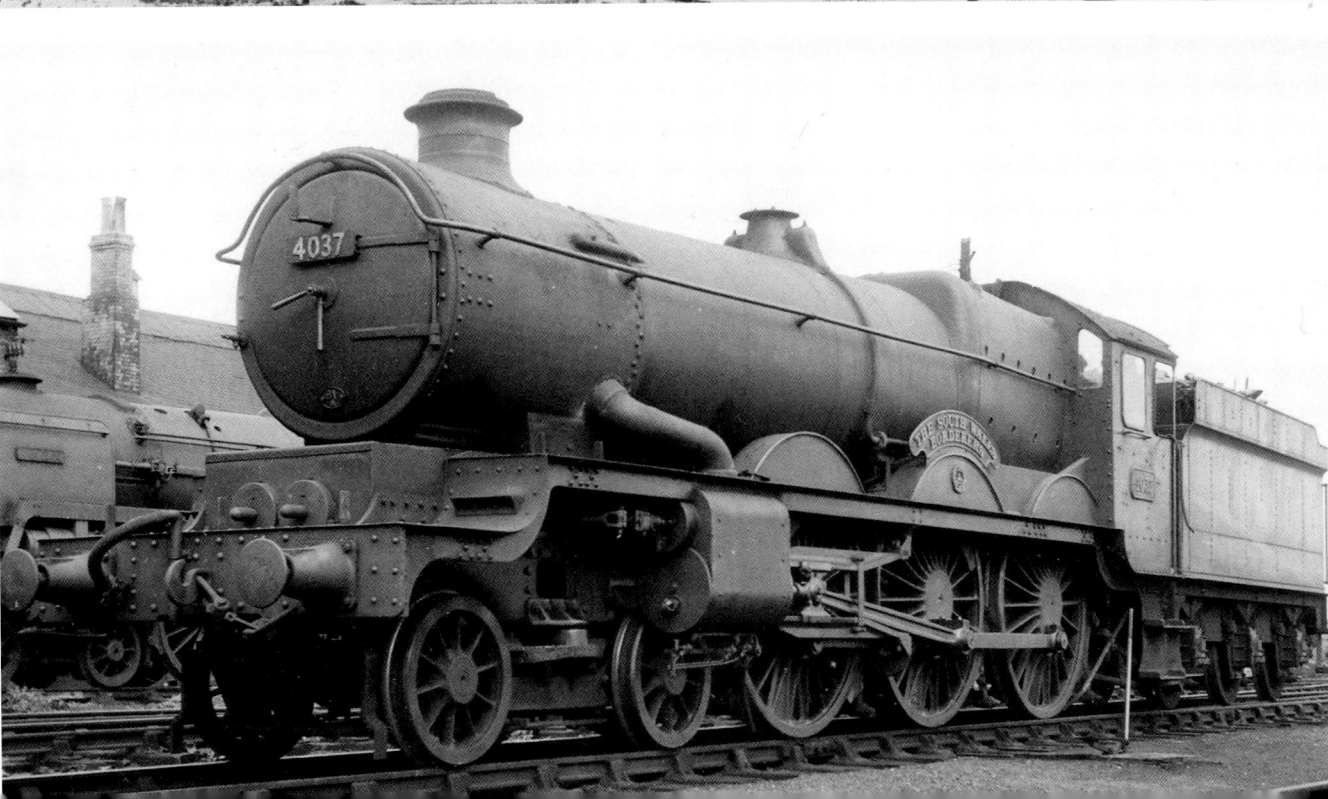

Penzance allocated
4087 *Cardigan Castle* received a new front end frame section as early as 1950 and is seen here unusually outside Cornwall on a schools excursion to London climbing Whiteball Bank, 19 May 1950.
(Author's Collection)

After 4087 and 4097, one of the first Castles to receive a new front end frame section was the rebuilt 'Star' 4037 (formerly *Queen Philippa*) renamed *The South Wales Borderers* in April 1937. It is seen here at Old Oak Common with Britannia 70024 *Vulcan* in the background, 26 July 1953. The inside cylinder cleating is now of rectangular box shape between the wider front end frame plates, but 4037 still has the original type of external steam pipes at this time. Strangely, the early type of valve spindle cover seems to indicate that the later pattern of semi plug piston valves had not been fitted. 4037 would go on to become the GW's highest mileage engine with nearly two and a half million miles in traffic since its construction in 1911. (MLS Collection)

The 1924 built 4082 renamed and renumbered since 1952 as 7013 *Bristol Castle* ex-works at Swindon, still in its 1924 form apart from the Collett 4,000 gallon tender, 8 May 1955. This would, however, be its last stint in this form and would receive a new frame front end at its next general overhaul in 1957. The cab has now been modified as outlined in chapter 2, resulting in the loss of the brass beading at the front corners.
(MLS Collection)

4073 *Caerphilly Castle* was slated for condemnation in 1955 having spent over thirty years in heavy top link work. However, its frames still appeared to be in good condition and it was reprieved until May 1960 when it was withdrawn and selected for preservation as part of the national collection. It is seen here at Ludlow on the 11.45am Manchester-Torquay, 1 August 1957.
(MLS Collection)

Likewise, 4074 *Caldicot Castle* was also planned for withdrawal in 1955, but surprisingly survived yet another Swindon Works visit in 1958, still with the original joggled frame though the inside cylinder cleating was altered in shape to the narrow box type. It has been fitted with the later arrangement of mechanical lubrication. In fact, 4074 has a 4-row superheat HD boiler and would be further enhanced in 1959 with a double chimney and would not be withdrawn until May 1963. It is seen here at its home depot, Landore, in 1958. Neyland's 1001 *County of Bucks* is in the background. (John Scott-Morgan/MLS Collection)

Landore's 4000 *North Star*, six months before withdrawal, stands at Cardiff General waiting to depart for Swansea, 24 November 1956. Despite the engine's age, it has been recently fitted with the later type of outside steam pipe casing. (R.O. Tuck/Rail Archive Stephenson)

Newton Abbot's 4077 *Chepstow Castle* after arriving at Shrewsbury with the 8am Plymouth-Liverpool lodging turn, 14 June 1957. (R.O. Tuck/Rail Archive Stephenson)

The Shrewsbury engine and crew's lodging turn to Newton Abbot, 5004 *Llanstephan Castle,* with the 9.5am Liverpool – Plymouth at Nantyderry with the Sugar Loaf mountain above Abergavenny as background, 22 March 1957. (R.O. Tuck/Rail Archive Stephenson)

Chester's 4076 *Carmarthen Castle* rebuilt with new front end frame section entering Shrewsbury station with a Birkenhead-Paddington train which it will work to Wolverhampton, 1957. (G.A. Coltas/MLS Collection)

Gloucester's 5042 *Winchester Castle* at Cardiff General with the 9.5am from Gloucester, c1956. 5042 would survive in deplorable condition to be one of the four last remaining Castles at Gloucester in 1965. (John Hodge)

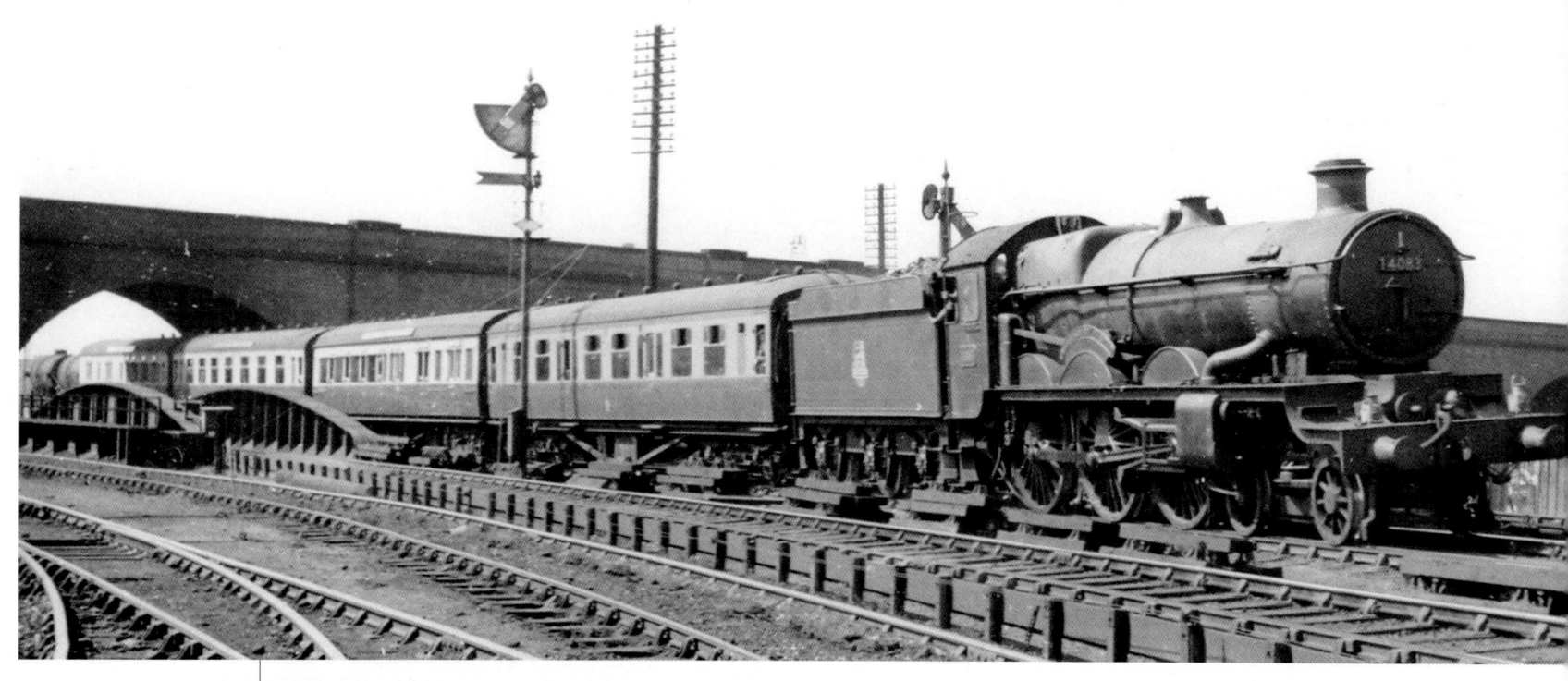

4083 *Abbotsbury* Castle passes its home depot of Stafford Road en route from Chester with a train from Wolverhampton, c1953. (MLS Collection)

I suffered this experience on the Saturday strengthened *Pembroke Coast Expresses* in 1960/1 when perfectly good Castles blowing off steam for most of the way, exhaust virtually silent, lost 15 minutes on the public timetable only for the driver, when challenged, to say the train had been retimed in the WTT and was on time. Luckily Mr Nock's experience with 4091's crew was different and, despite the load, the driver attempted to keep the public schedule. 4091 left Bath 5½ minutes late and struggled at first with 49mph at Box falling to 28½ on the 1 in 100 through Box Tunnel. Chippenham was passed at 60mph and on the 1 in 100 from Dauntsey speed fell from 57½ to 43½ before a signal check to 35 at Wootton Bassett. After a pws to 50 at Shrivenham 4091 was driven hard to run in the upper 60s rising to 71mph at Didcot and continuing at 68-69 until a 15mph p-way slack at Tilehurst. 66mph was then held from Twyford to Hanwell before a series of signal checks including a dead stand for a minute and a half at Kensal Green meant arrival was 3¾ minutes late (though early by the changed WTT time). Net time was only 109 minutes which showed a Castle had time in hand on the public schedule even with this load.

Within a year of the timetable accelerations, Castles had replaced 'Kings' on the *Bristolian*, apart from the down run on Mondays when the load was eight rather than the usual seven coaches. The Old Oak Common Castle on the down run would return on the 12noon Bristol and Bristol Bath Road would provide one of their Castles for the up service. Both depots used an ex-works Castle for several weeks – usually three months until the engine was due for its routine valves and pistons examination. The same engines would be associated with the service in the mid-1950s – I associate 5056, 7024, 7030 and 7036 from the London end and 7014, 7015, 7019 and 7034 from Bath Road in particular. I append below details of three runs with 5056 whilst still single chimneyed, the first during a spell on the *Bristolian* in 1957 and the other two during a second spell in 1959.

Resurgence in the 1950s • 187

		Paddington-Bristol *The Bristolian*							
		5056 *Earl of Powis*			5056			5056	
		248/263 tons			245/260 tons			248/265 tons	
		Driver Steer							
		22.10.1957			5.2.1959			20.5.1959	
Miles	Location	Times	Speeds		Times	Speeds		Times	Speeds
0	Paddington	00.00		T	00.00		2¼ L	00.00		½ E
1.3	Westbourne Park	03.26		½ E	02.57		1¼ L	03.10		1¼ E
5.7	Ealing	08.29	64		08.02	64		08.05	66
9.1	Southall	11.27	72	½ L	11.06	70	2¼ L	11.01	72/ pws 15*	½ E
13.2	West Drayton	14.52	75		14.32	77		16.42	63
18.5	Slough	18.57	78	1½ L	18.58 pws 30*		3¾ L	21.15	75	3¼ L
24.2	Maidenhead	23.28	75	2 L	24.40	72	5¼ L	25.49	76	3¾ L
31	Twyford	28.51	77	1¾ L	30.07	77		31.03	80
36	Reading	33.15	61* sigs	2¼ L	33.58	80	5¼ L	34.51	78	3¼ L
	Scours Lane	-	pws 15*		-			-	76
41.6	Pangbourne	40.07	62		38.09	78		39.10	77½
44.8	Goring	42.58	69		40.37	78		41.40	77
48.5	Cholsey	45.58	75/78		43.29	79		44.33	78
53.1	Didcot	49.37	75	1½ L	46.59	80	1¼ L	48.06	77½	½ E
56.5	Steventon	52.22	77/75	1¾ L	49.34	78	1¼ L	50.42	77½	½ E
60.4	Wantage Road	55.31	74		52.32	78		53.42	78
66.5	Uffington	60.33	72		57.11	77½		58.26	76
71.6	Shrivenham	64.37	75		60.59	80		62.19	78½
77.3	Swindon	69.18	72	2¼ L	65.26	77/ sigs 5*	¾ L	66.44	81	¾ E
82.9	Wootton Bassett	73.54	78		73.01	69		70.52	87
87.7	Dauntsey	77.27	88		76.41	91		74.09	94
94	Chippenham	82.00	75	3 L	80.55	85	4¼ L	78.28	80	¾ E
98.3	Corsham	85.45	68		84.06	77½		81.56	70½
101.9	Box	88.34	84		86.43	88		84.45	79
106.9	Bath	92.43	42*	3¾ L	91.17	slow*	4½ L	89.45	slow*	¼ L
113.8	Keynsham	99.54	69/ sigs 57*		97.41	76		95.48	70
116.7	St Anne's Park	102.47	66		100.22	easy		99.27	easy
118.3	Bristol Temple Meads	105.34 (100½ net)	½ L		103.42 (98 net)		1 L	102.38 (99½ net)		3 E

Other services received the 'refreshing' effect of the fast schedules, and P.G.Barlow timed a snippet with 4084 on the fast 7.50pm Paddington – Bristol one evening in 1955.

Paddington-Reading

7.50pm Paddington-Bristol

4084 *Aberystwyth Castle* **Bristol Bath Road**

8 chs, 267/3290 tons

29.6.1955

Miles	Location	Times	Speeds	
0	Paddington	00.00		
1.3	Westbourne Park	02.56		1 E
5.7	Ealing Broadway	08.09	61	
9.1	Southall	11.22	66	¼ E
13.2	West Drayton	14.55	71½	
18.5	Slough	19.06	75½	T
24.2	Maidenhead	23.46	74/75	¼ E
31	Twyford	29.26	pws 20*/55	
34.1	Sonning	35.31	pws 15*/51	
<u>36</u>	<u>Reading</u>	<u>38.11</u>	<u>(34 net)</u>	<u>3¾ L</u>

This was a *Bristolian* performance with an extra coach (the 7.50pm was the return working of the up *Bristolian* engine). Other similar performances could be found on trains like the 5.35pm Oxford-Paddington, booked over the 63.4 miles in the even hour. 4097 *Kenilworth Castle* with the usual six coaches, 210 tons gross, came up to London in 55¾ minutes in May 1957 sustaining 78-80mph from Goring to Twyford, increasing to 85 at Maidenhead. Landore's 4099 *Kilgerran Castle* hauled the down *South Wales Pullman* on 17 July 1959 and beat the 151 minute schedule to Newport by nearly eight minutes despite a 5mph bridge check near Hayes, a 20mph p-way renewal speed restriction at Langley, signal checks to 45mph at Reading, 20mph at Badminton and severe checks all the way from Pilning to the entrance of the Severn Tunnel. In between 4099 was hauling its 335 ton train at 70-74mph from Goring

Bath Road's 7015 *Carn Brea Castle* reverses off shed to collect the stock for the 4.30pm Bristol-Paddington *Bristolian*, from Malago Vale carriage sidings, 15 April 1958. (John Hodge)

to Swindon, and was climbing the 1 in 300 to Badminton at almost 60mph before the check there, then 80+mph at Winterbourne before more checks.

Paddington-Bristol two-hour trains had been restored in 1954 and a Bath Road Castle was diagrammed to the 11.45am Bristol up run. One of the 1926 built engines, 4096 *Highclere Castle*, worked the train on 22 January 1957 and with eight coaches, 295 tons gross, arrived at Paddington five minutes early (112 minutes net). Badminton was passed at 57mph, 84 at Little Somerford, and a steady 74mph was maintained from Shrivenham to a 40mph signal check at Steventon. The 70mph mark was crossed again at Cholsey and 72-73 sustained from there to Slough when the engine was eased to avoid too early an arrival.

In a different sphere of work, 4077 *Chepstow Castle* had command of the down *Cornish Riviera Express* between Plymouth and Penzance and was timed on both 12 July 1955 and 25 January 1956, keeping time on both occasions with a 10-coach 360 ton gross load. 26mph on the steepest 1 in 68 beyond St Germans, rising to 34 on the 1 in 106, and 33 on the 1 in 74 after Menheniot, and 34 on the 1 in 74/58 before Doublebois with a maximum of 61 was enough to cut the 52 minute schedule to Par by a minute. The awkward climb out of Par, four miles of mostly 1 in 60 to St Austell, was taken at 28 falling to 25 in July and a much better climb starting at 39mph and not falling below 30 in January enabled the difficult 29 minute schedule to Truro to be beaten by nearly two minutes on the second occasion. Three miles of 1 in 60 out of Truro to Chacewater was climbed by 4077 in July at 28mph and 34 in January 1956. Downhill after Redruth was taken easily with a maximum of 62mph on both occasions.

Another hard task given regularly to Castles was the through working from Newton Abbot to Shrewsbury by Newton Abbot and Shrewsbury Castles on alternate days. 4098 *Kidwelly Castle* of Newton Abbot was timed by O.S.Nock north of Bristol on 8 May 1957 with 13 coaches, 416/445 tons. It left Bristol 4 minutes late, slogged up Filton Bank at 20mph, allowed speed to rise to 70mph at Pilning before braking to 58mph at the tunnel entrance and worked hard on the climb from Caerleon to Pontypool Road arriving there in 27 seconds over the hour, a few minutes early. 4098 took water there and left on time, passing Abergavenny at 42mph, falling to 21 on the 1 in 82 and rising to 24½mph on the last 1 in 95 to Llanvihangel. 4098 took the train easily down to Hereford with nothing over 64mph reached in 46 minutes 42 seconds. The train waited time there, leaving on time at 1.30pm. With 60 on the level at Leominster, 66 at Woofferton, a long p-way check at Bromfield, the climb to Church Stretton was started at no more than 44mph. 4098 fell to 33mph but was then opened right out and made a magnificent climb accelerating its 445 ton train to 42 at Marsh Brook, falling to 39 on the last 1 in 112 and then actually accelerating again on the final stages to 41½mph. It then coasted down with a maximum of 70mph at Dorrington and was stopped unfortunately at Sutton Bridge Junction for over five minutes before arriving at Shrewsbury in exactly 75 minutes, two minutes late (but 65 minutes net). The train was taken onto Crewe by 45552 *Silver Jubilee* itself. It may be of interest to point out that all these runs described in the last couple of paragraphs were with 40XX series Castles built between 1924 and 1926.

Canton's 5007 *Rougemont Castle* passes Canton depot with the 2.2pm Old Oak Common-Fishguard milk and fish van empties, 10 December 1955. (John Hodge)

7022 *Hereford Castle* passing Canton depot with the down fish empties for Milford Haven, 25 July 1955. (R.O. Tuck/Rail Archive Stephenson)

Laira's 4077 *Chepstow Castle* with the up *Cornish Riviera Express* at Hayle in Cornwall, 14 June 1956. Note this 1924 engine with tall chimney but Hawksworth tender, and still with joggled frame. (R. Cogger/MLS Collection)

5017, formerly *St Donat's Castle,* renamed *The Gloucestershire Regiment 28th 61st* on 26 April 1954 in honour of the company's military bravery in the battle of the Imjin River in the Korean war. Allocated to Gloucester in October 1951, this locomotive remained a shed favourite at Gloucester depot until its withdrawal in September 1962. It is at Cardiff General awaiting the road with the 8.48am Fishguard-Paddington via Gloucester parcels train, 20 June 1959. (John Hodge)

One of Exeter's pair of Castles, the 1927 built 5003 *Lulworth Castle,* at Exeter St David's with a down express, c1956. It is still as built but would have the front end section of its frames renewed before its withdrawal in August 1962. (MLS Collection)

4088 of Laira with the 3.32pm Bristol – Plymouth parcels at Exeter St David's, 30 August 1955. (R.O. Tuck/Rail Archive Stephenson)

The record breaking 5006 *Tregenna Castle*, based at Old Oak Common in the mid-1950s, departing from Teignmouth station with a summer Saturday mid-morning train from Paddington, 14 August 1957. 5006 would receive new front end frames at its next major overhaul. (MLS Collection)

5097 *Sarum* Castle was Shrewsbury depot's choice for the Newton Abbot double-home diagram in the summer of 1955, working the 9.5am Liverpool and the 8am Plymouth on alternate days. The two photos show it running into Shrewsbury with the 8am Plymouth, 30 June 1955; and on the 8am Plymouth at Dawlish. (R.O. Tuck/Rail Archive Stephenson)

The Newton Abbot Castle that alternated with Shrewsbury's 5097 in the summer of 1955 was 5011 *Tintagel Castle*. It is seen here between Teignmouth and Dawlish, September 1955. (R.O. Tuck/Rail Archive Stephenson

Shrewsbury's 5050 *Earl of St Germans* drops down from Dinmore Tunnel towards Moreton-on-Lugg with the 9.5am Liverpool-Plymouth, 2 July 1954. (R.O. Tuck/Rail Archive Stephenson)

Laira's 5058 *Earl of Clancarty* emerges from Kennaway tunnel onto Dawlish's promenade with the 7.30am Penzance-Manchester, 5 July 1957. This train was booked with WR engines to Pontypool Road but was diagrammed for a Crewe 'Royal Scot' from Pontypool Road to Manchester. (L.G. Marshal/MLS Collection)

The first Hawksworth Castle, 5098 *Clifford Castle,* leans to the curve as it drops into Par station with the up *Cornish Riviera Express* on its Penzance-Plymouth leg, 28 June 1956. (A.W. Martin/MLS Collection)

On the same day Laira's other Hawksworth Castle, 7031 *Cromwell's Castle*, tackles the climb out of Par with the down *Cornish Riviera Express*, 28 June 1956. (A.W. Martin/MLS Collection)

Old Oak Common's 4097 *Kenilworth Castle*, with 4-row superheat boiler, heads the up *Torbay Express* at an unidentified location, 18 May 1957. (GW Trust)

The last up West of England service in the 1950s was the 1.20pm Penzance, 4.10pm from Plymouth. It was due into Paddington at 9.10pm and although it was not a reliable timekeeper, it was accelerated in the mid-1950s to arrive at 9pm after a 155 minute schedule from Taunton (142.7 miles) – not too onerous, but it was a heavy train, normally 13 coaches. Although booked for a King, when W. Alcock travelled on the footplate in 1957, it only had a Laira Castle, 5058 *Earl of Clancarty*. He described the run in the magazine *Steam World* in April 2000. He was accompanied by the crew, Driver Underhill and Fireman Moles of Laira and Inspector George Price who accompanied me on my first footplate experiences in the same year. The load from Plymouth to Newton Abbot was 277/300 tons, only just within the 280 ton limit for a Castle over the South Devon route, and Hemerdon was surmounted at 15mph at 60 per cent cut-off and full regulator(!) after a slowing to 35 just before the start of the 1 in 42. Thirty per cent and full regulator got the train over Dainton at 23mph and it was at a stand in Newton Abbot in 47 minutes 49 seconds, over three minutes early. The train was made up there to 13 coaches, 410/445 tons and after the Exeter stop, left there on time using 25/20/25 per cent cut off, to clear Whiteball summit at 38mph and was in Taunton after 76mph through Wellington in 36 minutes 52 seconds, on time. 5058 was taken easily over the level track near Athelney as the driver caught sight of a distant signal on, but 70mph at Somerton dropped to 56 at Langport, followed by a long p-way slack at 15mph at Keinton Mandeville. 30 per cent cut off and full regulator saw 5058 accelerate to 48 at Castle Cary falling to 34 only on the 1 in 81 to Brewham summit. Steam pressure dropped slightly to 200lbs psi from this

Landore's 5072 *Hurricane* is diverted via the Vale of Glamorgan line with a Sheffield-Swansea train. It is pictured at Porthkerry, 25 April 1954. (Rail Archive Stephenson)

Old Oak Common's 5084 *Reading Abbey* passes non-stop through Cardiff General on the centre road with the 4.25am Fishguard – Paddington boat train, including former LMS as well as GW coaches, 30 July 1955. (Rail Archive Stephenson)

Canton's 5020 *Trematon Castle* has steam to spare as it passes over the water troughs between Ludlow and Bromfield with the 2.24pm Shrewsbury-Bristol train, 4 June 1956. (R.O. Tuck/Rail Archive Stephenson)

effort but recovered by Westbury. Another heavy p-way slack at Edington before the 1 in 222 rise to Patney hindered the climb which was surmounted at 49mph with a further drop in pressure to 195lbs but it soon recovered once more as 5058 sped its train through Newbury at 80mph and despite these two severe slacks costing at least nine minutes, passed Reading at 8.20pm on time. Speed in the low 70s between Twyford and West Drayton set up the train for an early arrival in London, but signal checks at Southall and Ealing Broadway meant the arrival in Paddington was exactly at 9pm. The 142.7 miles from Taunton had been covered in 142 minutes net with 445 tons.

Other routes dominated by the Castles throughout the 1950s were the Gloucester and Worcester-Paddington expresses. On the South Wales route, the Landore Castles retained the fastest workings but Canton Castles shared the Cardiff-Paddington heaviest trains with Britannias, starting with 70025-70029 and ultimately acquiring the entire WR allocation of fifteen before they were replaced by 'Kings' and more double chimney Castles and moving on to the LMR. The Gloucester and Worcester trains normally loaded to 9-10 coaches and were easily encompassed by the Castles running in the high 60s or low 70s from Swindon or Didcot to and from London. 7007 *Great Western*, based at Worcester and still with single chimney, had 10 coaches for 360 gross tons on 10 June 1957, and completed the 27.4 miles from Oxford to Reading in 29½ minutes, with a top speed of 76½mph at Tilehurst. It then made an exceptional fast run over the last section in 35 minutes 39 seconds for the 36 miles from Reading to Paddington, with 73-75mph maintained from Maidenhead to Old Oak Common West, arriving early. A run with Worcester's rebuilt Star 5083 *Bath Abbey* was more typical. With 9 coaches, 320 tons gross it lost 8 minutes to Reading because of a signal stop at Hinksey barely out of Oxford and then a long 20mph p-way slowing at Radley. It just reached 70mph at Tilehurst before the Reading stop. Another p-way slack at Ruscombe Sidings delayed the train further but 5083 then ran steadily at 68-69mph to London, reached nearly ten minutes late. Worcester had at this time several of the rebuilt 'Abbeys' – 5083, 5086, 5090 and 5092.

Another Canton Castle, 5054 *Earl of Ducie*, is on the North & West route descending from Llanvihangel near Pontrilas with the 11.50am Swansea-Manchester train, 2 July 1955. (R.O. Tuck/Rail Archive Stephenson)

Landore's 4074 *Caldicot Castle* and another unidentified Landore Castle run into Cardiff General with the 2.30pm Swansea (4pm Cardiff)-Paddington. 4074 was probably released at Cardiff for a relief down working working back to Swansea or West Wales, c1957. 4074 has received a 4-row superheat boiler and mechanical lubricator and will be fitted with a double chimney a couple of years later. (John Hodge)

Another rare double-heading of two Castles on the 4pm Cardiff – Paddington, this time because of the addition of Hawksworth BCK No 7372, which was reserved for 'semi royal' duties, on this occasion carrying HRH Princess Margaret. Landore's 4099 *Kilgerran Castle* is being piloted by Canton's favourite Castle, 5099 *Compton Castle,* 26 February 1958. (John Hodge)

It's harvest time as Landore's 5043 *Earl of Mount Edgcumbe* passes an overloaded tractor and cart between Marshfield and Rumney River Bridge with the down *South Wales Pullman*, 25 July 1955.
(R.O. Tuck/Rail Archive Stephenson)

Canton's 5074 *Hampden* waits for the *Red Dragon* from Swansea which it will take over at Cardiff, returning from London on the 3.55pm Paddington *Capitals United Express*, 28 September 1956.
(R.O. Tuck/Rail Archive Stephenson)

Landore's 5077 *Fairey Battle* west of Cardiff near St Fagans with the 9.30am Manchester-Swansea, 29 September 1956. (R.O. Tuck/Rail Archive Stephenson)

Canton's 5099 *Compton Castle* at Cardiff General with a Gloucester-Swansea stopping train, 31 March 1956. 5099 would be transferred to Old Oak Common in November that year while the Canton shedmaster was on leave much to that gentleman's wrath, as he considered it Canton's best Castle. (Rail Archive Stephenson)

7023 *Penrice Castle* is being oiled at Canton shed before going up to Cardiff General to work the 4.45pm train to Paddington, 2 December 1956. Canton's 5925 *Eastcote Hall* is behind as well as another Castle.
(Rail Archive Stephenson)

Landore's 5051 *Earl Bathurst* arrives at Newport High Street with the up *Pembroke Coast Express*, c1958. 5051 was later preserved sometimes using its original name of *Dryslwyn Castle*.
(John Hodge)

Worcester's 7013 *Bristol Castle*, the former 4082, now fitted with new front end frames and valveless mechanical lubricator and reservoir beside the smokebox, runs into Paddington station with an express from Hereford and Worcester, 29 April 1957. (MLS Collection)

Swindon's 5000 *Launceston Castle*, clearly recently ex-works and fitted with higher superheat boiler and mechanical lubricator, arriving at Bristol Temple Meads with the 1.5pm from Paddington, c1958. (John Hodge)

4073 *Caerphilly Castle*, looking very smart, ready to go off Canton shed for its next turn of duty, c1959. (John Hodge)

Here is 4073 *Caerphilly Castle* still going strong on a relief Paddington-South Wales express at Newport High Street, 30 September 1959. (John Hodge)

Landore's 7012 *Barry Castle* on the turntable at Cardiff Canton, 29 April 1959. Although it looks in excellent condition here, along with 7016 and 7018 it had a dubious reputation when first built and was rarely seen on Landore shed's top-link workings to London. It was the last Castle (with Shrewsbury's 5032) to be seen by the London-based author when he was trainspotting in the early 1950s. (John Hodge)

Swindon's 5025 *Chirk Castle* – looking unusually smart for that depot – on the 3.50pm Whitland-Kensington milk train, 19 May 1957. 5025 was the initial trial Castle with improved draughting and later, when stationed at Oxford in the 1960s, was the author's regular steed for his commuting runs from Reading to Slough. (R.O. Tuck/ Rail Archive Stephenson)

The allocation of Castles at the beginning of the 1957 summer timetable was (change from 1954 shown):

Old Oak Common: 4082 (ex-7013), 4090, 5006, 5007, 5008, 5014, 5029, 5034, 5035, 5038, 5040, 5043, 5044, 5052, 5055, 5056, 5060, 5065, 5066, 5074, 5082, 5084, 5087, 5092, 5093, 5099, 7001, 7004, 7010, 7017, 7020, 7024, 7025, 7027, 7030, 7032, 7033, 7036 (38, +5)

Reading: 4085, 5036 (no change)

Oxford: 5012, 5026, 7008 (no change)

Bristol Bath Road: 4075, 4079, 4080, 4084, 4091, 4096, 5019, 5027, 5048, 5054, 5057, 5063, 5064, 5067, 5076, 5085, 5096, 7011, 7014, 7015, 7018, 7019, 7034, 7035 (24, no change)

Swindon: 5000, 5009, 5025, 5062, 5068, 7037 (6, -2)

Newton Abbot: 4037, 4098, 5005, 5011, 5024, 5028, 5053, 5059, 5071, 5078, 5079, 7000, 7029 (13, -3)

Taunton: 7031 (+1)

Exeter: 5091 (-1)

Plymouth Laira: 4077, 4086, 4087, 4088, 4089, 5003, 5021, 5049, 5058, 5069, 5072, 5089, 5098 (13, +7)

Penzance: 4099, 5023 (no change)

Stafford Road: 4083, 4092, 5010, 5015, 5022, 5031, 5032, 5045, 5047, 5070, 5075, 5088, 7026 (13, -3)

Shrewsbury: 5004, 5050, 5073, 5097 (no change)

Chester: 4076, 5033, 5061 (3, -1)

Worcester: 5037, 5081, 5083, 5086, 5090, 7005, 7007, 7013 (ex-4082) (8, +1)

Gloucester: 5017, 5018, 5042, 5094, 7006 (5, no change)

Cardiff Canton: 4073, 5001, 5020, 5030, 5046, 5095, 7022, 7023 (8, -7)

Swansea Landore: 4074, 4078, 4081, 4093, 4094, 4095, 4097, 5002, 5013, 5016, 5039, 5041, 5051, 5077, 5080, 7003, 7009, 7012, 7016, 7021, 7028 (21, +3)

Carmarthen: 7002 (-1)

Total (166, -1, ie 4000)

The largest changes in Castle allocation are explained by the concentration of all the WR's Britannias at Cardiff Canton, with Old Oak Common and Plymouth Laira receiving Canton's Castles in exchange.

Chapter 7
A NEW BEGINNING AND THE BEGINNING OF THE END

From the success of the double-chimney 'Kings' and the experimental redraughting at Swindon, it was decided to test a Castle with a double blastpipe. The engine selected was Landore's 7018 *Dryslwyn Castle* which had developed the unenviable reputation of being both sluggish and shy of steam. It was equipped with a double chimney in May 1956, whilst still retaining its three-row superheat boiler. It was subject to dynamometer tests on the West of England route, including the 12noon Paddington *Torbay Express,* and one of these early runs in July 1956 is recorded below:

Paddington-Exeter *Torbay Express*
7018 *Dryslwyn Castle*
9 chs, 310/330 tons

Miles	Location	Times	Speeds		Gradients
0	Paddington	00.00		T	
5.7	Ealing Broadway	09.04	60/sigs 45*		
9.1	Southall	12.26			
18.5	Slough	21.49	71		
24.2	Maidenhead	-	sigs 20*		
	Ruscombe Sidings	-	pws 20*		
36	Reading	47.35	40*	9½ L	
44.8	Aldermaston	56.59	65		
53.1	Newbury	64.39	68/64		
58.5	Kintbury	69.27	71		
61.5	Hungerford	72.05	61*		
66.4	Bedwyn	76.39	66		
70.1	Savernake	80.40	46/pws 10*		1/185 R, 1/106 R

		Paddington–Exeter *Torbay Express* 7018 *Drysllwyn Castle* 9 chs, 310/330 tons			
Miles	Location	Times	Speeds		Gradients
75.3	Pewsey	86.10			
81.1	Patney	93.28	70½		1/222 F
86.9	Lavington	97.52	87		L
94.6	Heywood Road Jcn	103.18	77/72	8¾ L	
97	Fairwood Road Jcn	105.12	74/60		
102.3	Blatchbridge Jcn	109.55	71		
108.5	Brewham summit	115.18	63		1/112 R, 1/107 R
115.1	Castle Cary	120.52	78/62*		1/98 F
122	Keinton Mandeville	124.57	76/71		
125.8	Somerton	129.23	78/74		1/264 R
130.8	Curry Rivell Jcn	133.08	88		1/264 F
138	Cogload Jcn	138.30	79		
142.7	Taunton	142.12	72	2¼ L	
149.8	Wellington	148.38	62		1/170 R, 1/90 R
153.6	Whiteball Box	152.58	47½ / 46	1 L	1/80 R
158.6	Tiverton Jcn	157.16	84/70		1/115 F
160.9	Cullompton	158.55	83 /eased 65		
166.4	Silverton	163.28	78		
170	Stoke Canon	166.27	74		
173.5	Exeter St David's	169.54	(net 156)	T	

On the level after Lavington 7018 developed a drawbar pull of 3.8 tons at 87mph and actual dhp per hour of 800. This rose to 4 tons and 950 dhp on the climb to Brewham and 1,050 dhp on the climb to Whiteball. However, 7018 was running well within its capabilities and water consumption was only 30 gallons a mile and firing rate 2,400lbs per hour. 7018 was also tested on the Bristol-Paddington route.

A further advance was made in April 1957 when 4090 *Dorchester Castle*, an engine with renewed front end, was equipped with a 4-row superheater boiler, extended smokebox and new elliptical shaped double-chimney, rather more handsome than 7018's rectangular shaped chimney. (7018 received the new style chimney and 4-row superheater boiler at its next Works visit in 1958.) 4090 first surprised onlookers with its maiden performance on a *Trains Illustrated* special in May when, coming up from Newport, it touched 93mph at Hullavington. It was then allocated to Old Oak Common and spent the whole of the summer of 1957 on the down *Bristolian* and the return 12noon Bristol, gaining such a reputation that the Old Oak drivers specially requested its return to that duty after its first valves and pistons examination in July. I have a number of logs from the Railway Performance Society archive (three recorded by P.G. Barlow) and I table several to show that it was not a one-off spectacular event, but repeated day after day during that summer.

7018 Drysllwyn Castle with new double chimney and 3-row superheat boiler tears down the gradient from Badminton in the 90s passing Hullavington, 1956. (Kenneth Leech/B. Hayward Collection)

Paddington-Bristol, *The Bristolian*

		4090 *Dorchester Castle*		4090		4090		4090		
		7chs, 246/265 tons		7 chs, 246/260t		7 chs, 246/265t		8chs, 280/300t		
		15.5.1957		28.5.1957		29.5.1957		17.6.1957		
Miles	Location	Times	Speeds	Times	Speeds	Times	Speeds	Times	Speeds	Schedule
0	Paddington	00.00		00.00		00.00		00.00		0
1.3	Westbourne Park	02.38		02.57	41	02.55		02.58	37	4
5.7	Ealing Broadway	07.31	68	07.51	63	07.48	63	08.10	62	
9.1	Southall	10.27	71	10.54	68	10.47	71	11.11	70	11
13.2	West Drayton	13.42	76	14.22	78/pws	14.10	77/pws	14.35	77	

		Paddington-Bristol, *The Bristolian*								
		4090 *Dorchester Castle*		4090		4090		4090		
		7chs, 246/265 tons		7 chs, 246/260t		7 chs, 246/265t		8chs, 280/300t		
		15.5.1957		28.5.1957		29.5.1957		17.6.1957		
Miles	Location	Times	Speeds	Times	Speeds	Times	Speeds	Times	Speeds	Schedule
18.5	Slough	18.02	77	19.46	60	18.50	64	18.33	81/79	17½
24.2	Maidenhead	22.42	76	24.52	72	23.48	74	22.55	80	21½
31	Twyford	27.40	pws 24*	30.21	76	29.23	72	28.00	80	27
36	Reading	33.18		36.49 ** sigs		35.03 sigs 15*		31.37	84	31
38.6	Tilehurst	-		40.07	60	38.38	60	33.33	81	
41.5	Pangbourne	39.10	68½	42.47	69	41.21	67	35.46	78	
44.7	Goring	41.54	73	45.31	72	44.06	70	38.15	76	
48.5	Cholsey	44.52	76½	48.31	76	47.09	74	41.08	77	
53.1	Didcot	48.27	77½	52.13	74	51.00	72	44.51	75	46
56.5	Steventon	51.06	76	55.02	72	53.53	70	47.35	73	48½
60.4	Wantage Road	54.12	76/78	58.14	74	57.09	71	50.45	74	
66.5	Uffington	57.06	76	63.06	76	62.18	72/71	55.50	71	
71.5	Shrivenham	63.10	76	67.01	78	66.28	75	59.58	74	
77.3	Swindon	67.03	75/sigs 60*	71.27	79	71.03	76	66.00	pws 15*	67
82.9	Wootton Bassett	72.17	80	75.33	85	75.18	84	71.51	73	
87.7	Dauntsey	75.46	90	78.48	97	78.36	95	75.28	90	
94	Chippenham	80.25	76½	82.48	88	82.43	86	80.18	sigs 48*	79
98.3	Corsham	83.56	72½	85.55	81	85.52	80/82	84.39	66	
101.9	Box	86.38	76½	88.32	84/76*	88.33	73*/77	87.43	74	
106.9	Bath	91.35	34*	92.44	45*	93.06	44*	92.28	34*	90½
113.8	Keynsham	98.25	71	99.14	76	99.45	76	99.16	77	
116.7	St Anne's Park	100.58	60	01.41	65*	102.08	66*	101.38	68*	
118.3	Bristol Temple Meads	104.26		105.04		105.13		105.10		105
		(net 101)		(net 98 ½)		(net 100 ½)		(net 101)		

** sig stand Kennet Bridge 15 secs
Reading pws 15 *

The much rebuilt 4090 *Dorchester Castle* with new frame front end, 4-row superheater boiler, double chimney, extended smokebox and Hawksworth tender on Swindon shed immediately after rebuilding, 7 April 1957. (R.O. Tuck/Rail Archive Stephenson)

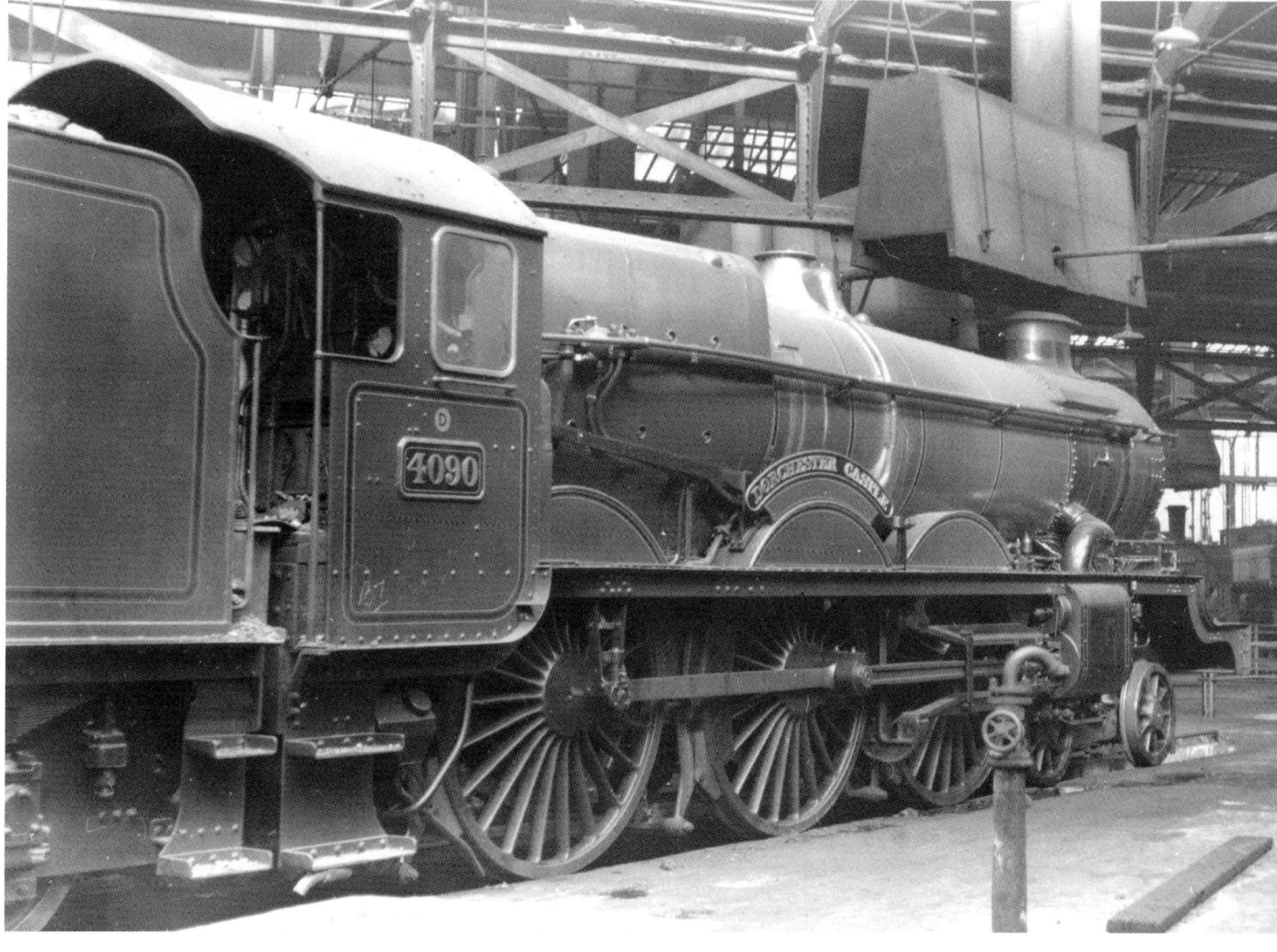

Note that 4090's performance with eight coaches was indistinguishable from the runs with seven. I have details of a further earlier run with 4090 on 30 April when it again completed the run in 105¼ minutes (102 net) with another top speed of 96mph at Dauntsey. At the time 5082 *Swordfish* was Old Oak Common's 'number 2' Castle allocated to the *Cambrian Coast Express,* but it deputised for 4090 the week the latter was in Old Oak's 'Factory' undergoing the routine three monthly V & P exam. Not to be put in the shade by 4090, it completed the 118 miles in 104 minutes 50 seconds (101 net) with 95mph at Dauntsey. The unknown recorder of the run on 15 May returned on the up *Bristolian* with Bath Road's 7019 *Fowey Castle,* and logged the run of 104 minutes 20 seconds, with maxima of 88mph at both Hullavington and on the level at Didcot. 4090 was still working the *Bristolian* in September 1957 and I have details of a run on 5 September when after delays before Reading it ran as before between 78 and 81mph between Didcot and Swindon and touched 92 at Dauntsey.

There were some very fast runs in the up direction during 1958 and 1959 before dieselisation with the 'Warships'. 7015 *Carn Brea Castle,* still in single chimney form, had unchecked runs in March and April 1958 in 101¼ and 100 minutes, when 97 and 96mph respectively were reached at Little Somerford and 85-88 sustained between Shrivenham and Cholsey with the standard 7-coach set. 7018 started its reign on the up *Bristolian* in June 1958 and on two runs an authenticated 'hundred' was reached, one of which was the fastest steam run recorded on the train.

One of the early Castles to be rebuilt with 4-row superheater and double chimney was Laira's 4087 *Cardigan Castle*, seen here still in single chimney form at Bristol Temple Meads with a class 'C' freight for the West of England, having earlier arrived with the 7.30am Penzance-Manchester, 31 July 1957. It was built in 1925 and by 1950 it had already been rebuilt with a new straight front end to the frame and rectangular inside cylinder casing still 'unstepped' as late as 1957. It was rebuilt with a double-chimney in February 1958 and is seen at Old Oak Common, 10 May 1961. In the mid-1950s, it was one of five Castles provided experimentally with the Davies & Metcalfe valveless mechanical lubricator and reservoir beside the smokebox on the driver's right hand side. The 'Dew' buffers are clear in the 1957 photo but replaced by the 'Turton' buffers in 1958. (GW Trust)

May:	4088, 5043, 7013 (ex-4082), 7023
June:	4097, 5088
July:	5057
August:	4080
September:	5061, 7019
October:	5084
November:	5069, 5095

1959
January:	5098
February:	5022, 7014
March:	7024
April:	4074, 5066
May:	5032
June:	5031, 5071, 7008
July:	5068, 5073, 7030
August:	7036
September:	5049
October:	5026, 7029
December:	7034

With the higher degree of superheating Hawksworth had decided to carry out lubrication trials with the 5098 series. The first two engines of the 'lot', 5098 and 5099, were equipped with the standard hydrostatic lubricator, whilst the remaining eight engines were segregated into four groups of two, each group being fitted with a different version of a basic lubrication system. This met some resistance from crews used to the hydrostatic system and complaints that some of the 70XX engines were 'sluggish' and the lubrication system was blamed. It was, as the feed rates were subsequently increased with consequent better results, and some of the Hawksworth Castles had superb reputations - both 5098 and 5099 were favourites at Laira and Canton respectively. As engines of earlier series received 4-row superheat boilers they too were provided with mechanical lubrication.

The other Castle rebuilt with a 4-row superheat boiler with extended smokebox, Landore's 4093 *Dunster Castle*, at Carmarthen shed, in May 1958. (MLS Collection)

7018 *Drysllwyn* Castle ex-works with 4-row superheater, the revised shape double-chimney in the form in which it would dominate the haulage of the up *Bristolian* in the Spring and Summer of 1958, at Bristol Temple Meads on the 5pm to Cardiff, 15 April 1958. (John Hodge)

7018 made a number of distinguished runs on the up *Bristolian* between May and September 1958 with at least two more 'hundreds' recorded between Hullavington and Little Somerford and four more between 96 and 98. The speeds were achieved with full regulator and cut-off between 20 and 22 per cent. A speed of 100mph on this train is also claimed for 5043 on 5 June as part of a 100 minute run (net 95½). 5057 *Earl Waldegrave* made the fastest net time of all when it left Bristol five minutes late and had a relaying check on the fastest stretch near Hullavington, but managed to arrive at Paddington 2½ minutes early in a net time of 93 minutes at an average speed of 75.7mph, the Swindon-Ealing stretch being run at 86.8. The average between Shrivenham and Goring was 94.5mph with around 99-100mph being achieved on level track near Wantage Road. A locomotive running inspector of Bath Road, J.F. Hancock, rode this train at least once a week as part of his normal duties and he recorded these details between December 1957 and November 1958. He rode on 36 occasions with 'King' 6018 (1), and Castles 5043 (1), 5067 (1), 5092 (1), 7011 (1), 7034 (1), 7035 (1), 5002 (2), 5057 (2), 7018 (11) and 7015 (14). The train arrived on time or early on 24 occasions and achieved a net time better than 105 minutes on 32 out of 36 runs – two recording 106½ (in rain & fog) and one (5092's only run) in heavy mist in 110 when it was also troubled with poor steaming. One other run was very late because of a hotbox on the coach of a preceding train. 22 of the runs had net times of 100 minutes or under.

In addition to 7018 and 4090, a further thirty-five Castles were fitted with 4-row superheater boilers and double chimneys between December 1957 and December 1959, as follows:

1957
December: 4093 (also with extended smokebox)

1958
January: 7022
February: 4087, 7004

		Bristol-Paddington, *The Bristolian* 7018 *Drysllwyn Castle*					
		7 chs, 247/265 tons 9.7.1958			7 chs, 247/260 tons July 1958		
Miles	Location	Times	Speeds		Times	Speeds	Gradients
0	Bristol Temple Meads	00.00			00.00		
1.6	Stapleton Road	03.44	45	1¼ E	04.00	40	1 E
2.5	Ashley Hill	-			05.20	34	
3.7	Horfield	06.59	37		-		
4.8	Filton Junction	08.42	44	¼ L	09.03	40*	½ L
6.2	Stoke Gifford East	10.43	43	¾ L	10.45	46	¾ L
9.1	Coalpit Heath	14.12	60		13.57	57	
13	Chipping Sodbury	17.54	64		17.25	73	
17.6	Badminton	21.52	71	¼ L	21.15	71	¼ E
23.4	Hullavington	26.01	93		25.21	96	
27.9	Little Somerford	28.47	100		28.05	102	
30.6	Brinkworth	30.29	92		29.45	93	
34.7	Wootton Bassett	33.54	60*	T	32.48	60*	1¼ E
40.3	Swindon	38.32	81	½ E	37.29	77	
46	Shrivenham	42.37	85		41.40	84	
51	Uffington	46.03	89		45.09	88	
53.7	Challow	47.51	90		46.55	89	
57.2	Wantage Road	50.06	92		49.15	90	
61.1	Steventon	52.40	93		51.55	88	
64.5	Didcot	54.55	92	4½ E	54.15	86	5¼ E
69.2	Cholsey	-			57.25	87	
72.9	Goring	60.27	90		59.57	90	
76.1	Pangbourne	62.42	86		62.13	86	
79	Tilehurst	64.42	86		64.13	87	
81.6	Reading	66.42	78	4¾ E	66.11	75*	5¼ E
86.6	Twyford	70.29	75	4½ E	70.00	80	5 E
93.4	Maidenhead	75.33	83	4½ E	75.03	82	5 E
99.1	Slough	79.57	80	4½ E	79.07	85	5¼ E
104.4	West Drayton	83.48	82		82.47	87	
108.5	Southall	86.53	79	4¼ E	85.45	84	5¼ E
111.9	Ealing Broadway	89.18	84		88.11	83	
114.3	Old Oak West Jcn	91.02	75		-	80	
116.3	Westbourne Park	93.07		8 E	91.45		9¼ E
117.6	Paddington	95.55		9 E	93.50		11¼ E

5066 *Sir Felix Pole* (previously *Wardour Castle*) undergoing rebuilding with 4-row superheat boiler and double chimney at Swindon Works, April 1959. A 'County' is in the next bay. (John Hodge)

The old and the new – Wolverhampton Stafford Road depot with single chimney 5072 *Hurricane* and rebuilt 'Star' 5088 *Llanthony Abbey* newly fitted with 4-row superheat boiler and double chimney, 14 September 1958. Note 5088's mechanical lubricator in front of steampipe. (MLS Collection)

There were, however, some experiments to improve lubrication. 7018 on its first overhaul after receiving the double chimney was provided with a 4-row superheater boiler and a mechanical lubricator set to provide 50% extra oil in running, and this engine became Bristol Bath Road's engine for the up *Bristolian* for months and many fine runs were recorded with it. Five locomotives – 4087, 4088, 5084, 7013 (ex-4082) and 7014 – were equipped with a Davies & Metcalfe lubricator with an extra 10 gallon oil reservoir which was placed on the right hand side of the smokebox. These were in place when the locomotives concerned received a 4-row superheater boiler and before double chimneys were fitted (see photos on pages 204 and 216). Despite 7018's new reputation and the fact that the Davies & Metcalfe engines were also strong engines and favourites for top link work, these experiments were not followed up and it may be that the extra cost with the plans for mass dieselisation well underway could not be justified.

The 'Alfloc' boiler water treatment was used at selected depots in hard water areas from the mid-1950s to reduce the build-up of scale on the boiler tubes and inner boiler surfaces. The treatment was added in the form of briquettes which were placed in a long feeder tube fitted adjacent to the tender water filling opening. The briquettes dissolved in the tender and the resulting solution was fed into the boiler through the injectors. An important part of the treatment was regular blowing down of the boiler to remove the scale and other impurities which the chemicals removed from the internal areas of the boiler. Locomotives receiving this treatment were fitted with 'Everlasting' (trade name) blow down valves located above the foundation ring at the front of the firebox. These valves were manually operated by a linkage operated by a removable lever which was inserted on a shaft at the right hand side motion bracket and normally stowed in the cab on the fireman's side panel. Because of the additional equipment 'treated' locos were usually grouped together at specific depots where dedicated pits were provided for the blow-down operation and where the firemen were trained in carrying out the procedure. Daily testing of the boiler water samples and associated adjustment of the briquette dosage were also additional requirements at these depots.

Stafford Road was in a hard water area and all the 'Kings' and half the Castles allocated there were 'Alfloc' locos. In later years many of the 70XX series allocated to Worcester were similarly treated. The daily dosage of briquettes would be added to the tenders by a boilersmith and on the London trips the fireman would carry out the blow-down procedure at Ranelagh Bridge, off the up working and again at Stafford Road at the end of the down working. Care had to be taken at Ranelagh Bridge to blow down before the engine was turned otherwise the noise raised by the expulsion of steam close to neighbouring flats would cause one irate woman to throw bottles and cans at the engine until the blowdown was complete! The boiler water sample would be taken and analysed by the factory chemist before the following day's working. Another additional fitting on 'Alfloc' locos was a tundish on the front of the left hand side tender toolbox. The treatment could cause the boiler to prime, when a large amount of boiler water could be lost through the safety valves. To counteract this an 'anti-foam' chemical would be poured by the fireman into the tundish where it would be fed into the tender sump and so into the boiler. An 'untreated' loco would require washing out weekly whereas a 'treated' engine could go two weeks and one Stafford Road locomotive being monitored went a month between each boiler washout.

From 7008 onwards the Castles were provided with the Hawksworth 4,000 gallon flush sided tenders similar to those designed for the 'Counties' but 6 inches less in width. These became in general use among the whole fleet of Castles and these were interchangeable not only at Works overhauls, but occasionally on sheds when tender defects arose. As will be noticed from the photographs, many of the early 40XX series had spells with the Hawksworth tenders as well as the 50XX and therefore many of the 70XX built with these tenders finished with Collett tenders. The self-weighing tender, No. 4127, was based on the Hawksworth Castle tender, holding 3,800 gallons of water and weighing almost 50 tons. It was coupled in August 1952 to 4084, September to November 1952 to 5081, November 1952 to January 1953 to 5007, January to July 1953 to 5090, July to September 1953 to 5080, and was seen attached to 7018 during the tests with the extra lubrication in 1958. After 1953 it seems to have been stored at Swindon and only used when specific relevant tests were authorised. There was one other unique tender which I've seen no records for. A Collett style 4,000 gallon tender 'No. 2856' had been rebuilt in 1950 with a 'Noral' aluminium alloy tank which weighed three tons less than the standard version and could be recognised by its smooth outline like the Hawksworth tenders. It was fitted for a short while to 5074 *Hampden* and by 1955 it was seen with 7008 *Swansea Castle,* had a short spell with 7022 *Hereford Castle* and finished behind 5020 *Trematon Castle.* It would appear to have been Hawksworth's experiment and was not developed although it continued to be in use until at least the end of 1962.

The first Castle withdrawal took place as early as March 1950, when 100A1 was condemned with a badly cracked frame. It was, of course, a rebuild of 4009 built in 1907 and therefore had a very respectable life of nearly 43 years. Two other 'Star' rebuilds were also early withdrawals, 4016 and 4032 in September 1951. 4000 *North Star* had a 51-year life to May 1957 and became one of the few WR steam engines to exceed two million miles in traffic (2,110,396 miles of which 1,191,592 was as a Castle).

5007 *Rougemont* Castle with self-weighing tender fitted to this engine between October 1952 and May 1953, at Cardiff General waiting to take over the 1.13pm Cardiff-Shrewsbury/Manchester, 10 January 1953.
(John Hodge)

Just three days later the self-weighing tender is seen attached to 5090 *Neath Abbey* standing at Worcester station with a Paddington express, 13 January 1953. (A. Donaldson/Kidderminster Railway Museum)

5080 *Defiant* with the self-weighing tender at Hereford, 31 August 1953. (L.B. Lapper/F.K. Davies/John Hodge Collections)

Laira's 7022 *Hereford Castle* at Bristol Temple Meads having just arrived with a train from Plymouth, 2 May 1959. It is attached to the Collett all-welded tender that was fitted for the longest time to 7008. (John Hodge)

The rebuilt *Great Bear*, 111, was withdrawn in July 1953, but the other rebuilt early 'Star', 4037, was not withdrawn until September 1962 and had accumulated the highest mileage of any GW engine at 2,429,722 miles. The earliest members of the Castle class as built, 4073 and 4074, were earmarked for withdrawal in 1955, but 4073 survived to 1960 and 4074 received 4-row superheat and double-chimney and was not withdrawn until May 1963. 4073 was recorded in April 1955 on the 8.20am Weston-super-Mare, running up from Bath in 106 minutes net, defying its fate, and 4074 having received its double chimney in April 1959, was Landore's engine on the down *Pembroke Coast Express* in August when it recorded 90mph in the middle of the Severn Tunnel. 5086 of the 'Star/Abbey' rebuilds was condemned in November 1958 and the first condemnation of a 'proper' Castle was 4091 *Dudley Castle*, withdrawn from Old Oak Common in January 1959. This engine had been of concern at Old Oak for a number of months seeming weak and off-beat, the remedy defying discovery (we used to joke that 4091 was the first GW 3-cylinder Castle). As a result of 100A1's withdrawal before 7028-7037 were constructed the total class size of 171 engines was never in service at the same time – 170 was the maximum.

The allocation of Castles at the end of 1959 was: (* = double chimney: change from 1957 shown)

Old Oak Common: 4075, 4082 (ex-7013), 4096, 5008, 5014, 5027, 5034, 5035, 5040, 5043*, 5044, 5052, 5054, 5056, 5060, 5065, 5066*, 5074, 5082, 5084*, 5087, 5093, 7001, 7004* 7010, 7013* (ex-4082), 7017, 7020, 7024*, 7025, 7027, 7030*, 7032, 7033, 7036* (35, -4)

Reading:	4092, 5010, 5018, 5036, 5061* (5, +3)	Plymouth Laira:	4087*, 5028, 5029, 5053, 5058, 5069*, 5098*, 5099, 7022*, 7031 (10, -3)	Cardiff Canton:	4073, 4084, 4086, 5021, 5095*, 7006, 7023* (7, -1)
Oxford:	5012, 5025, 5033, 7008* (4, +1)	Penzance:	4095, 5020 (no change)	Swansea Landore:	4074*, 4076, 4093*, 4094, 4097*, 4099, 5004, 5013, 5016, 5039, 5041, 5051, 5077, 5080, 5091, 7009, 7028, 7035 (18, -3)
Bristol Bath Road:	4079, 4081, 5015, 5048, 5062, 5073*, 5076, 5078, 5085, 5090, 5092, 5096, 5097, 7003, 7014*, 7018*, 7019*, 7034*(18, -6)	Stafford Road:	5019, 5022*, 5026*, 5031*, 5045, 5046, 5047, 5059, 5063, 5070, 5072, 5088*, 5089, 7026 (14, +1)		
Swindon:	5000, 5005, 5007, 5009, 5023, 5064, 5068*, 7037 (8, +2)	Banbury:	4078, 5057*, 7011 (+3)	Carmarthen:	4090*, 5006, 5030, 5067, 7012, 7016, 7021 (7, +6)
Newton Abbot:	4037, 4077, 4080*, 4083, 4098, 5003, 5011, 5024, 5032*, 5049*, 5055, 5079, 7029* (13, no change)	Shrewsbury:	5001, 5038, 5050, 7015 (no change)	Total (164, -2)	
		Chester:	(-3)		
		Worcester:	4088*, 4089, 5002, 5037, 5042, 5071*, 5081, 5083, 7002, 7005, 7007 (11, +3)		
Taunton:	(-1)				
Exeter:	5075 (no change)	Gloucester:	4085, 5017, 5094, 7000 (4, -1)		

The first impact of dieselisation on the allocation of Castles is apparent here. The initial tranche of Swindon built diesel hydraulic 'Warships' were being allocated to Bristol Bath Road and Plymouth Laira and the new diesel diagrams on Paddington - Bristol/West of England services saw a reduction of Castles at Laira,

Laira's 5020 *Trematon Castle* on an Exeter-Kingswear stopping train at Dawlish, 1958. For many years 5020 was a star engine at Canton where it was kept in spotless condition. Times have changed!
(J. Davenport/MLS Collection)

Bath Road and Old Oak Common. The redundancy of some 'Kings' at Laira saw them move to Old Oak Common and displace a few Castle turns there with sheds like Reading, Oxford, Swindon and Banbury gaining. An increase of six at Carmarthen, including Old Oak's star double chimney 4090, is puzzling. It was usual for Landore's high mileage Castles spending a few months there before major overhauls. One must assume some rediagramming of a few Landore turns and more parcels and milk train working via the Swansea District line. The Fishguard-Rosslare ferry traffic was building up, but the increase would soon be on the car roll-on roll-off ferry with the conversion of the *St David* in 1963. There does not appear to have been a policy to move the newly available double chimney Castles to depots with particularly demanding work. Both Old Oak and Bath Road appear to have enough for the 'crack' expresses, but depots with little top link work like Reading, Oxford, Swindon and Banbury have just retained engines previously there when the rebuilt engines returned from overhaul.

Newton Abbot's 5079 *Lysander* on the up *Torbay Express* leaving Kingswear beside the River Dart, 23 June 1958. (W. Potter/MLS Collection)

Exeter's 5075 *Wellington* crosses the Royal Albert Bridge into Saltash with a special train into Cornwall, 21 July 1959. (Stephen Sumerson/Rail Archive Stephenson)

Laira's 7006 *Lydford Castle* runs through Saltash station with the up *Cornish Riviera Express,* 21 July 1959.
(Stephen Sumerson/Rail Archive Stephenson)

Laira's 7022 *Hereford Castle* rescuing a failed 'Warship' diesel hydraulic leaving Par station with a down express for Newquay, summer 1959.
(R.M. Casserley Collection)

Old Oak Common's 7013 *Bristol Castle* (ex-4082) arriving at Bristol Temple Meads with the 12noon Penzance-Crewe Mail, 16 May 1959. (John Hodge)

5005 *Manorbier Castle*, reallocated to Old Oak Common in the Spring of 1958 as part of a reshuffle to equalise mileages between depots, heads the 9.40am Paddington-Kingswear past Stoke Canon station, 28 June 1958. (MLS Collection)

Landore's 5016 *Montgomery Castle* heads past Canton depot with the 8.50am Paddington *South Wales Pullman*, 27 February 1959. 5016 and its Landore crew will have worked up to Paddington the previous night with the *Pembroke Coast Express*. (John Hodge)

5091 *Cleeve Abbey* was a much travelled engine in the late 1950s. Seen here on a Chester-Shrewsbury stopping train, while based at Chester, 24 April 1957, it moved two months later to Exeter, Carmarthen and Landore in quick succession. (MLS Collection)

Stafford Road's 5047 *Earl of Dartmouth* eases round the curve through High Wycombe station with an up Wolverhampton express, c1959. (H.K. Harmon/Rail Archive Stephenson)

An unusually scruffy engine (for Canton), 5092 *Tresco Abbey*, heads the daily Fishguard-Paddington parcels train near Goring, 1960. 5092 would receive a double chimney in Works the following year. (J. Davenport/MLS Collection)

A pair of Swindon based Castles, 5000 *Launceston Castle* (leading) and 5023 *Brecon Castle*, head the Whitland-Kensington milk train past Cardiff Goods Shed, 28 April 1959. (John Hodge)

Laira's 5069 *Isambard Kingdom Brunel*, requested to power the Talyllyn Railway's AGM special, takes water at Ruabon before collecting the return train from Dukedogs 9004 and 9018, 18 April 1959. (H.D. Bowtell/MLS Collection)

A New Beginning and the Beginning of the End • 229

Worcester's 7005 *Sir Edward Elgar* at Battenhall Cutting, Worcester, with the 10.50am Hereford-Paddington, 30 May 1958. (Brian Penney)

Worcester's 7005 *Sir Edward Elgar* at Evesham with the 11.45am Worcester-Paddington, 7 June 1959. (Brian Penney)

Chapter 8
PERSONAL RECOLLECTIONS

My earliest memory of all which I hinted at in the preface was of a journey on Boxing Day 1944 when I accompanied my mother and four year old sister from Shirehampton near Avonmouth back to our home in East Molesey, nearest station, Hampton Court. I still have the ticket, the return half of a soldier's warrant ticket, child fare, duly date stamped. My father who was stationed in the army in the Bristol area saw us off at Temple Meads station and took me to see the engines of our train, for we were double-headed by a Castle and Hall. We must have dropped the Hall off at Swindon, for on arrival, only 4087 *Cardigan Castle* stood at the buffer stops, a puzzling mystery for a six year old. I started train spotting when I was eight (on the Brighton Belle en route to a seaside holiday on the South Coast) and was allowed to go alone to London trainspotting for the first time in early 1950 when I was eleven. That first day, after seeing the *Royal Scot* and its Duchess at Euston, I spent the rest of the morning entranced by the Kings and Castles at Paddington and can still see in my mind's eye a somewhat filthy 4082 *Windsor Castle* backing on to a Worcester train in platform 1, 5030 *Shirburn Castle* rolling in fast into platform 9 with the up *Red Dragon* and an immaculate Canton 5020 *Trematon Castle* standing at platform 2 with the 1.55pm to South Wales.

Every school holiday then was graced by at least one trainspotting trip to the London termini with mornings from around 11am until early afternoon being spent at Paddington. On Summer Saturdays I was tempted to stay well into the afternoon as it was so busy with unusual engines making an appearance. 4087 turned up in August 1952 on a Minehead - Paddington train and 4000 *North Star* backed on to the 4.10pm to Wolverhampton. 4087 turned up again in the summer of 1954 when it was based at Penzance with a holiday train from Newquay which I assume it only worked from Plymouth. Rebuilt 4032 *Queen Alexandra* arrived once just before its withdrawal and resplendent Canton Castles would appear for the 1.55 and 3.55pm Paddington-West Wales, 5006 *Tregenna Castle* on the 3.55 on one occasion.

I referred at the beginning of chapter 6 to my boyhood holidays in Devon in 1952 and 1953 and enjoying the sights of Castles at Newton Abbot and seen from the beach at both Goodrington Sands and Teignmouth, but the family holidays in 1954 were spent at Ilfracombe and in 1955 at Whitby. Around 1955/6 the London area experienced severe smogs or 'pea-soupers' as they were known. All lines into London were badly affected although with ATC equipment the WR suffered less delay from this cause than the other Regions. This was demonstrated in an extreme way in November 1956 when I'd been at Oxford attempting to win a scholarship (unsuccessfully) and rode a Worcester service back to Paddington on an appalling evening of dense fog. It was already dark and very misty at Oxford and the train arrived from Worcester a few minutes early. It stopped short and 7004 *Eastnor Castle* was uncoupled and disappeared into the night, and a burnished Castle backed two royal saloons onto the

Laira's 4087 *Cardigan Castle* arriving at Paddington with the 9.30am from Minehead, 9 August 1952. 4087 has the new front end frame section and also retains a tall chimney as originally built. (David Maidment)

front. Part of the platform had been cordoned off, and the mystery was solved when Princess Margaret was escorted to her saloon by the stationmaster. I could not get near enough to see the identity of our engine, and we set off with great gusto and I remember seeing the outline of our locomotive, the fire glowing in the mist, as we rounded the curve at Didcot to the main line. We were soon travelling in the upper 70s and the fog thickened as we got into the Thames Valley. To my surprise we roared through Reading unchecked and the fog was now dense. I started timing and speed increased gradually until around Ruscombe we were exceeding 80mph, although I could see nothing. Then I heard a frantic whistling, the brakes came full on and we ground to what appeared to be an emergency stop. I hung out of the window and at first I could see nothing but swirling fog. Then I just made out the parapet of a bridge. We were standing on Maidenhead bridge over the Thames. The silence was eerie. After a halt of three or four minutes we began slowly to resume speed and then, even though I was near the back of the train, the even beat of the Castle became very distinct and urgent. By Slough we were running at over 70mph again and speed increased to 75, 78 as we swept through what must have been Southall and Ealing, though I could still see nothing. I could not believe on such a night that we would be unchecked right through to the terminus but we were. We drew up in Paddington's No.8 platform just six minutes late. I waited until the princess had been driven away and the crowds had cleared and had access to the engine. It was Old Oak's 5040 *Stokesay Castle* in mint condition, buffers and cylinder covers burnished. I later learned that the driver and inspector had been overconfident and had been too quick to cancel the ATC warning and braked too late overrunning Maidenhead's starter signal.

In the summer of 1956, I joined a group of eight sixth-formers on a one week work experience course run by the Western Region to introduce to the participants the opportunities BR provided for operational management. The week was spent visiting railway installations in the Bristol area and at the end, after visiting relatives in the village of Wickwar, I returned in very sprightly fashion to London on the 12noon Bristol behind Old Oak Common's 7036 *Taunton Castle*, which had worked the down *Bristolian* that morning. I kept in touch with Rodney Meadows, the Bristol District Assistant Operating Superintendent who had been our chaperone for the week, and he fixed it for me to be employed at Old Oak Common from January to September 1957, my 'gap year' between school and college.

I therefore entered Old Oak Common that first January morning via the front gate with no guilt feelings looking over my shoulder to see if I'd get thrown out. I made my way down the long drive, past a couple of 47XX 2-8-0s resting from the night labours and cut through the shed across the main passenger turntable, where a number of Castles and a couple of Kings were clustered, to the main office and that of the shedmaster, Ray Sims. After issuing me with a denim overall he called a driver over and told him to show me round the shed. The driver had booked on for the 12noon *Torbay Express* and he took me to his engine, 5074 *Hampden*, which was just ex-works and had only been transferred to Old Oak when it had come out of Swindon the previous month. We climbed aboard 5074 and he eased it out of the No.1 roundhouse down to the coaling stage to top up with best Welsh Markham Colliery coal and then, while the fireman filled the tank with water, explained to me the workings of the shed and engines there. 5074, he said, now alternated with a Newton Abbot Castle on the *Torbay*, 4098 *Kidwelly Castle* was working from the Devon end. He took me to the huge blackboard by the drivers' booking on point where all the outgoing departures were just marked by time with space for the running foreman to chalk in the allocated locomotive. It became my ritual each day as I entered the shed to gaze at the board and see what engines were working, not only our own, but the 'foreign' engines that had come on shed overnight - engines from Laira, Bath Road, Landore. Most Canton, Gloucester, Worcester and Stafford Road engines had short turnrounds and were watered, turned and stabled at Ranelagh Bridge.

After a short spell in the Stores, I was moved to work for Billy Gibbs, the Chief Mechanical Foreman, in the Central Office placed literally in the middle of the shed between the four roundhouses. I was to cover the work of a clerk on long-term sick leave as 'Engine History Clerk' which meant that I looked after the engine record cards of all engines allocated to the depot, compiling mileage, oil and coal consumption from the drivers' tickets and stores and coal stage dockets before passing them to the Chief for allocating any necessary repairs. We had 36 Castles at that time, three having just been transferred to us as Billy Gibbs explained to me that a number of our engines had been in Swindon Works for several months and our availability was therefore poor. My job also involved preparing routine maintenance plans (boiler washouts and valves and piston exams) as well as shopping proposals for Swindon Works Heavy and Intermediate repairs.

Some of the Castles of the post-war build attained some incredibly high mileages between trips to Swindon works – I recall 5099 and 7020 in particular, the latter still on South Wales main line work with 116,000 miles on the clock since its previous shopping. By this time, its paintwork was nearly black from

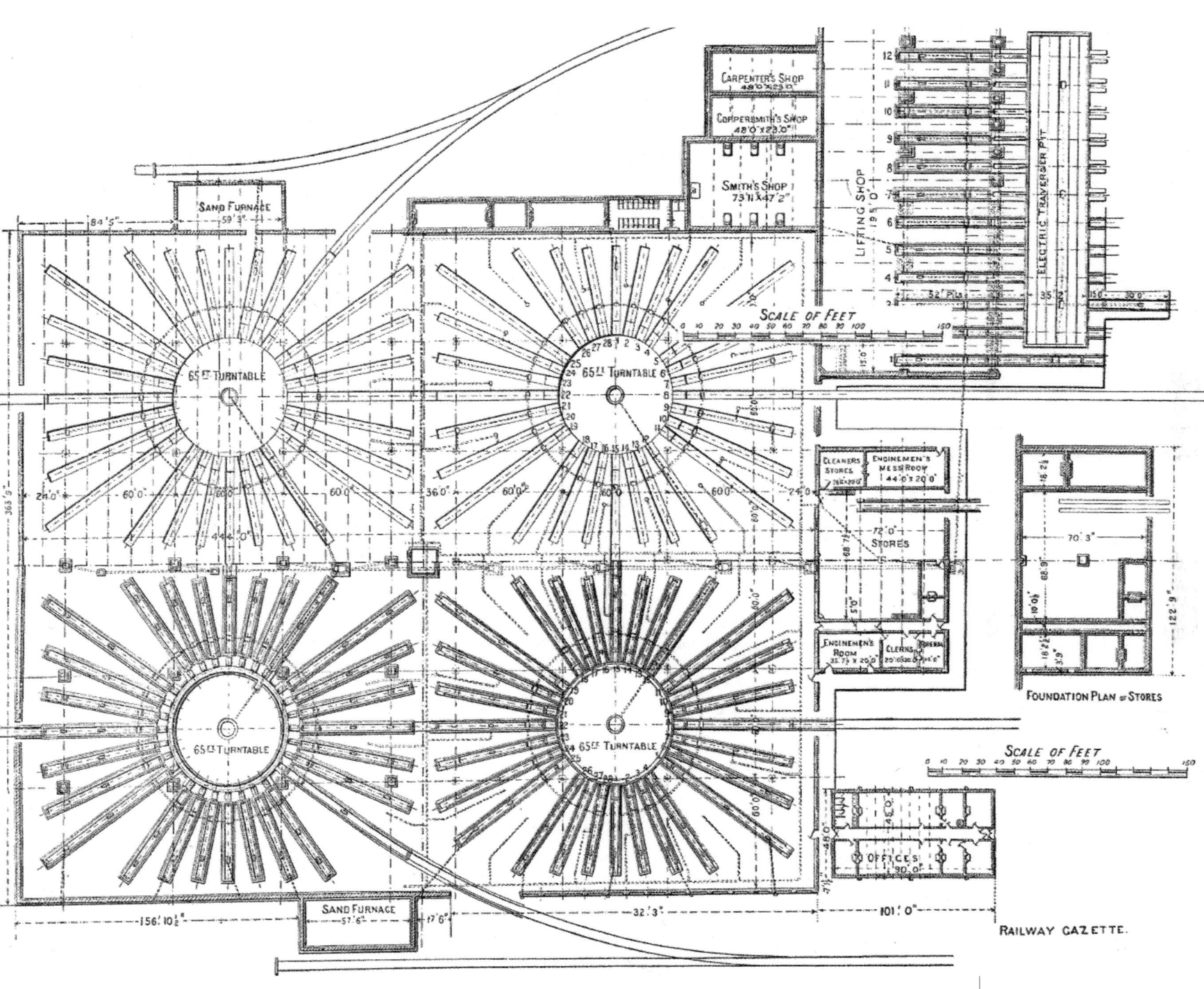

A plan of the layout of Old Oak Common motive power depot. The Central Office of the Chief Mechanical Foreman is the small square box in the bullseye of the four turntables. The chalked engine allocation list was on the wall of the office at the upper end of the right hand lower turntable. The shedmaster's office is in the block centre right and the 'Factory' is top right. The lower two turntables as a general rule held the main line passenger engines, freight engines top right and tank engines top left. (Railway Gazette)

the regular oily cleaning but it was a very shiny rather rich greeny-browny-black! Most Castles ran about 82-90,000 miles between Swindon visits, even some of the early 40XX, and 'Kings' were shopped after about 78-80,000 miles which they acquired very quickly as they averaged about 2,000-2,500 miles a week and there was no such thing as a light turn for a 'King'. I've mentioned the Swindon Works problem - I found that we'd seven Castles currently in Works, 5029, 5038, 5065, 5066, 5082, 7010, and 7030, with 7033 and 7036 stopped on shed waiting to go in. Two of them, 5029 and 7030, had been there nearly five months. With the two or three stopped for boiler washouts plus a couple in the Old Oak Factory for routine three monthly valve and piston examination or hot box repair, it meant even with the three extra Castles allocated to us at the end of 1956, we had at most twenty-three Castles available for traffic. This was tight enough for the winter timetable, but the Mechanical Foreman was worried about the summer when the number of diagrams for Castles always exceeded (especially on Saturdays) the full number of Castles allocated. During the late Spring of 1957 he had me go through the records and pull out all the details of the higher mileage engines that we would normally be proposing for Works repair before the end of the summer timetable. After half an hour of digging I produced the following, in order of priority:

5014, mileage 95,000, due Heavy General Repair

5092, mileage 90,000, due Heavy General Repair

7024, mileage 101,000, due Heavy Intermediate Repair

5055, mileage 88,000, due Heavy Intermediate Repair

5060, mileage 104,000, due Heavy Intermediate Repair

5099, mileage 106,000, due Heavy General Repair

7020, mileage 116,000, due Heavy Intermediate Repair

5044, mileage 89,000, due Heavy Intermediate Repair

Charles Collett had revised Swindon Works repair categories in the 1930s by introducing the 'Intermediate' repair enabling Castles to extend their mileage between Heavy General Repairs to 200-250,000 miles, a much greater figure than on other UK railways. As a result of my research Billy Gibbs instructed me to prepare shopping proposals immediately for 5014 and 5092. 5092 had been reported by drivers as 'rough riding' and was on 'restricted working' and must not be rostered for fast passenger trains. Although 5060, 5099, 7020 and 7024 had over 100,000 miles he knew that all had been running without any major complaints or heavy casual repairs, so he marked them off to wait for the autumn. I was asked to check recent repair cards for 5044 and 5055 and when I found no record of repetitive faults, he decided that they could wait also unless either suffered a major failure. He decided that we could also push the three-monthly valves & pistons exam for engines due in the peak summer period back a couple of months.

We had received 4090 *Dorchester Castle* back from Swindon in April complete with 4-row superheater and double-chimney and by May she had become our regular engine on the *Bristolian,* back on the 12noon Bristol. 5082 *Swordfish* returned from its Swindon overhaul in May and became our other 'picked' engine for the *Cambrian Coast Express,* a hard out and back turn to Shrewsbury, but one which paid the crew well as footplate crews got extra pay for every ten miles over 140 a day. I got to know the drivers' views about our engines as I not only saw the daily repair dockets that got returned by drivers after each journey, but I also heard the gossip as drivers visited Billy Gibbs and complained about their engines or asked for a special job on a favourite. The reaction to our rebuilt 4090 was incredible. Driver after driver asked Billy what he'd done to her, though it was of course the rebuilding at Swindon that became the model for future rebuilds. 'Never had a Castle like this one!' was the general opinion. 'I did 95 down Dauntsey yesterday' said one *Bristolian* driver, 'and I wasn't even pushing her. We could have done the ton easily.' There were some other favourites too. Billy Gibbs always seemed to select engines for VIP or royal work from a pool that included 5035, 5040, 5056, 7001, 7024, 7027, 7030, 7032, 7033 or 7036. There were some weaker engines too. We got Bristol's 4091 later and one or two of the 40XX were rough-riding though strong. 5006 (the former record-breaker) and 5007 got the reputation of being weak and a few foreign engines came in accompanied by some choice epithets. Newton Abbot's

4090 *Dorchester* Castle, a year after its *Bristolian* exploits, banished to the tank engine turntable to receive repairs to its dismantled motion, July 1958. (David Maidment)

5003 'couldn't pull the skin off a rice-pudding' and some of the 70XX had the reputation of being sluggish or poor steamers - 7000, 7012, 7016, 7018, 7029. 7018 was chosen for the first double-chimney experiment because of its poor performance. 7029 was of course also transformed by the double-chimney conversion. Problems with some engines were quickly cured at Works visits but for some unaccountable reason, good or bad, some engines' reputations followed them for years.

There were some regulars we saw day-in, day-out. Laira used to send up a high mileage Castle on the West of England milk train which would return on the 3pm Kensington milk empties. 4077 *Chepstow Castle* and 'King' 6008 (the latter on restricted working) were regulars although my old favourite, 4087 of Laira, put in an occasional experience. One morning in June 1957 I came across it sizzling happily at the exit of the shed as I came into work and I asked the driver if I could come up. It was booked off shed for the fast 9.30am Paddington to Plymouth and when I explained my affection for the engine, I got told in no uncertain

4087 Cardigan Castle at Old Oak Common in June 1957. It was built in 1925 and by 1950 it had already been rebuilt with a new straight front end to the frame and rectangular inside cylinder casing still 'unstepped' as late as 1957. In the mid-1950s it was one of five Castles provided experimentally with the Davies & Metcalfe valveless mechanical lubricator and reservoir seen beside the smokebox. 4087 already has a 4-row superheater and just seven months later would be one of the first Castles to receive a double chimney. It is one of the few Castles retaining the taller single chimney at this late stage. It was based at Laira/Penzance for many years, one of the last two based at Laira until February 1963. It was withdrawn in October 1963. (David Maidment)

Old Oak Common's selected engine for the *Cambrian Coast Express* in 1957, 5082 *Swordfish*, seen here with the up train at Birmingham Snow Hill, 31 August 1957. (M. Mensing)

7001 *Sir James Milne* at Swindon on the occasion of the author's first official footplate trip, June 1957. He fired 7001 from this point to the top of Sapperton bank. (David Maidment)

terms that 'an old 'forty' like this is no good for a hard Plymouth job, she's too rough!' She obviously had enough steam and left the shed on time and within a year she'd joined 4090 as one of the early double-chimney converts and became one of Laira's star engines.

Ray Sims called me into his office around this time to ask me how I was getting on, and then, to my pleasant surprise, asked me if I would like an 'official' footplate trip. Of course I was delighted and Ray selected the morning Gloucester turn, 11.5 out returning on the 4pm Gloucester, and chose a good recently ex-works 7001 *Sir James Milne* for my first experience as he guessed I would be initiated into the art of firing. I was accompanied by Inspector George Price and was duly inducted at Swindon and fired to Sapperton summit. Luckily the engine rode superbly and despite missing the firehole door a couple of times, mistiming my swing, I soon got the hang of it and we sailed over the summit with steam to spare. On

Stafford Road well known driver, Bert Griffiths, and fireman Forrester who welcomed me on their 5032, seen on completion of the run at Paddington, 21 August 1957. (David Maidment)

the return trip the Inspector goaded the driver to give me an experience of speed - we had kept time easily up to then without exceeding about 72mph – and we shot out of Reading and I experienced the crossings at the west end of Slough station at somewhere between 80 and 85mph. Such working was very economical, little more than 30 gallons of water and 32-33lbs of coal per mile and of course by the time the regulator was opened fully on the last stretch the fireman was already running the fire down to keep the engine quiet under Paddington roof.

Two months later, Ray Sims offered me a second footplate trip and I chose to go to Wolverhampton with a double-chimney 'King' (6015). As the inspector had mistakenly expected me on the 9.10 Paddington (my pass was for the 9 o'clock) I was at a loose end at Wolverhampton and just showed my pass to Stafford Road driver Bert Griffiths and fireman Forrester and was welcomed on board their Stafford Road single-chimney 5032 *Usk Castle,* one of the only three I'd never seen as a trainspotter (the others were 100A1 and Landore's 7012). The train was the 11.35am from Wolverhampton with a heavy thirteen coach load including a horsebox which restricted our speed to 60mph before Banbury where it was detached. It must have been needed very urgently to delay a train such as this. Once we'd got rid of it, Bert Griffiths grinned and we were off in a hurry, now with twelve coaches. We tore down below Bicester at around 86-87mph and went hard up to Saunderton, followed by another high 80 down through Denham.

5032 *Usk* Castle of Stafford Road which gave me an excellent footplate ride from Wolverhampton, 21 August 1957.
(David Maidment)

I used my first 'free pass' to travel to Swansea on the overnight 12.45am newspaper train behind 5084 and returned on the *South Wales Pullman*, seen here ready for departure at Swansea High Street behind Landore's 5077 *Fairey Battle*, August 1957.
(David Maidment)

Worcester's 7005 *Lamphey Castle* a few months before it was renamed *Sir Edward Elgar* at Old Oak Common, polished up to work the 6.45pm train to Oxford and Worcester on which a member of the royal family would be travelling, 27 May 1957. (David Maidment)

Long-time Old Oak Common resident, 5044 *Earl of Dunraven,* at its home depot, June 1957. (David Maidment)

5032 had been equipped with 4-row superheater and mechanical lubricator, but not yet the double chimney it would acquire later. Griffiths clearly had complete confidence in the engine which steamed perfectly despite the hard work and rode as well as 7001 had done.

I went back to Old Oak during the college vacation in the summer of 1958 and for the first few weeks resumed my role in the Central Office until the resident clerk returned. An event of interest that I learned there had been the decision in early 1958 by the WR Motive Power Department to review all top link engine allocations in order to equalise mileages so that no depot had all the low or high mileage locos - this mainly applied to the Castles. It was a golden opportunity to get rid of any black sheep and much effort was made to hang on to the favourites. We had received 4096, 5001, 5005, 5010 and 5027 and we'd had to lose 5029, 5038, 5055, 5092 and 7006 although somehow we didn't manage to lose 4091. We held onto our 'stars', those I mentioned earlier.

5043 *Earl of Mount Edgcumbe* waiting to be coaled after dropping the fire at Old Oak Common having worked the down *Bristolian* and 12noon Bristol return, September 1958. I enjoyed a footplate trip on it to Swindon the following day on the Saturday equivalent. (David Maidment)

In 1958, I spent more time acting as the Running Foreman's Assistant in the main office block. I was actually in charge of booking the engines out to their jobs as well as receiving other depot messages about incoming locos turning round at Ranelagh Bridge. Although I tried to manipulate some turns, in fact my scope for choice was very limited. We had the practice of keeping the best locos on the same turns for weeks (as opposed to the ER method of allocating specific engines to crews). The top link engines got best Welsh coal – Oakdale or Markham – whilst the freight (and some 'foreign' engines) went to the other side of the coaling stage and got briquettes or worse. I could choose which Castle to banish to Ranelagh Bridge to act as standby – one of my predecessors, I was told, had regularly dispatched 4037 when it was at Old Oak (around 1955-6) to stand there in the knowledge that it looked superb with its huge polished nameplate, but such was its reputation for rough riding that no foreign crew would think of taking it unless their steed was a total failure!

Our star engines in the Summer of 1958 were 5043 *Earl of Mount Edgcumbe* working the *Bristolian*, 7013 *Bristol Castle* (the erstwhile 4082) on the out and return *Cambrian Coast Express* and 5093 *Upton Castle* alternating with a Newton Abbot Castle on the *Torbay*. The first two were from the increasing number of double chimney Castles. Newly double-chimneyed 5057 *Earl Waldegrave* had at length replaced 7018 *Drysllwyn Castle* on the up *Bristolian*, a Bath road turn, and 4087 and 4097 *Kenilworth Castle* were much in evidence on Laira and Landore turns respectively. I had one 'unofficial' footplate run in 1958 - I was invited to join 5043, our *Bristolian* engine, on the Saturday morning equivalent as far as Swindon, and found everything straightforward with no trouble at all in running the heavy summer load stopping at Reading. Little did I know then that I'd be travelling behind 5043 on the *Bristolian* in 2010.

At the end of my college spring term after exams in 1959 and 1960, I treated myself to a weekly season ticket between Paddington and Reading and spent the day timing steam runs between the two stations. I kept records of the following trains, and only ignored diesel hauled or DMU services used to fill in to be in the right position for the next steam service. The dominance of Castles on the WR 1959 and 1960 summer timetables is apparent, for of the 85 runs I recorded, 62 were hauled by Castles – and it was consistent between the two years, 32 out of 43 and 30 out of 42. The variety of depots from which the engines came was extensive – Old Oak Common, Reading, Oxford, Bristol Bath Road, Swindon, Newton Abbot, Laira, Worcester, Gloucester, Cardiff Canton, Swansea Landore. Only Castles from Stafford Road of the main depots were excluded. Punctuality, particularly in 1959, was poor although little of the time loss could be blamed on the engines. In 1959 there was a severe speed restriction over a bridge being rebuilt at Hayes, and most trains were therefore late at Reading as the recovery time inserted to cater for planned permanent way speed restrictions was inserted in schedules west of Reading. Driving was erratic in that some drivers were content to accept lateness through delays whilst others responded with vigorous driving to try to recoup lost time.

Of the 62 Castle runs only one had time booked against the engine. That was a bad one when 5093 *Upton Castle* was clearly already ailing as it arrived at Reading on the 10.30am Swansea amid a haze of brown smoke and the blower hard on. The crew continued with it rather than request the assistance of the Reading standby pilot (a 63XX) and dropped a further 15 minutes, keeping going but suffering signal checks as the train had lost its path as well as struggling to make 60mph. The driver complained that the engine was overdue for boiler washout, the tubes being badly blocked. 5093 was normally a good engine, having been Old Oak Common's selection for regular use on the *Torbay Express* the previous year. The other engines did not fare so well. A 'Hall', a 'County' and a 'Britannia' dropped time, a 'King' failed completely and a 'Warship' running on one engine had the assistance of a Taunton 'Hall' (that is 5 out of 23 runs with other classes!). Two other trains were running late as a result of an earlier failure, a late running 'Hall' replacing a failed Canton 'Britannia' and another up service delayed by 15 minutes through the failure of Gas Turbine 18000 ahead.

Record of runs Paddington – Reading, 15-20 June 1959					
Train	Load	Loco	Act time	Net time	Punctuality
Mon 15/6/59					
08.55 West Wales	13	7009 *Athelney Castle* 87E	44.10	40.00	4L
13.18 Bristol	10	5062 *Earl of Shaftesbury* 82A	39.48	36.45	T
17.05 Bristol	10	5958 *Knolton Hall* 81A	48.55	40.30	16L (dep 7L)
Tues 16/6/59					
10.05 Bristol/Glos	9	5064 *Bishop's Castle* 82C	50.15	41.00	10¼ L
13.18 Bristol	10	5062 *Earl of Shaftesbury* 82A	50.35	39.00	10½ L
15.18 W'hampton	12	6960 *Raveningham Hall* 81D	Semi-fast, not timed		
18.35 Gloucester	11	5007 *Rougemont Castle* 85B	Not timed		
Wed 17/6/59					
08.55 West Wales	12	4097 *Kenilworth Castle* 87E	46.55	42.30	7L
11.15 Gloucester	9	5052 *Earl of Radnor* 81A	42.00	38.45	2L
14.55 Swansea	9	5964 *Wolseley Hall* 82C	45.03	40.00	5L
18.35 Gloucester	11	6019 *King Henry V* 81A	46.40	40.30	6¾ L
Thurs 18/6/59					
08.55 West Wales	12	5080 *Defiant* 87E	47.31	41.30	7 ½ L
11.30 Plymouth	9	5058 *Earl of Clancarty* 83D	51.25	39.45	11½ L
14.15 Gloucester	10	4085 *Berkeley Castle* 85B	40.35	37.00	½ L
17.05 Bristol	10	6920 *Barningham Hall* 81A	48.24	43.30	8½ L
20.05 Bristol	10	D804 *Avenger* 83D	38.24	36.00	1½ E
Fri 19/6/59					
08.55 West Wales	12	5016 *Montgomery Castle* 87E	44.25	40.00	4½ L
11.30 Plymouth	9	5028 *Llantilio Castle* 83D	40.57	37.45	1L
14.15 Gloucester	9	7000 *Viscount Portal* 85B	40.40	37.30	¾ L
Sat 20/6/59					
09.15 Weston–s-Mare	14	5034 *Corfe Castle* 81A	48.35	SO stopped at Ealing B'way	
13.55 West Wales	12	1012 *County of Denbigh* 82C	49.15	44.00	9¼ L
18.35 Gloucester	12	6019 *King Henry V* 81A	40.57	38.00	1L

Record of runs Reading – Paddington, 15th – 20th June 1959

Train	Load	Loco	Act time	Net time	Punctuality
Mon 15/6/59					
11.15 arr ex W'mouth	8	6955 *Lydcott Hall* 82D	49.00	38.00	10L
15.20 arr ex Worcs	10	5042 *Winchester Castle* 85A	44.00	39.00	3L
16.15 Gloucester	9	5044 *Earl of Dunraven* 81A	42.01	37.30	T
Tues 16/6/59					
11.45 arr ex Swansea	13	5056 *Earl of Powis* 81A	49.15	43.00	6L
15.00 arr ex Glos	11	5094 *Tretower Castle* 85B	44.36	38.30	6L
15.00 Bristol	9	4082 *Windsor Castle* 81A	43.41	40.00	6L
17.25 Bristol	9	5085 *Evesham Abbey* 82A	40.36	36.30	2L
Wed 17/6/59					
10.30 arr ex Swindon	8	1019 *County of Merioneth* 82C	42.36	36.15	2L
14.15 arr ex Oxford	9	7008 *Swansea Castle* 81F	45.38	39.00	14½ L
16.47 arr ex Worcs	8	4089 *Donnington Castle* 85A	40.49	35.00	2E
19.20 arr ex Swansea	11	5004 *Llanstephan Castle* 87E	Not timed		
Thurs 18/6/59					
10.40 arr ex F'guard	9	4093 *Dunster Castle* 87E	51.23	36.30	10L
13.00 arr ex Swansea	13	70024 *Vulcan* 86C	45.18	42.30	8L
16.47 arr ex Worcs	8	4088 *Dartmouth Castle* 85A	43.22	37.30	½ E
19.20 arr ex Swansea	10	5091 *Cleeve Abbey* 87E	46.47	39.45	17L
21.25 arr ex Bristol	8	5090 *Neath Abbey* 82A	43.36	38.15	T
Fri 19/6/59					
10.30 arr ex Swindon	9	5008 *Raglan Castle* 81A	43.26	38.30	7L
13.00 arr ex Swansea	13	70029 *Shooting Star* 86C	43.48	41.15	10½ L
16.47 arr ex Worcs	7	5958 *Knolton Hall* 81A	44.10	40.00	5L
Sat 20/6/59					
08.20 Penzance	13	4078 *Pembroke Castle* 82A	55.50	40.00	13L (7E at Rdg)
15.00 Bristol	10	5035 *Coity Castle* 81A	39.25	35.30	4E
21.30 arr ex Bristol	11	7006 *Lydford Castle* 83D	50.30	38.30	13L

Gloucester's 4085 *Berkeley Castle* at Paddington before departure with the 2.15pm to Gloucester and Cheltenham, 18 June 1959. The run to Reading was vigorous, almost keeping time despite the bridge slowing at Hayes. 4085 was in excellent ex-works condition and seemed to have restored its reputation having been based at Reading almost since its construction and considered one of the weaker engines of the class. It had been seen that morning roaring through Reading on the centre road with the up *Cheltenham Spa Express*. (David Maidment)

4089 *Donnington Castle* running through Reading station with the 5.15pm Paddington-Worcester /Hereford *Cathedrals Express*, 17 June 1959. 4089 had given me one of the fastest journeys of the week running up from Reading to Paddington earlier that afternoon in 40¾ minutes, 35 minutes net with a sustained 83mph from Maidenhead to Slough and was one of the few trains that week that actually arrived in Paddington early. (David Maidment)

Landore's 5004 *Llanstephan Castle* on arrival at Paddington on the 7.20pm arrival from South Wales, 17 June 1959. (David Maidment)

Old Oak's 5008 *Raglan Castle* running in ex-works on a Swindon diagram, a morning train from Bristol and Gloucester that combined at Swindon, 19 June 1959. The train I had just arrived on, the 8.55am Paddington, is seen disappearing towards South Wales and I just had time to take this photo and rush under the connecting underground passage to travel to London in the lovely old saloon coach next to the engine where I enjoyed the full force of the crisp exhaust as we ran strongly up to Paddington. It was running a few minutes late or I would have not made the connection. 6141 is departing with a local for Didcot. (David Maidment)

Newton Abbot's ex-works 5003 *Lulworth Castle* at the head of the 9.5am to Bristol at Paddington, 22 June 1960. The 8.55am to South Wales and the 9.5 ran from adjacent platforms and at the start of each day I had a choice between the Landore Castle on the 8.55 or anything on the 9.5 (varying from a Penzance 'County' to a Laira or Bath Road Castle). (David Maidment)

Swindon's 5023 *Brecon Castle* and an unidentified Landore Castle double head the 2.55pm Paddington to Swansea, 16 May 1960. This was a regular working, the Swindon Castle coming up in the morning on the 10.30am arrival from Gloucester and Swindon and returning ahead of a Landore Castle as far as Swindon. In my travels a month later I experienced the pairing of 5000 (Swindon) and 5080 (Landore) and three days later 5009 (Swindon) and 4094 (Landore). (MLS Collection)

7007 *Great* Western brings the 2.57pm Reading semi-fast train into Paddington station, February 1958. (David Maidment)

Worcester's 7025 *Sudeley Castle* enters Reading station with an afternoon Paddington-Worcester/Hereford *Cathedrals Express*, June 1960. (David Maidment)

Record of runs Paddington – Reading, 20-25 June 1960					
Train	Load	Loco	Act time	Net time	Punctuality
Mon 20/6/60					
09.05 Bristol	11	1008 *County of Cardigan* 83G	49.08	42.00	9L
11.30 Plymouth	9	6002 *King William IV* 83D	39.39	39.00	½ E
13.40 Bristol	11	5078 *Beaufort* 82A	40.02	38.00	T
17.05 Bristol	10	6019 *King Henry V* 81A	80.45	loco failed	41L
Tues 21/6/60					
08.55 West Wales	11	4076 *Carmarthen Castle* 87E	42.39	39.00	2½ L
11.15 Gloucester	8	5037 *Monmouth Castle* 81A	42.58	40.00	3L
14.55 Swansea	13	5080 *Defiant* 87E (d/h)	37.28	37.28	1½ E
		5000 *Launceston Castle* 82C			
Wed 22/6/60					
09.05 Bristol	11	5003 *Lulworth Castle* 83A	39.34	39.34	½ E
12.45 Worcester	9	7007 *Great Western* 85A	46.29	40.30	6½ L
16.38 W'hampton	10	7914 *Lleweni Hall* 81D	45.02	41.30	½ E
Thurs 23/6/60					
09.15 Worcester	8	5042 *Winchester Castle* 81A	38.06	37.45	2E
11.15 Gloucester	8	5065 *Newport Castle* 81A	36.17	36.00	4E
13.40 Bristol	11	5073 *Blenheim* 82A	41.33	38.00	1½ L
17.05 Bristol	10	5082 *Swordfish* 81A	44.42	41.30	4¾ L
Fri 24/6/60					
09.05 Bristol	11	7022 *Hereford Castle* 83D	43.08	40.00	3L
11.30 Plymouth	9	6025 *King Henry III* 81A	47.53	36.15	8L
14.55 Swansea	14	4094 *Dynevor Castle* 87E (d/h)	41.18	38.15	1¼ L
		5009 *Shrewsbury Castle* 82C			
Sat 25/6/60					
09.05 Bristol	14	6010 *King Charles I* 81A	42.40	42.40	1½ E
12.45 Worcester	9	5014 *Goodrich Castle* 81A	40.31	40.31	½ L
17.20 Reading	9	5018 *St Mawes Castle* 81D	stopping train		T

Record of runs Reading – Paddington, 20-25 June 1960					
Train	Load	Loco	Act time	Net time	Punctuality
Mon 20/6/60					
11.15 arr ex W'mouth	8	5974 *Wallsworth Hall* 82D	44.21	36.00	2½ L
13.15 arr ex W'mouth	11	4074 *Caldicot Castle* 81D	52.14	40.15	10L (3E Rdg)
15.10 arr ex Swansea	12	5057 *Earl Waldegrave* 81A	42.24	38.15	1L
19.20 arr ex Swansea	10	5030 *Shirburn Castle* 87E	49.08	41.00	6L
Tues 21/6/60					
10.30 arr ex Swindon	11	5000 *Launceston Castle* 82C	43.08	36.45	6L
13.30 arr ex Worcs	8	7002 *Devizes Castle* 85A	46.02	37.00	7¾ L
17.35 arr ex Bristol	10	6028 *King George VI* 81A	41.45	37.15	11½ L
Wed 22/6/60					
10.30 arr ex Swindon	10	5023 *Brecon Castle* 82C	41.10	37.15	1L
15.10 arr ex Swansea	12	5093 *Upton Castle* 81A	60.17 loco failing		31L
Up W of E	12	D832 *Onslaught* 83D (d/h)	44.22	38.00	40L (D832 1 eng)
		4904 *Binnegar Hall* 83B			
Thurs 23/6/60					
10.30 arr ex Swindon	10	5068 *Beverston Castle* 82C	42.37	37.30	10L
Local from Reading		7016 *Chester Castle* 86C	Not timed		T
15.00 arr ex Glos	11	5081 *Lockheed Hudson* 85A	43.04	37.15	10½ L
19.45 arr ex W.Wales	9	4099 *Kilgerran Castle* 87E	41.58	38.45	15L
Fri 24/6/60					
10.30 arr ex Swindon	10	5009 *Shrewsbury Castle* 82C	39.38	38.30	4L
13.15 arr ex W'mouth	11	5036 *Lyonshall Castle* 81D	48.35	41.45	15¾ L (2L Rdg)
17.43 FO arr ex B'tol	13	5087 *Tintern Abbey* 81A	37.02	37.02	3E
Sat 25/6/60					
11.15 arr ex W'mouth	9	7917 *North Aston Hall* 82D	41.43	36.30	T
15.20 arr ex Swansea	12	6943 *Farnley Hall* 86C	53.52	41.30	54L
20.05 arr ex Bristol	12	1009 *County of Carmarthen* 82A	39.10	38.30	2L

I joined the railway as a permanent staff member in August 1960 and returned to Old Oak Common as part of my management training in April 1962, but those stories will be covered in a later book to be published in a few months' time, *Great Western Castle 4-6-0 Locomotives – The Final Years, 1960-1965*.

CASTLE PORTRAITS FOR MODELLERS

With 171 locomotives built over twenty-seven years and modified and rebuilt during a further decade, it is perhaps not surprising that that there was so much variety in the detail and painting embellishments – so much so, in fact, that a Castle enthusiast could often tell the identity of a particular locomotive as it approached before its number could be read. This detail can be important for modellers who wish to reproduce a particular favourite or most appropriate engine for their layout and I'm therefore bringing together here a number of 'Castle' portraits to identify most of the differences.

4079 *Pendennis Castle* as built with Churchward 3,500 gallon tender, 'joggled' frames, tall chimney, steam pipes before later revised enlarged shape, brass beading to cab edge, and GW livery of 'Great Western' with crest on the tender, photographed in 1924. It was withdrawn in May 1964 after failing at Westbury on the 9 May 1964 high speed special and was purchased for preservation. The brass beading to the cab edge was later removed from the 4073-5012 series. (F. Moore/MLS Collection)

Castle Portraits for Modellers • 253

5010 *Restormel Castle* as built in July 1927, at Old Oak Common. It has straight frames over the front bogie and wider inside cylinder cleating, but is otherwise similar to 4079 above. (F.K. Davies/John Hodge Collections)

4088 *Dartmouth Castle* as built in 1925 and supplied with a Collett 3,500 gallon 'intermediate' tender, seen at Plymouth North Road, 8 August 1925. (P.J.T. Reed/F.K. Davies & John Hodge Collections)

4075 *Cardiff* Castle of Old Oak Common at Canton shed, 9 October 1960. It has a Collett 4,000 gallon tender, has the redesigned slightly larger outside steam pipes and has no cab edge brass beading. It has the slightly shorter chimney that was adopted from 5044 onwards and then on most boilers of all the series later. Livery is the final BR 'Standard Green' of 1957-1965. (R.O. Tuck/Rail Archive Stephenson)

111 *Viscount* Churchill, the 1924 rebuilding of *The Great Bear*, at Old Oak Common, c1949. It is in early BR livery and before provision of smokebox number- or shed-plate. The initials PDN (indicating Old Oak Common allocation) can just be made out on the platform angle (hanging bar) just behind the bufferbeam. (E.V. Fry/Rail Archive Stephenson)

Castle Portraits for Modellers • 255

5001 *Llandovery* Castle built in August 1926 and photographed at Cardiff General station waiting to take over a London express, 9 February 1956. It retains a 2-row superheat boiler and design of the original inside cylinder cleating which is the width of the frame as on the 4093-5012 series with the straight frame plates without joggle. The cab has no brass beading to the leading edge. It has the later curved external steam pipes redesigned to reduce cracking and steam leakage. It also has the post-5044 shorter chimney, a Collett 4,000 gallon tender and BR livery pre-1957, and silver painted buffers normally associated with Landore Castles. However, 5001 was based at Canton between 1939 and 1958, received a 4-row superheater and double chimney in July 1961 and was withdrawn in February 1963 from Old Oak Common. (R.O. Tuck/Rail Archive Stephenson)

4098 *Kidwelly* Castle, a long time Newton Abbot engine of the 4093-5012 series with straight frames dished over the bogie wheels and the first inside cylinder cleating design but wider than the 4073-4092 series. Like all engines of the 4073 – 5012 series, it has lost its original brass beading to the cab edge. It retains the 2-row superheater and hydrostatic oil lubrication, has the modified steam pipes and a Hawksworth 4,000 gallon tender. It has the original taller chimney. Livery is with the late BR emblem, 24 June 1958. It was withdrawn in December 1963 from Old Oak Common by which time it had a Collett tender. (MLS Collection)

The standard 2-row superheat Castle of the 5013-5097 series, 5024 *Carew Castle*, as built in April 1934, and photographed in April 1956. This series was built with straight frames and the inside cylinder cleating was a rectangular box – later from the mid-1950s there would be a shallow central raised section added to the top of the cleating to clear modified exhaust channels. It has the original pre-5044 taller chimney. All engines from 5013 retained the brass beading to the cab front corners until withdrawal. It has the Collett 4,000 gallon tender. 5024 is at its long time home depot of Newton Abbot. It was withdrawn in May 1962. (J.F. Davies/Rail Archive Stephenson)

Canton's 5021 *Whittington Castle* at Cardiff General waiting to take over the 12noon to Paddington, 11 October 1960. It is a standard Castle of the 5013-5097 series with shorter post-5044 style chimney and Hawksworth tender. It is fitted with a high superheat boiler and mechanical lubricator placed in front of the steam pipe to give greater accessibility to the inside motion. 5021 was built in August 1932 and withdrawn from Canton shed in September 1962, the month when twenty-six Castles were withdrawn. (John Hodge)

Rebuilt 'Star' 5092 *Tresco Abbey* of Worcester photographed in the early 1950s at Old Oak Common. It was built as a 'Star' in 1923 and rebuilt as a Castle in April 1938. It retained the 'joggled' frame of the Stars and the 4073-4092 series, but the inside cylinder casing is a rectangular but narrower than the 5013-5097 series. It would get the ribbed step later and was one of the last of the class to be provided with 4-row superheater and double-chimney in October 1961. It still retains the original slimmer outside steam pipes but has the short chimney. It was withdrawn in July 1963. (MLS Collection)

June 1946 built Hawksworth 3-row superheat 7005 *Lamphey Castle* as built with Collett 4,000 gallon tender. It still has the first style steam pipes and plain rectangular inside cylinder casing and the mechanical lubricator can be seen behind the steam pipe. The locomotive was renamed *Sir Edward Elgar* in August 1957. It is seen here at Worcester in August 1953 where it resided for almost its entire life, before withdrawal in September 1964. (MLS Collection)

7007 *Great* Western, the last Castle built in July 1946 before nationalisation and renamed from *Ogmore Castle* in January 1948. It was also the last Castle constructed with a Collett tender, but by this photograph taken in August 1956 it had acquired a Hawksworth tender, as was fitted to 7008 onwards when built. It still has the 'unstepped' inside cylinder casing and has the GW coat of arms on the centre splasher. It has the later style steam pipes and is seen at Worcester, its home depot from 1950 onwards. (H.D. Bowtell/MLS Collection)

4076 *Carmarthen* Castle, contrasting with the photo of 4079 taken in 1924. By August 1961 4076 has been rebuilt with a new front end frame recognisable by the full width rectangular inside cylinder cleating. It has a Collett 4,000 gallon tender and later style steam pipes but retains a 2-row superheat boiler and the modified and unbeaded cab front edge of the early series. The engine is seen ex-works at Swindon before returning to Landore depot and acquiring white painted buffer faces. Note that the brass safety valve cover has been painted over. (MLS Collection)

5004 Llanstephan Castle of Landore on the up *Pembroke Coast Express* at Cardiff General, September 1958. Note the dish over the leading bogie wheel of the renewed front end frame section of this engine of the 1926/7 series built with the straight frame but renewed in the mid-1950s. Note also the unusual inclusion of a Southern coach at the front of a chocolate and cream named train set. 1013 *County of Dorset* is in the background. (John Hodge)

Landore's 4094 *Dynevor Castle* at Cardiff Canton shed, c1960. It has been rebuilt with a new front end frame section and is seen from the left hand fireman's side. Livery is post-1957 BR emblem, with the (fading) Landore embellishment of silver painted buffers. (John Hodge)

The first double chimney Castle, 7018 *Drysllwyn Castle*, at Old Oak Common, September 1957. The stark straight-sided double chimney is very clear. It was fitted to a 3-row superheat boiler, all subsequent engines fitted with reshaped double chimneys had 4-row superheated boilers. 7018 was booked on this occasion for the fast 7.15pm Paddington-Bristol, but just before it went off shed, the driver reported injector problems and the remaining 'Star' 4056 *Princess Margaret* was a last minute replacement which got no further than Southall as it was in dreadful condition and was scrapped without turning another wheel in traffic. (David Maidment)

4090 *Dorchester* Castle, the first to receive a 4-row superheater and double chimney in April 1957. It was also one of two to have an extended smokebox (the other was 4093, although 5068 acquired one of these boilers later). It has a new frame front end and modified stepped inside cylinder cleating and Hawksworth tender. It has the later style steam pipes and unbeaded cab front edges. The double chimney is the new style oval shape and not the rectangular straight-sided double chimney of 7018. All Castles apart from 7018 received this style as did 7018 also in 1958 when its 3-row superheater HC boiler was replaced with a 4-row HD one. Although it cannot be seen in this photo, the mechanical lubricator was placed in front of the right hand side steam pipe. It is seen outside the Old Oak Common 'Factory' in the summer of 1957, awaiting its 3-monthly valves and pistons examination after working the down *Bristolian* regularly since May. (MLS Collection)

Castle Portraits for Modellers • 261

Hawksworth's first of the new run of Castles built in May 1946, 5098 *Clifford Castle*, at its home depot, Laira, in June 1960. It is coupled to a Collett tender as built but was rebuilt with 4-row superheat boiler and double chimney in January 1959. The mechanical lubricator is behind the later type external steam pipe. The raised step of the inside cylinder cleating is very clear in this photograph. (MLS Collection)

Rebuilt 'Star' 5084 *Reading Abbey* at Cardiff General waiting with coaches to add to the 8am Cardiff to Paddington (the Fishguard boat train), having worked down on the 12.45am Paddington newspaper train (I travelled on that train with 5084 just two weeks later), 23 July 1957. 5084 has been rebuilt with new front end frame section and is one of the five engines with a Davies & Metcalfe valveless mechanical lubricator, also Hawksworth tender. It would receive a 4-row superheat boiler and double chimney in October 1958. (R.O. Tuck/Rail Archive Stephenson)

Swindon's 4088 *Dartmouth Castle* at Cardiff Canton, Spring 1962. It was built in 1925 and rebuilt with 4-row superheater and double chimney in May 1958. In the mid-1950s it was one of five Castles provided experimentally with the Davies & Metcalfe valveless mechanical lubricator and 10 gallon oil reservoir seen beside the smokebox. It was withdrawn in May 1964. (John Hodge)

4085 *Berkeley Castle* was transferred from Gloucester to Old Oak Common after an overhaul in the winter of 1960 when it exchanged its Collett tender for a Hawksworth example. Note that although it retains the original 'joggled' frame, the inside cylinder cleating is of the narrow 'block' type, similar to 4074 and 4077 and some of the 'Abbey' series of rebuilt 'Stars'. It is at Swindon shed after arrival with an excursion from Paddington, 18 September 1960. (Brian Stephenson)

4074 *Caldicot* Castle also received a 4-row superheat boiler whilst retaining its original joggled frame and in April 1959, four years after it had been earmarked for withdrawal, it received a double chimney. Its modified inside cylinder cleating with added chequer plate front corner can be seen in this photograph. The mechanical lubricator is in front of the later style steam pipe. 4074 is seen at Fosse Road operating from Reading shed in August 1962. It was withdrawn in May 1963.
(MLS Collection)

Five Castles were equipped for oil burning between 1946 and 1948. 100A1 *Lloyds* was one of them, with the modified Collett tender carrying the fuel tank. The others were 5039, 5079, 5083 and 5091. Only 5091 had the fuel tank mounted on a 3,500 gallon tender. 100A1 is seen here at Old Oak Common in 1946 still in GW livery and with the wartime cab window plate covering.
(W. Potter/MLS Collection)

Above: **The lone** Castle that was streamlined in 1935 by a reluctant Collett under pressure from the GW Board and Publicity Department. 5005 *Manorbier Castle* is seen with the full streamlining to cylinders and front end as constructed in 1935. The cover over the cylinder and front end was removed within a couple of years because of overheating. Unlike the streamlined King, 6014, 5005 did not retain the V-shaped cab when the rest of the streamlining was removed by the end of the war. The photo was taken in May 1935 at Old Oak Common. The only thing it retained from its streamlining was the knob and stand in front of the inside cylinder casing where the GW train identification number frame could be mounted. This is still visible in the photo of 5005 on page 225. (J.H.L. Adams/Online Transport Archive/Rail Archive Stephenson)

Right: **The cab** controls and layout of 5022 *Wigmore Castle* seen at Swindon Works after a general overhaul, 7 April 1957. Note the simple fireman's wooden tip-up seat – the driver was provided with a similar one on the right hand side. (R.O. Tuck/Rail Archive Stephenson)

COLOUR SECTION

Paddington-Penzance

Newton Abbot's 5059 *Earl St. Aldwyn* departs from Teignmouth with the up *Devonian* for Wolverhampton, c1956. (R.C. Riley)

5078 *Beaufort* with a down express emerges from the Parson's Rock Tunnel, Dawlish, onto the Teignmouth sea wall, 4 September 1954. (Peter Gray/GW Trust)

5003 *Lulworth* Castle struggles up Dainton bank with the Crewe-Plymouth mail train, 29 July 1953. (Peter Gray/GW Trust)

Shrewsbury's 5004 *Llanstephan Castle* pulls away from Dawlish station with the 7.15am Liverpool-Plymouth, 13 July 1957. (Peter Gray/GW Trust)

5078 *Beaufort* departs from Dawlish with a down express, c1957. (Peter Gray/GW Trust)

Newton Abbot's 5059 *Earl St. Aldwyn* passing Dawlish Warren with the up *Torbay Express*, 3 July 1957. (R.C. Riley)

Old Oak Common's 4096 *Highclere Castle* with the down *Torbay Express* between Goodrington and Churston, 3 September 1958. (Michael Hale/GW Trust)

Bath Road's 7003 *Elmley Castle* struggles up the gradient past the holiday makers on Goodrington Sands beach with the Sunday 2.20pm stopping train from Exeter to Kingswear, 5 July 1959. (Peter Gray/GW Trust)

270 • GREAT WESTERN CASTLE CLASS 4-6-0 LOCOMOTIVES – 1923–1959

5055 *Earl of Eldon* at Hackney approaching Newton Abbot with the down *Devonian*, 24 July 1959. (Peter Gray/GW Trust)

Paddington-Swindon-Bristol

An Old Oak Common favourite, 5035 *Coity Castle,* departs from Paddington past the parcels 1A platform with a Bristol express, c1958. (R.C.Riley)

Worcester's 5037 *Monmouth Castle* draws empty stock from Paddington back to Old Oak Common carriage sidings after earlier arriving with a Worcester express, while Old Oak Common's 5084 *Reading Abbey* backs over the flyover from Old Oak shed to collect the 3.38pm Paddington-Plymouth parcels train, 18 October 1957. (R.C. Riley)

4077 *Chepstow Castle* at Bristol Temple Meads with the 10.15am arrival from Plymouth, 25 May 1959. (Peter Gray/GW Trust)

Bath Road's immaculate 5085 *Evesham Abbey* draws the empty stock for the 4.30pm *Bristolian* into Temple Meads platform, 3 June 1959. (Dr J.A. Coiley)

5090 *Neath Abbey* with a Bristol-Paddington express near Corsham, May 1959. (Derek Penney)

Paddington-Gloucester, Worcester & S.Wales

5034 *Corfe Castle* 'assisted by a 'Hall'' climbing to Sapperton Tunnel with a Cheltenham-Paddington express, 10 September 1949. (Mark Yarwood/GW Trust)

Gloucester's 5017 *The Gloucestershire Regiment 28th 61st* leaves Paddington 1A platform with the 2.20pm van train to Shrewsbury via Oxford, 3 October 1959. (R.C. Riley)

Landore's 7016 *Chester Castle* at Twyford with the 11.55am Paddington-West Wales express, 24 May 1959. (K.L. Cook/Rail Archive Stephenson)

Worcester's 5037 *Monmouth Castle* heads the 5.15pm Paddington-Hereford *Cathedrals Express* through Tilehurst, c1959. (Ken Wightman)

Paddington-Wolverhampton & Chester

Stafford Road's 5075 *Wellington* accelerates the 4.10pm Paddington-Wolverhampton past Denham Golf Club Halt, 15 June 1957. (R.C. Riley)

Stafford Road's 4083 *Abbotsbury Castle* departs from Wolverhampton Low Level with the *Cornishman* for Bristol and Penzance, 14 June 1957. (Michael Hale/GW Trust)

On Shed

Old Oak Common's long time resident 5044 *Earl of Dunraven* stands at the entrance to the Old Oak roundhouses outside the shedmaster's office, with the Senior Running Foreman, H.G.Coles, observing, c1956.
(H.G. Coles observing, c1956. R.C.Riley.)

Rebuilt 'Star', the original 4000 *North Star* at its home depot of Wolverhampton Stafford Road, c1956. (Colour Rail)

Colour Section • 277

Old Oak Common's 5010 *Restormel Castle* is coaled at Landore depot, 4 January 1959. (Peter Gray/GW Trust)

Nameplates

Above left: **Nameplate of** 4079 *Pendennis Castle*. (GW Trust)

Above middle: **Nameplate of** 5076 *Gladiator*, formerly *Drysllwyn Castle*. (GW Trust)

Above right: **Nameplate of** 5017 *The Gloucestershire Regiment 28th 61st*, formerly *St Donat's Castle*. (GW Trust)

Above left: **Nameplate of** 7007 *Great Western,* formerly *Ogmore Castle.* (GW Trust)

Above middle: **Nameplate of** 7029 *Clun Castle* with Hornby model of *Bristol Castle* on the running platform. The model is 1/76 scale of the loco on which it rests. It enjoyed a trip on the footplate of 5043 during the *Bristolian* run in 2010. (Bob Meanley)

Above right: **Nameplate of** 7037 *Swindon.* (GW Trust)

Models

The Hornby Dublo model of 7013 *Bristol Castle* that was given to Bob Meanley as a Christmas present in 1957 and inspired his love of the 'Castles'. It is reflected in the polished running platform of the preserved 7029. (Bob Meanley)

David Maidment has at least a dozen '00' models of Castles, and this is his favourite, 4087 *Cardigan Castle,* as built in 1925. It is a Wills body kit on a scratch built chassis professionally painted and in the livery and with the 3,500 gallon tender as built. (David Maidment)

4087 *Cardigan* Castle as an Airfix model rebuilt with 'Crownline' double chimney, name and number plates, valveless mechanical lubricator, and Hawksworth tender as the locomotive ran between 1961 and its withdrawal in October 1963. (David Maidment)

7018 *Drysllwyn* Castle, the first to receive a double chimney in 1956, as a Fulgurex brass model, detailed and professionally repainted. (David Maidment)

The last member of the class, 7037 *Swindon*, built in 1950, produced as a specially commissioned model for the GW 175 celebrations by Swindon STEAM Museum, 2010. (David Maidment)

Bob Meanley's 'O'gauge model of 5043 *Barbury Castle* in its as built condition (1936) in the 1934 GW livery prior to being renamed *Earl of Mount Edgcumbe*. This and the model of 7029 are both by Masterpiece Models. Bob has for some years acted as engineering advisor to Masterpiece. The boss was called Michael Brooks who commissioned the first build of Castles which included the model of 5043 in the picture. Having it named Barbury Castle was through a desire to have a model in original condition and it was actually made before Tyseley returned 5043 to traffic. (Bob Meanley)

Bob Meanley's 'O'gauge model of 7029 *Clun Castle* with double chimney in final BR livery. The model of 7029 is somewhat newer and was part of a batch of Castles commissioned by the current owner of Masterpiece Models, John Borkowski. They were commissioned to represent various engines of the 5098 class, with over 100 being made. The builder is a company in South Korea called SJ Models. Their attention to detail is just stunning and they have an insatiable appetite for getting the detail right, much of it being derived from genuine Castle detail drawings. Accordingly, smokebox doors and toolbox lids open, tank filler lids open, all of the inside Walschaert motion is in there, it works, and it drives the outside rocking levers, wheels are all sprung, the firedoors slide, and even the chain for securing the handbrake handle is there. (Bob Meanley)

APPENDIX

Dimensions

Cylinders (4)	16in x 26in
Coupled wheel diameter	6ft 8 ½ in
Bogie wheel diameter	3' 2in
Boiler pressure	225lb psi
Heating surface	2,280.7sqft (2,258sqft 5098 cl with 3-row superheat)
Grate area	29.36sqft
Axleload	19¾ tons
Weight - Engine	79 tons 17 cwt
- Tender	46 tons 14 cwt
- Total	126 tons 11 cwt
Water capacity	4,000 gallons
Coal capacity	6 tons
Tractive effort	31,625lbs

Weight diagram

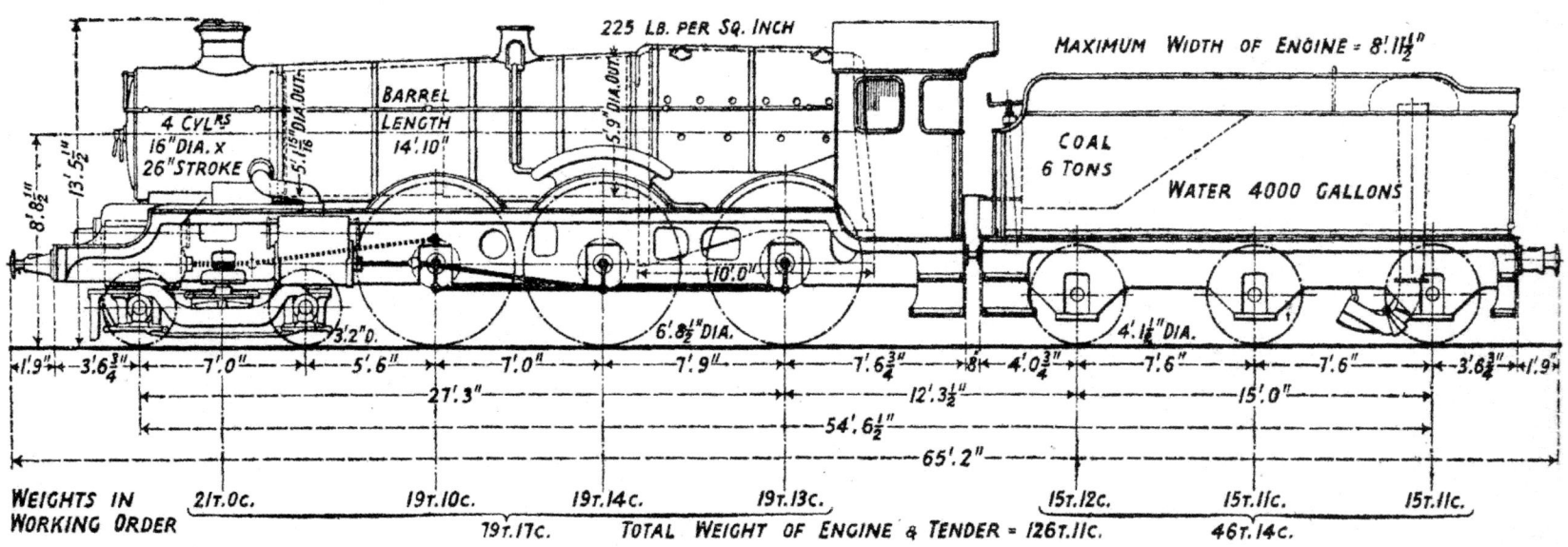

Statistics

No.	Built	Name	Double chimney	Withdrawn	Mileage
111	9/24	*Viscount Churchill*		7/53	1,989,628**
		(was *The Great Bear* from 1908)			
4000	11/29	*North Star*		5/57	2,110,396**
4009	4/25	*Shooting Star*		3/50	1,974,651**
	1/36	100A1 *Lloyds*			
4016	10/25	*Knight of the Golden Fleece*			
	2/38	*The Somerset Light Infantry (Prince Albert's)*		9/51	1,972,559**
4032	10/25	*Queen Alexandra*		/51	1,981,335**
4037	6/26	*Queen Philippa*		9/62	2,429,722**
	4/37	*The South Wales Borderers*			
4073	8/23	*Caerphilly Castle*		5/60 Preserved	1,910,730
4074	12/23	*Caldicot Castle*	4/59	5/63	1,844,072
4075	1/24	*Cardiff Castle*		11/61	1,807,802
4076	2/24	*Carmarthen Castle*		2/63	1,697,895
4077	2/24	*Chepstow Castle*		8/62	1,823,488
4078	2/24	*Pembroke Castle*		7/62	1,917,380
4079	3/24	*Pendennis Castle*		5/64 Preserved	1,758,398
4080	3/24	*Powderham Castle*	8/58	8/64	1,974,461
4081	3/24	*Warwick Castle*		2/63	1,894,998
4082	4/24	*Windsor Castle*	5/58	2/65	1,898,571
		7013 *Bristol Castle* from 2/52			
4083	5/25	*Abbotsbury Castle*		12/61	1,677,060
4084	5/25	*Aberystwyth Castle*		10/60	1,674,812
4085	6/25	*Berkeley Castle*		5/62	1,651,000
4086	6/25	*Builth Castle*		4/62	1,791,633
4087	6/25	*Cardigan Castle*	2/58	10/63	1,812,341
4088	7/25	*Dartmouth Castle*	5/58	5/64	1,848,430*
4089	7/25	*Donnington Castle*		9/64	1,876,807
4090	8/25	*Dorchester Castle*	4/57	6/63	1,848,646
4091	8/25	*Dudley Castle*		1/59	1,691,856
4092	8/25	*Dunraven Castle*		12/61	1,718,879
4093	5/26	*Dunster Castle*	12/57	9/64	1,842,985*
4094	5/26	*Dynevor Castle*		3/62	1,881,886
4095	6/26	*Harlech Castle*		12/62	1,695,899
4096	6/26	*Highclere Castle*		2/63	1,958,378
4097	6/26	*Kenilworth Castle*	6/58	12/60	1,713,966

No.	Built	Name	Double chimney	Withdrawn	Mileage
4098	7/26	Kidwelly Castle		12/63	1,723,879
4099	8/26	Kilgerran Castle		9/62	1,873,985
5000	8/26	Launceston Castle		10/64	1,870,200*
5001	8/26	Llandovery Castle	7/61	2/63	1,885,495
5002	8/26	Ludlow Castle		9/64	1,817,218
5003	5/27	Lulworth Castle		8/62	1,698,751
5004	6/27	Llanstephan Castle		4/62	1,854,704
5005	6/27	Manorbier Castle		2/60	1,731,868
5006	6/27	Tregenna Castle		4/62	1,812,966
5007	6/27	Rougemont Castle		9/62	1,854,951
5008	6/27	Raglan Castle	3/61	9/62	1,798,646
5009	7/27	Shrewsbury Castle		10/60	1,708,246
5010	7/27	Restormel Castle		10/59	1,684,146
5011	7/27	Tintagel Castle		9/62	1,732,565
5012	7/27	Berry Pomeroy Castle		4/62	1,625,965
5013	7/32	Abergavenny Castle		7/62	1,525,662
5014	7/32	Goodrich Castle		2/65	1,615,297*
5015	7/32	Kingswear Castle		4/63	1,554,288
5016	7/32	Montgomery Castle	2/61	9/62	1,480,896
5017	7/32	St Donat's Castle		9/61	1,598,851
	4/54	The Gloucestershire Regiment 28th 61st			
5018	7/32	St. Mawes Castle		3/63	1,503,642
5019	7/32	Treago Castle	3/61	9/62	1,521,335
5020	8/32	Trematon Castle		11/62	1,636,749
5021	8/32	Whittington Castle		9/62	1,446,936
5022	8/32	Wigmore Castle	2/59	6/63	1,546,104
5023	4/34	Brecon Castle		2/63	1,479,168
5024	4/34	Carew Castle		5/62	1,351,161
5025	4/34	Chirk Castle		11/63	1,401,530
5026	4/34	Criccieth Castle	10/59	11/64	1,209,457*
5027	5/34	Farleigh Castle	4/61	11/62	1,465,365
5028	5/34	Llantilio Castle		5/60	1,345,291
5029	5/34	Nunney Castle		12/63 Preserved	1,523,415
5030	6/34	Shirburn Castle		9/62	1,413,084
5031	6/34	Totnes Castle	6/59	10/63	1,434,409
5032	6/34	Usk Castle	5/59	9/62	1,288,968

No.	Built	Name	Double chimney	Withdrawn	Mileage
5033	5/35	Broughton Castle	10/60	9/62	1,160,197
5034	5/35	Corfe Castle	2/61	9/62	1,250,714
5035	5/35	Coity Castle		5/62	1,444,261
5036	6/35	Lyonshall Castle	12/60	9/62	1,304,430
5037	6/35	Monmouth Castle		3/64	1,500,851
5038	6/35	Morlais Castle		9/63	1,438,862
5039	6/35	Rhuddlan Castle		6/64	1,380,564
5040	7/35	Stokesay Castle		10/63	1,414,142
5041	7/35	Tiverton Castle		12/63	1,383,804
5042	7/35	Winchester Castle		6/65	1,339,221
5043	3/36	Barbury Castle	5/58	12/63 Preserved	1,400,817
	9/37	Earl of Mount Edgcumbe			
5044	3/36	Beverston Castle		4/62	1,377,644
	9/37	Earl of Dunraven			
5045	4/36	Bridgwater Castle		9/62	1,383,737
	9/37	Earl of Dudley			
5046	4/36	Clifford Castle		9/62	1,358,388
	8/37	Earl Cawdor			
5047	4/36	Compton Castle		9/62	1,225,670
	8/37	Earl of Dartmouth			
5048	5/36	Cranbrook Castle		8/62	1,327,811
	8/37	Earl of Devon			
5049	5/36	Denbigh Castle	9/59	3/63	1,282,965
	8/37	Earl of Plymouth			
5050	5/36	Devizes Castle		9/63	1,135,797
	8/37	Earl of St. Germans			
5051	5/36	Drysllwyn Castle		5/63 Preserved	1,316,659
	8/37	Earl Bathurst			
5052	5/36	Eastnor Castle		9/62	1,396,894
	7/37	Earl of Radnor			
5053	6/36	Bishop's Castle		7/62	1,293,786
	8/37	Earl Cairns			
5054	6/36	Lamphey Castle		10/64	1,412,394
	9/37	Earl of Ducie			
5055	6/36	Lydford Castle		9/64	1,439,975
	9/37	Earl of Eldon			

No.	Built	Name	Double chimney	Withdrawn	Mileage
5056	6/36	Ogmore Castle	11/60	11/64	1,434,833*
	9/37	Earl of Powis			
5057	7/36	Penrice Castle	7/58	9/64	1,273,324
	10/37	Earl Waldegrave			
5058	5/37	Newport Castle		3/64	1,224,735
	9/37	Earl of Clancarty			
5059	6/37	Powis Castle		6/62	1,054,062
	10/37	Earl St. Aldwyn			
5060	6/37	Sarum Castle	8/61	4/63	1,316,240
	10/37	Earl of Berkeley			
5061	6/37	Sudeley Castle	9/58	9/62	1,020,412
	10/37	Earl of Birkenhead			
5062	6/37	Tenby Castle		8/62	1,143,143
	11/37	Earl of Shaftesbury			
5063	6/37	Thornbury Castle		2/65	1,235,058
	1937	Earl Baldwin			
5064	7/37	Tretower Castle	9/58	9/62	1,155,986
	9/37	Bishop's Castle			
5065	7/37	Upton Castle		2/63	1,222,961
	9/37	Newport Castle			
5066	7/37	Wardour Castle	9/58	9/62	1,339,619
	4/56	Sir Felix Pole			
5067	7/37	St Fagans Castle		9/62	1,192,663
5068	6/38	Beverston Castle	3/61	9/62	1,081,514
5069	6/38	Isambard Kingdom Brunel	11/58	2/62	1,217,505
5070	7/38	Sir Daniel Gooch		3/64	1,139,354
5071	7/38	Clifford Castle	6/59	10/63	1,150,913
	9/40	Spitfire			
5072	7/38	Compton Castle		10/62	1,055,942
	11/40	Hurricane			
5073	7/38	Cranbrook Castle	5/59	2/64	995,495
	11/40	Blenheim			
5074	7/38	Denbigh Castle		5/64	1,142,187
	1/41	Hampden			
5075	8/38	Devizes Castle		9/62	1,068,502
	10/40	Wellington			

No.	Built	Name	Double chimney	Withdrawn	Mileage
5076	8/38	Drysllwyn Castle		9/64	1,121,080
	1/41	Gladiator			
5077	8/38	Eastnor Castle		7/62	1,089,166
	10/40	Fairey Battle			
5078	5/39	Lamphey Castle	12/61	11/62	1,038,165
	1/41	Beaufort			
5079	5/39	Lydford Castle		5/60	1,008,175
	1/41	Lysander			
5080	5/39	Ogmore Castle		4/63 Preserved	1,117,030
	1/41	Defiant			
5081	6/39	Penrice Castle		10/63	1,208,003
	1/41	Lockheed Hudson			
5082	6/39	Powis Castle		7/62	1,161,413
	1/41	Swordfish			
5083	11/22	Bath Abbey	Reb.6/39	1/59	1,822,834**
5084	12/22	Reading Abbey	Reb.4/37	10/58	7/62	2,017,118**
5085	12/22	Evesham Abbey	Reb.7/39		2/64	2,112,594**
5086	12/22	Malvern Abbey	Reb.12/37		11/58	1,871,501**
	12/37	Viscount Horne			
5087	1/23	Tintern Abbey	Reb.11/40		8/63	2,029,151**
5088	1/23	Llanthony Abbey	Reb.2/39	6/58	9/62	1,879,955**
5089	1/23	Margam Abbey	Reb.11/39		11/64	2,097,247**
	11/39	Westminster Abbey			
5090	2/23	Neath Abbey	Reb.4/39		5/62	2,058,275**
5091	2/23	Cleeve Abbey	Reb.12/38		10/64	1,921,723**
5092	2/23	Tresco Abbey	Reb.4/38	10/61	7/63	1,968,877**
5093	6/39	Upton Castle		9/63	1,145,221
5094	6/39	Tretower Castle	6/60	9/62	948,540
5095	7/39	Barbury Castle	11/58	8/62	1,122,493
5096	7/39	Bridgwater Castle		6/64	1,103,607
5097	7/39	Sarum Castle		3/63	993,804
5098	5/46	Clifford Castle	1/59	6/64	826,525
5099	5/46	Compton Castle		2/63	863,411
7000	5/46	Viscount Portal		12/63	824,873
7001	5/46	Denbigh Castle	9/60	9/63	838,604
	2/48	Sir James Milne			

No.	Built	Name	Double chimney	Withdrawn	Mileage
7002	6/46	Devizes Castle	7/61	3/64	837,626
7003	6/46	Elmley Castle	7/60	8/64	773,642
7004	6/46	Eastnor Castle	2/58	8/64	876,349
7005	6/46	Lamphey Castle		9/64	869,370
	8/57	Sir Edward Elgar			
7006	6/46	Lydford Castle	6/60	12/63	789,052
7007	7/46	Ogmore Castle	6/61	2/63	851,649
	1/48	Great Western			
7008	5/48	Swansea Castle	6/59	9/64	483,663*
7009	7/48	Athelney Castle		3/63	671,920
7010	7/48	Avondale Castle	10/60	1/64	662,192
7011	7/48	Banbury Castle		2/65	748,635
7012	8/48	Barry Castle		11/64	667,408*
7013	7/48	Bristol Castle		9/64	712,286*
		4082 Windsor Castle from 2/52			
7014	7/48	Caerhays Castle	2/59	2/65	765,282*
7015	9/48	Carn Brea Castle	5/59	4/63	636,439
7016	9/48	Chester Castle		11/62	672,533
7017	9/48	G.J. Churchward		2/63	724,589
7018	6/49	Drysllwyn Castle	5/56	9/63	614,259
7019	6/49	Fowey Castle	6/58	2/65	680,454*
7020	6/49	Gloucester Castle	2/61	9/64	610,143*
7021	6/49	Haverfordwest Castle	11/61	9/63	673,241
7022	6/49	Hereford Castle	12/61	6/65	733,069*
7023	7/49	Penrice Castle	5/58	2/65	730,636*
7024	7/49	Powis Castle	3/59	2/65	731,344*
7025	8/49	Sudeley Castle		9/64	685,916*
7026	8/49	Tenby Castle		10/64	636,668*
7027	9/49	Thornbury Castle		8/63 Preserved	728,843
7028	5/50	Cadbury Castle	10/61	12/63	624,626
7029	5/50	Clun Castle	10/59	12/65 Preserved	618,073*
7030	6/50	Cranbrook Castle	5/59	2/63	637,339
7031	6/50	Cromwell's Castle		7/63	749,715
7032	6/50	Denbigh Castle	9/60	9/64	666,374*
7033	7/50	Hartlebury Castle	7/59	2/63	605,219
7034	8/50	Ince Castle	12/59	6/65	616,584*

No.	Built	Name	Double chimney	Withdrawn	Mileage
7035	8/50	Ogmore Castle	1/60	6/64	580,346*
7036	8/50	Taunton Castle	8/59	9/63	617,653
7037	8/50	Swindon		3/63	519,885

* Mileage to 12/63 only.
** Including mileage as 'Star' or 'The Great Bear'

Shed Codes

81A Old Oak Common	83A Newton Abbot	84A Stafford Road	86C Canton
81C Southall	83B Taunton	84E Tyseley	87A Neath
81D Reading	83C Exeter	84G Shrewsbury	87E Landore
81F Oxford	83D Laira	84K Chester	87F Llanelli
82A Bristol Bath Road	83G Penzance	85A Worcester	87G Carmarthen
82B St Philip's Marsh		85B Gloucester	88L Cardiff East Dock
82C Swindon		85C Hereford	
82D Westbury			

No.	First Allocation	1935	1947	1953	1955	1959
111	Old Oak Common	81A	81A	-	-	-
4000	Swindon	84G	84A	84A	84A	-
4009/ 100A1	Old Oak Common	81A	81A	-	-	-
4016	Old Oak Common	82A	83A	-	-	-
4032	Laira	83D	83D	-	-	-
4037	Stafford Road	81A	81A	81A	81A	83A
4073	Old Oak Common	81A	81A	82A	82A	86C
4074	Old Oak Common	83C	87E	87E	87E	87E
4075	Old Oak Common	81A	81A	82A	82A	82A
4076	Old Oak Common	87E	81A	84K	84K	87E
4077	Old Oak Common	83A	83A	83A	83D	83A
4078	Old Oak Common	81A	87E	87E	87E	82A
4079	Old Oak Common	84A	85C	85B	84A	82A
4080	Old Oak Common	83G	82A	82D	82A	83A
4081	Old Oak Common	82A	87E	87E	87E	82A
4082 (as 7013)	Old Oak Common	81A	85B	82C	81A	81A

No.	First Allocation	1935	1947	1953	1955	1959
4083	Old Oak Common	83D	86C	84A	84A	83A
4084	Laira	87E	82A	82A	82A	82A
4085	Laira	83C	81D	81D	81D	85B
4086	Laira	82A	85A	83D	83D	83D
4087	Laira	81A	83D	83G	83D	83D
4088	Laira	83D	83D	83D	83D	85A
4089	Old Oak Common	84A	82A	83D	83D	85A
4090	Old Oak Common	83A	83D	81A	84A	81A
4091	Old Oak Common	86C	82A	82A	82A	81A
4092	Old Oak Common	83D	85A	84A	84A	81D
4093	Old Oak Common	86C	82A	87E	87E	87E
4094	Old Oak Common	83D	86C	82A	84A	87E
4095	Laira	83D	87E	87E	87E	83G
4096	Laira	87E	82A	82A	82A	81A
4097	Old Oak Common	82A	83G	81A	81A	87E
4098	Old Oak Common	83C	83A	83A	83A	83A
4099	Old Oak Common	81A	83A	83A	83G	87E
5000	Old Oak Common	83D	81A	82A	82A	82C
5001	Old Oak Common	84A	86C	86C	86C	84G
5002	Old Oak Common	86C	87E	87E	87E	82C
5003	Old Oak Common	86C	83B	83C	83C	83A
5004	Taunton	86C	81A	81A	81A	87E
5005	Old Oak Common	81A	86C	86C	86C	82C
5006	Old Oak Common	87E	87E	86C	81A	87G
5007	Laira	83D	86C	86C	86C	82C
5008	Laira	81A	81A	84A	84A	81A
5009	Laira	83D	83D	82C	82C	82C
5010	Old Oak Common	86C	86C	84A	84A	81D
5011	Newton Abbot	83D	83A	83A	83A	83A
5012	Newton Abbot	86C	83C	81F	81F	81F
5013	Newton Abbot	83C	87E	87E	87E	87E
5014	Laira	83A	81A	81A	81A	81A
5015	Canton	83C	84A	84A	84A	82A
5016	Old Oak Common	83A	87E	87E	87E	87E
5017	Taunton	83A	82C	85B	85B	85B

GREAT WESTERN CASTLE CLASS 4-6-0 LOCOMOTIVES – 1923–1959

No.	First Allocation	1935	1947	1953	1955	1959
5018	Old Oak Common	81A	84A	85B	85B	81D
5019	Swindon	83A	82A	82A	82A	84A
5020	Laira	86C	86C	86C	86C	83G
5021	Laira	83A	84G	83C	83C	83D
5022	Old Oak Common	81A	81A	84A	84A	84A
5023	Old Oak Common	81A	81A	83G	83D	82C
5024	Laira	83A	82A	83A	83A	83A
5025	Old Oak Common	81A	82A	82A	82A	81F
5026	Newton Abbot	83A	83C	81F	81F	84A
5027	Old Oak Common	81A	81A	84A	82A	81A
5028	Laira	83D	83A	83A	83A	83D
5029	Old Oak Common	81A	81A	81A	81A	83A
5030	Exeter	83C	86C	86C	86C	87G
5031	Stafford Road	84A	84A	84A	84A	84A
5032	Shrewsbury	84G	84G	84A	84A	83A
5033	Stafford Road	84A	84K	84K	84K	81F
5034	Newton Abbot	83A	83A	81D	81A	81A
5035	Canton	86C	81A	81A	81A	81A
5036	Canton	86C	81A	81D	81D	81D
5037	Old Oak Common	81A	81A	82A	85A	85A
5038	Old Oak Common	81A	81A	81A	81A	84G
5039	Old Oak Common	81A	81A	87G	87E	87E
5040	Old Oak Common	81A	81A	81A	81A	81A
5041	Laira	83D	83D	83A	83A	87E
5042	Old Oak Common	81A	85B	85B	85B	85A
5043	Old Oak Common	-	81A	87G	87G	81A
5044	Old Oak Common	-	81A	81A	81A	81A
5045	Old Oak Common	-	81A	84A	84A	84A
5046	Canton	-	86C	86C	86C	84A
5047	Landore	-	83A	83A	84A	84A
5048	Bristol Bath Road	-	82A	82A	82A	82A
5049	Worcester	-	86C	86C	86C	83A
5050	Worcester	-	83C	84G	84G	84G
5051	Landore	-	87E	87E	87E	87E
5052	Canton	-	86C	86C	86C	81A
5053	Shrewsbury	-	84G	84G	83A	83A

No.	First Allocation	1935	1947	1953	1955	1959
5054	Old Oak Common	-	81A	81A	86C	82A
5055	Old Oak Common	-	81A	81A	81A	83A
5056	Old Oak Common	-	81A	81A	81A	81A
5057	Newton Abbot	-	83D	83D	82A	82A
5058	Newton Abbot	-	83A	83D	83D	83D
5059	Exeter	-	83C	83A	83A	84A
5060	Stafford Road	-	83D	81A	81A	81A
5061	Shrewsbury	-	84G	84K	84K	81D
5062	Stafford Road	-	83A	82C	82C	82A
5063	Worcester	-	85A	85A	82A	84A
5064	Newton Abbot	-	84G	82A	82A	82C
5065	Exeter	-	81A	81A	81A	81A
5066	Old Oak Common	-	81A	81A	81A	81A
5067	Old Oak Common	-	82C	82A	82A	87G
5068	Bristol Bath Road	-	82C	82C	82C	82C
5069	Old Oak Common	-	81A	82A	83D	83D
5070	Old Oak Common	-	84A	84A	84A	84A
5071	Newton Abbot	-	83A	83A	83A	85B
5072	Newton Abbot	-	87E	87E	87E	84A
5073	Laira	-	84G	84G	84G	82A
5074	Old Oak Common	-	82A	Stored	86C	81A
5075	Stafford Road	-	84A	84K	84K	83D
5076	Exeter	-	82A	82A	82A	82A
5077	Old Oak Common	-	83B	86C	82A	87E
5078	Laira	-	83A	83A	83A	82A
5079	Old Oak Common	-	82C	83A	83A	83A
5080	Old Oak Common	-	86C	86C	86C	87E
5081	Stafford Road	-	81A	81A	85A	85A
5082	Bristol Bath Road	-	82A	81A	81A	81A
5083	Landore*	-	82C	82C	82C	85A
5084	Bristol Bath Road*	-	82A	82C	82C	81A
5085	Old Oak Common*	-	81A	82A	82A	82A
5086	Stafford Road*	-	84G	85A	85A	82C
5087	Old Oak Common*	-	81A	81A	81A	81A
5088	Shrewsbury*	-	84A	84A	84A	84A
5089	Landore*	-	87E	86C	87E	84A

No.	First Allocation	1935	1947	1953	1955	1959
5090	Laira*	-	83D	85A	85A	82A
5091	Bristol Bath Road*	-	82A	84G	84G	87E
5092	Gloucester*	-	85A	85A	81A	82A
5093	Old Oak Common	-	87E	81A	81A	81A
5094	Newton Abbot	-	83A	82A	82A	85B
5095	Laira	-	83D	81A	81A	86C
5096	Bristol Bath Road	-	82A	82A	82A	82A
5097	Shrewsbury	-	84G	84G	84G	84G
5098	Stafford Road	-	83C	83D	83D	83D
5099	Old Oak Common	-	81A	86C	86C	86C
7000	Newton Abbot	-	83A	83A	83A	85B
7001	Canton	-	86C	81A	81A	81A
7002	Landore	-	87E	87E	87E	85A
7003	Landore	-	87E	87E	87E	82A
7004	Gloucester	-	85B	81A	81A	81A
7005	Worcester	-	85A	85A	85A	85A
7006	Shrewsbury	-	84G	85B	85B	83D
7007	Stafford Road	-	84A	85A	85A	85A
7008	Oxford	-	-	81F	81F	81F
7009	Landore	-	-	87E	87E	87E
7010	Oxford	-	-	81A	81A	81A
7011	Bristol Bath Road	-	-	82A	82A	82A
7012	Landore	-	-	87E	87E	87E
7013 (as 4082)	Old Oak Common	-	-	81A	85A	81A
7014	Swindon	-	-	82A	82A	82A
7015	Swindon	-	-	82C	82C	84A
7016	Canton	-	-	82C	86C	86C
7017	Swindon	-	-	86C	81A	81A
7018	Landore	-	-	87E	87E	82A
7019	Bristol Bath Road	-	-	82A	82A	82A
7020	Canton	-	-	86C	86C	81A
7021	Landore	-	-	87E	87E	87G
7022	Canton	-	-	86C	86C	83D
7023	Canton	-	-	86C	86C	86C
7024	Old Oak Common	-	-	81A	81A	81A

No.	First Allocation	1935	1947	1953	1955	1959
7025	Old Oak Common	-	-	81A	81A	81A
7026	Stafford Road	-	-	84A	84A	84A
7027	Laira	-	-	81A	81A	81A
7028	Landore	-	-	87E	87E	87E
7029	Newton Abbot	-	-	83A	83A	83A
7030	Old Oak Common	-	-	81A	81A	81A
7031	Laira	-	-	83D	83D	83D
7032	Old Oak Common	-	-	81A	81A	81A
7033	Old Oak Common	-	-	81A	81A	81A
7034	Bristol Bath Road	-	-	82A	82A	82A
7035	Shrewsbury	-	-	84G	85B	87E
7036	Old Oak Common	-	-	81A	81A	81A
7037	Swindon	-	-	82C	82C	82C

* as Castle

Detailed costs of construction for Lot 303 (5043-5067)

Prefix	Description	Material	Wages	Establishment charges	Total
25 Engines					
1	Frames, Angles, Cross-stays & Stiffeners	£2,949	£1,390	£1,209	£5,548
2	Cylinders with covers	£4,678	£1,333	£1,170	£7,181
3	Horns & Ties	£875	£384	£253	£1,512
4	Axleboxes	£1,889	£713	£423	£3,025
5	Wheels	£12,084	£1,466	£1,486	£15,036
6	Pony trucks, & Bogie work	£4,042	£1,596	£1,006	£6,644
7	Brake Gear	£2,049	£798	£505	£3,352
8	Slide Bars	£2,062	£1,078	£661	£3,801
9	Valve & Reversing Gear	£5,659	£4,227	£2,585	£12,471
10	Smokebox	£1,418	£694	£452	£2,564
11	Sandboxes	£242	£255	£158	£655
12	Crossheads & Slippers	£4,366	£2,372	£1,510	£8,248
13	Springs	£1,524	£376	£282	£2,182
14	Cabs	£751	£844	£512	£2,107
15	Steam Fountains	£1,772	£127	£76	£1,975
16	Smokebox Steam Pipes	£1,340	£1,047	£506	£2,893
17	Assembly & Erection	£3,287	£7,610	£3,973	£14,870

Prefix	Description	Material	Wages	Establishment charges	Total
	Trial expenses	£100	£100		
	Scrap value retained	- £1,157	- £1,157		
Total (Engines)		**£49,830**	**£26,311**	**£16,869**	**£93,010**
25 Boilers					
	Copper tubes	£5,012			
	Copper Stays	£540			
	Boiler tubes	£3,185			
	Superheater tubes	£924			
	Steel boiler plate	£2,175			
Total (Boiler)		**£17,879**	**£6,188**	**£4,144**	**£28,211**
Total (Locomotive)		**£67,709**	**£32,499**	**£21,014**	**£121,222**
Average per locomotive					**£4,848**
25 x 4,000 gallon Tenders					
1	Frames, Angles & Stiffeners	£2,075	£852	£746	£3,673
2	Horns & Ties	£217	£55	£48	£320
3	Axleboxes	£388	£145	£104	£637
4	Wheels	£4,394			£4,394
5	Brake Gear	£1,116	£626	£442	£2,184
6	Springs	£551	£159	£110	£820
7	Tank	£2,480	£3,091	£2,068	£7,639
8	Cab connection	£107	£56	£37	£200
9	Cocks & Valves	£144	£41	£27	£212
10	Pipes	£247	£121	£56	£424
11	Assembly, Erecting & Painting	£1,015	£2,073	£887	£3,975
	Scrap value retained	- £259			- £259
Total (Tenders)		**£12,475**	**£7,220**	**£4,527**	**£24,222**
Average per Tender					**£969**
Average per Loco & Tender					**£5,817**

Derivation of names:

100A1 *Lloyds* — Lloyds Register was set up in 1760 to validate, certificate and accredit shipping. The first Register of Shipping was produced in 1764, the classification of hulls by letter (A was the best) and fittings by a number (1 was the best), hence A1 was the top classification for hull and fittings.

111 *Viscount Churchill* — Chairman of the GWR Board from 1908 until his death in 1934.

4000 *North Star* — Pole star indicating true north.

4016 *The Somerset Light Infantry (Prince Albert's)* Army Regiment from 1685-1959.

4032 *Queen Alexandra* — Danish princess married to Prince of Wales in 1863 and Queen of King Edward VII from 1902-1910.

4037 *The South Wales Borderers* Infantry regiment from 1881 – 1969 when absorbed into the Royal Regiment of Wales.

4073 *Caerphilly Castle* — Building commenced in 1268, second largest castle in the United Kingdom.

4074 *Caldicot Castle* — Stone mediaeval castle in Monmouthshire, dating from 1100, fell into ruin from around 1600 and restored in the twentieth century.

4075 *Cardiff Castle* — Eleventh century motte & bailey castle built on the site of a Roman fort, rebuilt in stone in the twelfth century, and completely rebuilt and extended in Victorian Gothic style by 3rd Marquess of Bute in the nineteenth century.

4076 *Carmarthen Castle* — Norman castle built in 1094, current ruins from 1105, extended in the thirteenth century.

4077 *Chepstow Castle* — The oldest surviving post-Roman stone fortification in Britain, construction commencing in 1067.

4078 *Pembroke Castle* — Construction started in 1093, expanded in the twelfth century, part dismantled in the Civil War and restored after 1928.

4079 *Pendennis Castle* — Built in 1539 near Falmouth in response to threats to south coast from France and Spain at time of Henry VIII.

4080 *Powderham Castle* — Built by the Courtenay family in 1391, it is near Exeter beside the Rive Exe.

4081 *Warwick Castle* — Built as a motte & bailey castle in 1068 and rebuilt in stone in the twelfth century.

4082 *Windsor Castle* — Built as a motte & bailey castle in eleventh century and rebuilt in stone in the twelfth century and occupied by the monarch from Henry I onwards, the longest occupied palace in Europe.

4083 *Abbotsbury Castle* — Site of an Iron Age fort near the village of Abbotsbury west of Dorchester.

4084 *Aberystwyth Castle* — Edwardian castle built around 1277 on site of an earlier bailey castle.

4085 *Berkeley Castle* — Located at Berkeley in Gloucestershire beside the Severn, construction commenced in eleventh century.

4086 *Builth Castle* — Now only mound and ditches remain of castle built in reign of Edward I near Builth Wells, Powys. Castle was destroyed by fire in the seventeenth century.

4087 *Cardigan Castle* — Constructed in the twelfth century in the town centre, but ruined until restored in the twenty-first century.

4088 *Dartmouth Castle* — Built in 1388 guarding the mouth of the River Dart.

4089 *Donnington Castle* — Constructed in 1386 and demolished in 1646 during the Civil War, just a gatehouse remaining, it is situated in the village of Donnington north of Newbury.

4090 *Dorcester Castle* — Constructed in 1154 but already abandoned by 1290 and in ruins in fifteenth century, a gatehouse was constructed in 1790 alongside the remaining walls. Maiden Castle, two miles from Dorchester, is an older and bigger site.

4091 *Dudley Castle* — Built in 1066 in Dudley in the West Midlands, it is now ruined and is the site of a zoo.

4092 *Dunraven Castle* — Built in 1803 near Southerndown, Glamorgan, 5 miles from Bridgend, it was demolished by its owner in 1963 (rumoured to avoid tax duties).

4093 *Dunster Castle*		Constructed as a motte & bailey castle in the eleventh century and rebuilt in stone in the twelfth, in the village of Dunster, Somerset.
4094 *Dynevor Castle*		Built in the twelfth century on the site of an earlier fort, overlooking the River Tywi near Llandeilo.
4095 *Harlech Castle*		Built by Edward I from 1282 during his invasion of Wales on a rock cliff overlooking the sea, a few miles north of Barmouth.
4096 *Highclere Castle*		A Victorian country house 5 miles south of Newbury, a location for the TV series *Downton Abbey*.
4097 *Kenilworth Castle*		Norman castle added to in Tudor times in Kenilworth between Coventry and Leamington.
4098 *Kidwelly Castle*		Norman castle constructed around 1200 overlooking the River Gwendraeth at Kidwelly between Llanelly and Carmarthen.
4099 *Kilgerran Castle*		13th century ruined castle at Cilgerran above the River Teifi (on the former Whitland – Cardigan branch).
5000 *Launceston Castle*		A Norman motte & bailey castle constructed in 1067 near Launceston, Cornwall.
5001 *Llandovery Castle*		Constructed in 1116 and fell into ruins in the fourteenth century.
5002 *Ludlow Castle*		Founded in 1075, partly ruined overlooking the River Teme.
5003 *Lulworth Castle*		Early seventeenth century mock castle in Dorset, south of Wool.
5004 *Llanstephan Castle*		Built in the twelfth century on site of an Iron Age fort at the head of the River Tywi in Carmarthenshire.
5005 *Manorbier Castle*		Norman castle on the coast 5 miles south west of Tenby.
5006 *Tregenna Castle*		Built in the eighteenth century at St Ives and became a hotel owned by the GWR.
5007 *Rougemont Castle*		Is in fact Exeter Castle built in 1068 within the city walls.
5008 *Raglan Castle*		Late mediaeval castle in Raglan village, Monmouthshire.
5009 *Shrewsbury Castle*		Sandstone castle in the city built in 1070.
5010 *Restormel Castle*		Thirteenth century castle overlooking the Fowey River, near Lostwithiel, Cornwall.
5011 *Tintagel Castle*		Mediaeval fortress on the cliffs of Tintagel, North Cornwall, associated with the Arthurian legends.
5012 *Berry Pomeroy Castle*		Fifteenth century mansion, abandoned around 1700, near Totnes.
5013 *Abergavenny Castle*		Constructed in 1087 and in the town centre.
5014 *Goodrich Castle*		A Norman castle near the village of Goodrich in Herefordshire.
5015 *Kingswear Castle*		Constructed from 1491 to defend access to the River Dart opposite Dartmouth Castle.
5016 *Montgomery Castle*		Norman castle, now ruined, in Montgomery, Powys.
5017 *St. Donat's Castle*		Mediaeval castle between Southerndown and Llantwit Major in the Vale of Glamorgan, now a Sixth Form College. *The Gloucestershire Regiment 28th 61st* renamed April 1954 after the infantry regiment formed in 1694, renamed in 1782 and amalgamated as present title in 1881.
5018 *St. Mawes Castle*		Fort built by Henry VIII opposite Pendennis Castle to defend the coast against threatened invasions from France and Spain.

5019 *Treago Castle*	A fortified manor house built around 1500 in St Weonards, Herefordshire.
5020 *Trematon Castle*	A Norman fortress overlooking the Plymouth Sound at Saltash.
5021 *Whittington Castle*	Thirteenth century castle in Whittington village near Oswestry.
5022 *Wigmore Castle*	Norman castle of 1067, dismantled during the Civil War, at Wigmore in north west Herefordshire.
5023 *Brecon Castle*	Norman castle in town of that name (named after a village near Rouen).
5024 *Carew Castle*	Norman castle built on the site of an Iron Age fort on the Carew River leading to the Milford Sound, Pembrokeshire.
5025 *Chirk Castle*	Constructed in 1295 in North Wales defending the entrance to the Ceiriog Valley.
5026 *Criccieth Castle*	Built in 1230 by Llywelyn the Great on the Cambrian line in Criccieth, near Portmadog.
5027 *Farleigh Castle*	Constructed in 1377, 9 miles south of Bath (also known as Farley Castle and Hungerford Castle).
5028 *Llantilio Castle*	Norman castle in Llantilio Crossenny, Monmouthshire, also known as the 'White Castle'. It is part of a trio which includes Grosmont and Skenfrith Castles, neither of which were used for GWR names.
5029 *Nunney Castle*	Mediaeval castle constructed in the fourteenth century at Nunney, Somerset.
5030 *Shirburn Castle*	Fourteenth-century castle in the village of Shirburn, Oxfordshire.
5031 *Totnes Castle*	Norman motte & bailey castle in Totnes on the River Dart.
5032 *Usk Castle*	Norman castle, c1120, on site of a Roman fortress on the town and river of the same name, Monmouthshire.
5033 *Broughton Castle*	Mediaeval moated manor house, c1306, in Broughton south west of Banbury. Home of the Fiennes family (incl ex-WR General Manager).
5034 *Corfe Castle*	Eleventh-century ruins on hill on Swanage Heritage Railway, Isle of Purbeck.
5035 *Coity Castle*	Norman castle, late eleventh-century, in Coity village north of Bridgend.
5036 *Lyonshall Castle*	Fort built in 1090 at Lyonshall village near Kington, Herefordshire.
5037 *Monmouth Castle*	Important border castle in the centre of Monmouth, damaged in the Civil War.
5038 *Morlais Castle*	Thirteenth-century castle near Merthyr Tydfil above the Taff Gorge.
5039 *Rhuddlan Castle*	Edward I castle constructed in 1277 at Rhuddlan, Denbighshire.
5040 *Stokesay Castle*	Thirteenth-century fortified manor house near Craven Arms and visible from the North & West line.
5041 *Tiverton Castle*	Mediaeval castle dismantled in the Civil War and converted to country house on banks of River Exe, Tiverton.
5042 *Winchester Castle*	Norman castle of 1067 – the Great Hall has been seat of Hampshire County Council.
5043 *Earl of Mount Edgcumbe*	5th earl was GWR director. Mount Edgcumbe is near Plymouth.
5044 *Earl of Dunraven*	Family seat Kilgobbin House, County Adare, Ireland. Also owned Dunraven Castle (see 4092). 6th Earl was GWR director.
5045 *Earl of Dudley*	Family seat – Dudley Castle (see 4091). 3rd Earl was Conservative MP for Wednesbury.
5046 *Earl Cawdor*	Family seat – Castlemartin – Pembrokeshire. Was Chairman of GWR.

5047 *Earl of Dartmouth*	Family seats – Marsden, West Yorkshire and Sandwell, West Bromwich.	
5048 *Earl of Devon*	Family seat – Powderham Castle (see 4080).	
5049 *Earl of Plymouth*	Family seat – Hewell Grange, Herefordshire, now Oakly Park, Bromfield.	
5050 *Earl of St. Germans*	Family seat – Port Eliot, Saltash.	
5051 *Earl Bathurst*	Family seat – Bathurst, Sussex.	
5052 *Earl of Radnor*	Family seat is at Longford Castle, Wiltshire.	
5053 *Earl Cairns*	Family seat at Bolehyde Manor, near Chippenham.	
5054 *Earl of Ducie*	Family seat at Tortworth Court, Gloucestershire.	
5055 *Earl of Eldon*	Eldon was in the County Palatinate of Durham.	
5056 *Earl of Powis*	Family seat is Powis Castle, near Welshpool (7024).	
5057 *Earl Waldegrave*	Family seat is at Chewton Mendip, Somerset.	
5058 *Earl of Clancarty*	An Irish title, family seat is Garbally Court, Ballinasloe, County Galway.	
5059 *Earl St. Aldwyn*	Family seat at Coln St Aldwyns, Gloucestershire.	
5060 *Earl of Berkeley*	Family seat is Berkeley Castle, Gloucestershire (4085).	
5061 *Earl of Birkenhead*	Lord High Chancellor of Great Britain and member of 1924 Olympic Committee.	
5062 *Earl of Shaftesbury*	Family seat is at Wimbourne St Giles, Dorset.	
5063 *Earl Baldwin*	Prime Minister of the United Kingdom, 1923-1929 and 1935-1937.	
5064 *Bishop's Castle*	Constructed in 1087 to defend the Shropshire village from the Welsh, ruined in the 17th century and little now remains.	
5065 *Newport Castle*	Constructed in 14th century to control movement on the River Usk.	
5066 *Wardour Castle*	Castle is in Wardour, Wiltshire, 15 miles west of Salisbury. Was partly destroyed in the Civil War.	
Sir Felix Pole	Renamed in April 1956 after the GWR General Manager from 1921-1929.	
5067 *St Fagans Castle*	Elizabethan Manor at St Fagan's west of Cardiff, built around the late 1500s. Now contains National History Museum.	
5068 *Beverston Castle*	Mediaeval stone fortress built in 1229 in the village of Beverston, Gloucestershire.	
5069 *Isambard Kingdom Brunel*	First Civil & Mechanical Engineer, Great Western Railway.	
5070 *Sir Daniel Gooch*	Superintendent of Locomotive Engineers GWR 1837-1864 and Chairman, 1865-1889.	
5071 *Spitfire*	Supermarine Spitfire powered by Rolls-Royce Merlin engine. Including the Seafire variant over 23,000 built.	
5072 *Hurricane*	Hawker Hurricane, single engined, from 1938, and 14,533 were built, 12 survive.	
5073 *Blenheim*	Bristol Blenheim light fighter/bomber from 1935, 4,422 built.	
5074 *Hampden*	Handley Page Hampden twin engine bomber, from 1936, 1,430 built.	
5075 *Wellington*	Vickers Wellington long range bomber from mid-1930s, 11,461 built.	
5076 *Gladiator*	Gloster Gladiator, the last RAF biplane fighter, 747 built.	
5077 *Fairey Battle*	Fairey Aviation single engine light bomber, 2,185 built from 1936-40.	

5078 *Beaufort*	Bristol Beaufort twin-engined torpedo bomber, 2,000 built from 1939, including 700 built in Australia.
5079 *Lysander*	Westland Lysander, single-engined light aircraft able to use small airstrips, 1,786 built from 1936.
5080 *Defiant*	Boulton Paul Defiant, single-engined turret fighter, 1,064 built from 1937.
5081 *Lockheed Hudson*	American twin-engined light bomber, 2,941 built 1938-43.
5082 *Swordfish*	Fairey Swordfish was a torpedo bomber biplane, 2,391 built 1936-44.
5083 *Bath Abbey*	Former Benedictine monastery founded in the 7th century, and rebuilt in the 10th, 12th and 16th centuries.
5084 *Reading Abbey*	Founded in 1121, destroyed in 1538, ruins stand in town centre.
5085 *Evesham Abbey*	Founded in 700, but now only wall and other fragments remain.
5086 *Viscount Horne*	Chairman of Great Western Railway, 1934-40.
5087 *Tintern Abbey*	Founded in 1131, the ruined abbey stands on the banks of the River Wye.
5088 *Llanthony Abbey*	Augustinian fourteenth century priory in the Vale of Ewyas in the Brecon Beacons.
5089 *Westminster Abbey*	Gothic, formally titled the Collegiate Church of St Peter at Westminster.
5090 *Neath Abbey*	Founded as a Cistercian monastery, now substantial ruins near Neath.
5091 *Cleeve Abbey*	Founded as a Cistercian monastery in the 12th century near Washford, Somerset. Converted in 1536 into a country house.
5092 *Tresco Abbey*	A Benedictine abbey founded in 964, and Priory of St Nicholas in 1114, on the island of Tresco in the Scilly Isles.
5093 *Upton Castle*	Small thirteenth-century fortified mansion on a creek of the Carew River, near Tenby, modernised in the eighteenth century.
5094 *Tretower Castle*	Twelfth-century motte & bailey castle, Tretower Court built in fourteenth century, in the village of Tretower, Powys County.
5095 *Barbury Castle*	Iron Age hill fort on the Ridgeway route near Swindon.
5096 *Bridgwater Castle*	Thirteenth century fortification, replaced in the seventeenth century by a mansion.
5097 *Sarum Castle*	Iron Age fort in Old Sarum, two miles north of Salisbury.
5098 *Clifford Castle*	Motte & bailey castle built in 1070 overlooking the River Wye four miles north of Hay-on-Wye, Herefordshire.
5099 *Compton Castle*	Fifteenth-century fortified manor house in Marldon, near Paignton in Devon.
7000 *Viscount Portal*	Chairman of the Great Western Railway, 1945-47.
7001 *Sir James Milne*	General Manager of the Great Western Railway, 1929-47.
7002 *Devizes Castle*	Motte & bailey castle built in 1080, rebuilt in stone in 1120, and rebuilt in neo Norman/Gothic style in the nineteenth century.
7003 *Elmley Castle*	Norman mediaeval Castle in village of Elmley near Bredon Hill.
7004 *Eastnor Castle*	Nineteenth century 'mock' castle two miles from Ledbury, Herefordshire.
7005 *Lamphey Castle*	Retreat of the bishops of St David's, Pembrokeshire, most dated 1328-47.

	Sir Edward Elgar	Renamed August 1957 – English composer, born Worcester, 1857-1934.
7006	*Lydford Castle*	Norman fort of 1068, replaced by a second castle in Lydford, Devon in 1195.
7007	*Great Western*	Renamed on the first day of nationalisation, 1 January 1948.
7008	*Swansea Castle*	Founded in 1106 and rebuilt in the thirteenth century, little remains in the city centre.
7009	*Athelney Castle*	Iron Age hill fort and King Alfred monument on the 'Isle of Athelney' near Bridgwater.
7010	*Avondale Castle*	The only known castle of this name is also known as Strathaven Castle in South Lanarkshire. No building of this name described as a castle or stately home is found on the GWR.
7011	*Banbury Castle*	Motte & bailey castle built in 1135 in Banbury, though no ruins remain.
7012	*Barry Castle*	Ruined gatehouse in the Romilly district of Barry. Was a fortified manor house in the thirteenth century.
7013	*Bristol Castle*	Norman castle in the city, of which only the moat now remains under Castle Park.
7014	*Caerhays Castle*	A castellated manor house near St Michaels Caerhays, Cornwall.
7015	*Carn Brea Castle*	Fourteenth-century building remodelled as hunting lodge in castle style, in the eighteenth century.
7016	*Chester Castle*	Built in 1070 in the south west of the City walls overlooking the River Dee.
7017	*G.J.Churchward*	Chief Mechanical Engineer, GWR, 1902-1922.
7018	*Drysllwyn Castle*	Native Welsh castle from 1197 above the River Tywi between Llandeilo and Carmarthen.
7019	*Fowey Castle*	Built to protect Fowey Harbour by Henry VIII, also known as St Catherine's Castle.
7020	*Gloucester Castle*	A Norman motte & bailey castle, replaced by a stone castle and demolished in 1790. No castle remains are now visible.
7021	*Haverfordwest Castle*	Commenced in 1120 and completed 1290, castle is in the town centre.
7022	*Hereford Castle*	Founded in 1052, rebuilt in the twelfth century, demolished in the 1650s.
7023	*Penrice Castle*	Thirteenth century castle on the Gower peninsular, with mansion added in 1770.
7024	*Powis Castle*	Mediaeval castle and mansion near Welshpool, in Powys.
7025	*Sudeley Castle*	Fifteenth century castle on site of a twelfth century fort, near Winchcombe, Gloucestershire. Still has residents.
7026	*Tenby Castle*	Founded in the twelfth century, a fortification on a headland overlooking the town of Tenby.
7027	*Thornbury Castle*	A Tudor country house built in 1511 in Thornbury, South Gloucestershire.
7028	*Cadbury Castle*	Iron Age hill fort at South Cadbury, five miles from Yeovil and has associations with the Arthurian legends.
7029	*Clun Castle*	Norman fortification rebuilt as a Marcher castle in the twelfth century, in Clun, Shropshire on the Welsh border.
7030	*Cranbrook Castle*	Iron Age hill fort overlooking the Teign Valley near Moretonhampstead and two other castles at Prestonbury and Wooston.
7031	*Cromwell's Castle*	Built in 1651 on the island of Tresco in the Scilly Isles after Parliamentary invasion and named after Oliver Cromwell.

7032 *Denbigh Castle*	Thirteenth century castle built by Edward I on rock above Denbigh town.
7033 *Hartlebury Castle*	Fortified manor house of the thirteenth century, in Hartlebury, Worcestershire.
7034 *Ince Castle*	Manor House built in 1642 three miles from Saltash, Cornwall.
7035 *Ogmore Castle*	Twelfth century castle on the River Ewenny at Ogmore-by-Sea near Bridgend.
7036 *Taunton Castle*	Dates from the Anglo-Saxon period, later a priory, now a museum.
7037 *Swindon*	Named in 1950 by Princess Elizabeth on a Swindon Works visit.

The Great Western Publicity Department seems to have been struggling for names of castles in GWR territory when it built the 70XX series, with at least twelve (7004, 7010-7015, 7020, 7022, 7027, 7034 & 7036) having a dubious claim apart from the GWR's wish to include the name of some of its key locations. Other 70XX had names previously used and discarded from the 'Earls' and 'RAF planes', with Ogmore Castle being used four times (5056, 5080, 7007 and 7035). They omitted perfectly good GW located castles at Skenfrith and Grosmont in Monmouthshire and Prestonbury and Wooston in the Teign Valley as well as ones intended but never used:

Wallingford – eleventh-century royal castle beside the Thames
Oystermouth – Norman castle on Swansea Bay, Mumbles
Hatherop – sixteenth-century castle near Coln St Aldwyn in Gloucestershire, now a school
Picton – thirteenth-century castle at Uzmaston near Haverfordwest
Wilton – twelfth-century castle near Ross-on-Wye.

BIBLIOGRAPHY

Allen, Cecil J., *Locomotive Practice & Performance,* Trains Illustrated, Ian Allan Ltd, 1950-1965
Bartlett, Steve, *Worcester's Locomotive Shed,* Pen & Sword, 2020
Bradshaw, David, *The GWR's two million mile club,* Steam Days, April 2020
Cook, Kenneth J., *Swindon Steam 1921-1951.* Ian Allan, 1972
Holcroft, H., *An outline of Great Western Locomotive Practice, 1837-1947,* Locomotive Publishing Co., 1957
Holden, Bryan and Leech, Kenneth, *A Century in Steam,* Irwell Press, 1992
Langston, Keith, *British Steam GWR Collett Castle Class,* Pen & Sword, 2015
Maidment, David, *A Privileged Journey,* Pen & Sword, 2015
Maidment, David, *An Indian Summer of Steam,* Pen & Sword, 2015
Nelson, Ronald, *Locomotive Performance, A Footplate Survey,* Ian Allan, 1979
Nock, O.S., *British Locomotives from the Footplate,* Ian Allan, 1950
Nock, O.S., *Fifty Years of Western Express Running,* Edward Everard Ltd., 1954
Nock, O.S., *Four Thousand Miles on the Footplate,* Ian Allan, 1952
Nock, O.S., *The GWR Stars, Castles & Kings, Vol 1,* David & Charles, 1967
Nock, O.S., *The GWR Stars, Castles & Kings, Vol 2,* David & Charles, 1970
Nock, O.S., *The Steam-hauled Bristolian,* Railway Magazine, March 1969
Ransome-Wallis, P., *On Engines in Britain and France,* Ian Allan, 1957
RCTS, *The Locomotives of the Great Western Railway, Part Eight, Modern Passenger Classes,* RCTS, 1953
Reed, Brian, *Loco Profile No.3 – Great Western 4-Cylinder 4-6-0s,* Hylton Lacy Publishers Ltd.,1967
Rutherford, Michael, *Castles & Kings at Work,* Book Club Associates/Ian Allan Ltd., 1982
Tuplin, W.A., *Great Western Steam,* George Allen & Unwin, 1958
Waters, Laurence, *Great Western Star Class Locomotives,* Pen & Sword, 2017

INDEX

100mph runs
    4086, 1939, Honeybourne, 120-121
    5043, 1958, Dauntsey, 214
    5052, 1937, Severn Tunnel, 121
    5057, 1958, Wantage Road, 214
    7018, 1958, Little Somerford, 213

ATC, 99, 151, 230

Bibliography, 301
Bristolian, 92, 112-113, 186-187, 209-214

Castle class construction, 25-26, 35, 56, 59, 66-69, 73, 88, 90, 99, 145, 152, 282-288
Castle class detailed construction cost (5043-5067), 293-294
Castle class design, 20-55
    Axles & bearings, 21, 34-35
    Bogie, 21-22, 31
    Boiler, 23-24, 35-37
    Brake system, 24, 47
    Buffers, 47
    Cab & controls, 24-25, 47-49
    Chimneys, 51, 208-209, 214-215, 282-288
    Compound proposal, 66-67
    Coupling rods, 43
    Cross-section, 27-29
    Cylinders & motion, 20, 22, 27-28, 39-41
    Dimensions, 20, 88, 281
    Drawings, 20, 26-34, 36-38, 40, 42-43, 45-46, 48-51
    Firebox, 23-24, 28
    Frames, 20-21, 26, 32-33, 67, 178

    Liveries, 54-55, 152, 154
    Lubrication, 44-46, 215, 218
    Piston Valves, 42
    Safety valves, 51
    Sanding gear, 47
    Smokebox, 38-39
    Spark arrestor, 52
    Speedometers, 50
    Steam pipes, 39
    Streamlining, 93-94
    Superheaters, 35, 38, 52, 145, 149, 214-215
    Tenders, 25, 53-54, 59, 66, 68, 90, 170, 218-221
    Weight diagram, 281
    Wheels, 21, 30, 67, 69
    Whistle, 51
Castle class maintenance
    Alfloc Water Treatment, 218
    Delayed, 164
    Old Oak Common, 232, 234
    Wartime problems, 144-145
Castle class mileages, 91, 164, 166, 221, 232, 234, 282-288
Castle class naming, 20, 56, 59, 67, 69-70, 76, 99-100, 145-146, 152, 282-288, 294-301
Castle class operation
    Accidents & damage,
    Dolphin Junction, 135
    Enemy damage, 135
    Allocations
    1924, 60-61
    1926, 78
    1927, 71
    1932, 88
    1935, 99, 112

    1939, 129
    1940-1944, 134-135
    1950, 155-156
    1954, 176-177
    1954, Impact of Britannias, 178, 199
    1957, 207, 241
    1959, 221-223
    1959, Impact of dieselisation, 222
    By locomotive from building to 1959, 288-293
Holiday traffic
    1952-53, 159,
    1957, 164
Castle class performance
    Accelerated schedules
        1952, 170
        1954, 175, 177-178
    Efficiency, 59, 64
    Paddington – Reading survey, 1959, 242-244
    1960, 250-251
    Postwar performance, 149, 151, 164
    Retiming for excess loads, 178, 186
    Run descriptions (no logs)
        Bristol – Shrewsbury
            4098, 1957, 189
            5072, 1940, 138-139
            5080, 1942, 141
        Oxford – Paddington
            5040, 1956, 230-232
        Paddington – Bristol route
            4076, 1934, 118
            4090, 1957, 212
            4091, 1932, 86, 1955, 186
            4096, 1957, 189
            5000, 1931, 84
            5003, 1929, 84

5012, 1928, 78
5023, 1937, 114
5038, c1949, 151
5039 (oil), 1947, 147
5044, 1936, 112
7015, 1958, 212
7018, 1958, 212
7019, c1950, 151, 1957, 212
7034, 1954, 176
Paddington – Penzance route
  4077, 1955, 189
  4094, 1936, 92
  5004, 1930, 81
  5058, 1957, 197, 199
  5079 (oil), 1947, 147
  5098, 1949, 149
  7036, c1949, 151
Paddington – Swansea route
  4078, 1954, 176
  4083, 1928, 78
  4089, 1937, 122
  4090, 1928, 78
  5057, 1951, 170
  5069, 1951, 170
  5074, 1955, 176
Paddington – Wolverhampton/Chester route
  4016, 1926, 78
  4082, 1926, 78
  4088, 1930, 78
  5006, 1931, 87
  5022, 1940-44, 144
  5032, 1957, 238
  5033, 1940-44, 144
  5061, 1940-44, 144
  5066, 1940-44, 144
Paddington – Worcester/Gloucester routes
  5083, 1957, 199
  7001, 1957, 237-238
  7007, 1957, 199
Tests & experiments
  4074, 58-59
  5025, ID, 175
  5049, 5087, 5098, 1949, 149
  5055, ATC, 99
  5056, ATC, 151
  5098, 147-148
  7018, 208
  Wartime decelerations, 135, 138
Castle class rebuilds,
  From Stars, 12, 39, 73, 77, 100, 112, 129
  From *Great Bear*, 73
Castle class specific references
  100A1, 7
  4085, 88
  4087, 6, 216, 230
  4090, 209, 234
  4091, 135, 140
  5005, 93-94
  5025, 7
  5032, 238-239, 241
  5039, 7
  5043, 7
  5055 test, 99
  5067, 114
  7001, 237-238
  7029, 7
Castle class withdrawals, 219, 221, 282-288
Cheltenham Flyer, 84-85, 92, 114

Drivers
  Griffiths, Bert, 238
  Steer, Percy, 187
  Street, F.W., 85, 112-114

Engineers
  Chapelon, André, 145
  Churchward, George Jackson, 8, 17
  Collett, Charles, 16-18
  Cook, Kenneth, 18-19
  Dean, William, 8
  De Glehn, Alfred, 10
  Ell, S.O, 145
  Goss, Professor, 8
  Hannington, R.G, 19
  Hawksworth, Frederick, 18
  Smeddle, Robert Alfred, 19

Firemen
  Forrester, 238

Funeral Trains,
  1910, 13
  1952, 166-169

Locomotive cost comparisons, 119
Locomotive Exchanges
  1910, 12-13
  1925, 61-66,
  1948, 152
Log Tables
  Bristol – Shrewsbury
  4000, 1934, 120
  5032, 1934, 120
  5032, 1940, 141
  5060, 1941, 141
  5086, 1942, 141
  Crewe – Carlisle
  5000, 1926, 69
  Kings Cross – Leeds
  4079, 1925, 62
  Oxford – Paddington
  4097, 1957, 188
  Various, 128
  Paddington – Bristol route
  4074, 1924 test, 58-59
  4082, 1938, 119
  4084, 1955, 188
  4087, 1935, 92
  4090, 1957, 210-211
  5005, 1932, 85-86
  5006, 1932, 84-85
  5018, 1935, 92
  5019, 1938, 113
  5037, 1937, 113-114
  5038, 1937, 113
  5039, 1937, 84-85
  5040, 1939, 113
  5042, 1935, 92
  5056, 1938, 113-114, 1957, 187, 1959, 187
  5066, 1937, 113
  5067, 1937, 113-114
  5080, 1939, 113
  7018, 1958, 213
  Paddington – Penzance route
  4074, 4472, 1925, 63
  4090, 1930, 80-81

4098, 1951, 169-170
7018, 1956, 208-209
Paddington – Swansea route
4079, 1937, 122
4097, 1933, 122
4099, 1959, 188
5014, 1937, 122
Paddington – Wolverhampton route
4080, 1929, 79
4082, 1929, 79
Paddington – Worcester route
4086, 1939, 121

Oil burning, 52-53, 146
Old Oak Common Mechanical Foreman's Office, 232-233, 235
Old Oak Common Running Foreman's Office, 241-242
Other locomotive classes
  Specific locomotive references
  40, 11
  98, 8
  100, 8
  4005, 12-13
  4042, 13
  8293 (8F) 135, 140
  18000, 159
  18100, 159
  Saint class
  Timeline, 16
  Star class
  General, 12
  Timeline, 16
  Withdrawals, 91, 100

Photographs (Black & White)
  Locations
  All Stretton, 143
  Badminton, 71
  Barry, 109, 129-131
  Birmingham Snow Hill, 236
  Box, 180
  Bristol Bath Road, 75, 110, 179, 188, 204
  Bristol Stapleton Road, 106, 115-116

Bristol Temple Meads, 15, 83, 93, 96, 104-105, 143, 176, 214, 216, 221, 225
Bromfield, 198
Bushey troughs, 12
Cardiff Canton, 178, 189-190, 203, 205-206, 226, 228, 254, 259, 262
Cardiff General, 166, 183, 185, 191, 198, 200-202, 219, 255-256, 259, 261
Carmarthen, 215
Challow, 172
Cheltenham Malvern Road, 151
Chippenham, 179
Cogan, 109
Creech St Michael, 175
Darlington, 58
Dawlish, 171, 195, 222
Dawlish Warren, 193
Dinas Powis, 132
Dinmore, 194
Dolphin Junction, 136, 140
Evesham, 229
Euston, 70
Exeter St David's, 14, 111, 161, 191-192
Filton Junction, 106, 108
Flax Bourton, 95, 107
Fosse Road, 263
Goodrington Sands, 160, 162
Goring, 227
Goring troughs, 96, 116-117, 150
Grantham, 66
Hadley Wood, 65
Harringay, 65
Hayle, 190
Hereford, 219
High Wycombe, 157, 227
Hullavington, 210
Iver, 82, 117
Kensal Green, 74
Kings Cross, 64
Kingswear, 223
Laira, 70, 261
Landore, 183
Leamington, 87, 146
Leebotwood, 142

Ludlow, 182
Marshfield, 165, 174, 201
Miskin, 123, 137
Nantyderry, 184
Newport, 203, 205
Newton Abbot, 159-162, 255-256
Norton Fitzwarren, 98, 124-125, 127, 163
Nottingham Victoria, 13, 74
Old Oak Common, 10, 12, 57, 71-73, 77, 88, 91, 94, 144, 148, 181, 212, 216, 235-236, 240, 254, 257, 260, 263
Paddington, 10, 60, 71-72, 76, 82, 90, 153, 180, 204, 231, 238-239, 241, 245-246, 248-249, 253,
Par, 154, 195-196, 224
Patchway, 83, 94, 100-104
Pilning, 105, 109
Plymouth North Road, 253
Pontrilas, 174, 199
Rattery, 171
Reading, 245, 247, 249
Ruabon, 228
Rumney River Bridge, 206
St Fagans, 145, 202
Saltash, 163, 223-224
Saltford, 152
Saltney Junction, 89
Saunderton, 118
Shrewsbury, 112, 164-166, 184-185, 193
Somerton, 95
Sonning, 156-157
Southall, 138
Southcote Junction, 150
Stafford Road, 15, 77, 186, 217
Steventon, 115
Stoke Canon, 225
Stratford-on-Avon, 147
Subway Junction, 13
Swansea, 239
Swindon, 75-76, 86, 93, 110-112, 128, 154, 158, 168, 182, 217, 237, 258, 262, 264
Taunton, 67, 98

Teignmouth, 172, 192, 194
Warwick, 139, 149
Westbourne Park, 155
Westbury, 97
Westerleigh Junction, 107
Whiteball, 125-127, 181
Windsor branch, 168
Wolvercote Junction, 173
Worcester, 219, 229, 257-258
Worle Junction, 14
Vale of Glamorgan, 136, 197
Yate, 108

Locomotives
40, 11, 12
98, 9
100, 9
100 A1, 76, 83
100 A1 (oil), 148, 263
102, 10
103, 10, 11
111, *Great Bear*, 73-74
111, Castle, 74-75, 144, 160, 254
184, 9
4000, 77, 143, 165, 183
4004, 13
4005, 12
4007, 14
4009, 75, 129
4016, 77
4021, 13
4037, 130, 181
4043, 14
4053, 178
4056, 15
4061, 15
4063, 111
4065, 112
4073, 56, 67, 124, 142, 182, 205
4074, 60, 183, 200, 263
4075, 125, 254
4076, 57, 164, 185, 258
4077, 184, 190
4079, 64-66, 108-109, 165-166, 252
4080, 60, 100, 171
4082, 58, 70, 95
4082 (ex-7013), 167-168
4083, 186

4084, 130
4085, 71, 245, 262
4086, 71
4087, 89, 181, 216, 231, 236
4088, 192, 253
4089, 101, 172, 245, 262
4090, 71, 163, 212, 235, 260
4091, 140
4092, 82
4093, 215
4094, 151, 259
4095, 123
4097, 101, 196
4098, 72, 107, 255
4099, 82, 107, 131-133, 200
4977, 165
5000, 68, 70, 147, 204, 228
5001, 72, 87, 91, 102, 142, 145, 255
5002, 90, 102
5003, 95, 191, 248
5004, 126, 184, 246, 259
5005, 93-94, 225, 264
5006, 86, 192
5007, 96, 189, 219
5008, 138, 247
5010, 89, 136-137, 253
5011, 194
5012, 88, 109, 161
5014, 127
5015, 139
5016, 127, 226
5017, 173, 191
5018, 173
5019, 179
5020, 198, 222
5021, 128, 154, 160, 256
5022, 97, 115, 127, 264
5023, 228, 248
5024, 162, 171, 256
5025, 152, 176, 206
5028, 106, 125, 161
5029, 96, 109
5030, 126
5032, 103, 238-239
5034, 162
5035, 118
5039, 105

5039 (oil), 149
5040, 105
5042, 184
5043, 103, 115, 136, 201, 241
5044, 97, 133, 240
5045, 132
5047, 98, 172, 227
5048, 174
5050, 194
5051, 203
5052, 131, 138
5053, 98, 110, 150
5054, 199
5056, 110, 116
5058, 104, 195
5063, 117
5064, 106
5066, 217
5069, 228
5070, 111, 117
5072, 197, 217
5074, 163, 180, 201
5075, 223
5076, 100, 170
5077, 178, 202, 239
5079, 223
5080, 137, 219
5082, 236
5083, 104, 123
5084, 198, 261
5086, 143
5088, 112, 217
5089, 150, 166
5090, 219
5091 (oil), 148
5091, 226
5092, 227, 257
5097, 159, 193
5098, 195, 261
5099, 200, 202
5925, 203
6141, 247
7001, 147, 177, 237
7004, 168
7005, 229, 240, 257
7006, 224
7007, 146, 157, 249, 258

7011, 153
7012, 206
7013 (ex-4082), 168, 182, 204, 225
7014, 155-156
7015, 188
7017, 153
7018, 174, 210, 214, 260
7022, 190, 221, 224
7023, 178, 203
7025, 157, 249
7027, 180
7031, 196
7032 (as 7037), 154
7037, 158, 175
8293 (8F), 140

Photographs (Colour)
  Locations
  Bristol Bath Road, 271-272
  Churston, 269
  Corsham, 272
  Dainton, 266

Dawlish, 266-267
Dawlish Warren, 268
Denham Golf Club, 275
Goodrington Sands, 269
Hackney, 270
Landore, 277
Old Oak Common, 271, 276
Paddington, 270, 273
Sapperton, 273
Stafford Road, 276
Teignmouth, 265
Tilehurst, 274
Twyford, 274
Wolverhampton, 275
  Locomotives
4000, 276
4077, 271
4083, 275
4096, 269
5003, 266
5004, 267

5010, 277
5017, 273
5034, 273
5035, 270
5037, 271, 274
5044, 276
5055, 270
5059, 265, 268
5075, 275
5078, 266-267
5084, 271
5085, 272
5090, 272
7003, 269
7016, 274
Nameplates, 277-278
Models, '0' gauge, 280
Models, '00' gauge, 278-279

Wartime traffic levels, 135
Wembley Exhibition, 1924-5, 57
World Power Conference, 57